TEACHER'S BOOK

BARBARA GARSIDE

ADVANCED
OUTCOMES

**HEINLE
CENGAGE Learning**

Australia • Brazil • Japan • Korea • Mexico • Singapore • Spain • United Kingdom • United States

**HEINLE
CENGAGE Learning**

Outcomes *Advanced Teacher's Book*
Barbara Garside

Publisher: Jason Mann

Senior Commissioning Editor: John Waterman

Development Editor: Heidi North

Senior Marketing Manager: Ruth McAleavey

Content Project Editor: Amy Smith

Production Controller: Denise Power

Cover and text designer: Studio April

Compositor: Q2AMedia

© 2012 Heinle, Cengage Learning

ALL RIGHTS RESERVED. No part of this work covered by the copyright herein may be reproduced, transmitted, stored or used in any form or by any means graphic, electronic, or mechanical, including but not limited to photocopying, recording, scanning, digitalising, taping, Web distribution, information networks, or information storage and retrieval systems, except as permitted under Section **107 or 108 of the 1976 United States Copyright Act**, or applicable copyright law of another jurisdiction, without the prior written permission of the publisher.

> For permission to use material from this text or product, submit all requests online at **cengage.com/permissions**.
> Further permissions questions can be emailed to **permissionrequest@cengage.com**.

ISBN: 978-1-111-21237-7

Heinle, Cengage Learning EMEA
Cheriton House, North Way, Andover, Hampshire
SP10 5BE United Kingdom

Cengage Learning is a leading provider of customised learning solutions with office locations around the globe, including Singapore, the United Kingdom, Australia, Mexico, Brazil and Japan. Locate our local office at **international.cengage.com/region**

Cengage Learning products are represented in Canada by Nelson Education Ltd.

Visit Heinle online at **elt.heinle.com**
Visit our corporate website at **cengage.com**

Printed in China by R. R. Donnelley
1 2 3 4 5 6 7 8 9 10 – 16 15 14 13 12

CONTENTS

INTRODUCTION TO *OUTCOMES* TEACHER'S BOOK	4
01 CITIES	8
02 CULTURE AND IDENTITY	14
03 RELATIONSHIPS	20
04 POLITICS	26
Review 01	32
05 NIGHT IN, NIGHT OUT	36
06 CONFLICT	42
07 SCIENCE AND RESEARCH	48
08 NATURE	54
Review 02	60
09 WORK	62
10 HEALTH AND ILLNESS	68
11 PLAY	74
12 HISTORY	80
Review 03	86
13 NEWS AND THE MEDIA	88
14 BUSINESS AND ECONOMICS	94
15 FASHION	100
16 DANGER AND RISK	106
Review 04	112
INTRODUCTION TO WRITING IN *OUTCOMES*	114
Writing Lessons 1–8	116
COMMUNICATION ACTIVITIES	
Teacher's Notes	120
Photocopiable Communication Activities	128
Grammar Reference Answer Key	160
Audio Track Listing	166

INTRODUCTION

WHAT'S IN *OUTCOMES* STUDENT'S BOOK?

16 units based round common topics Each unit has three interlinked 'lessons' of 50–90 minutes. The unit contents give clear practical outcomes. The first lesson teaches language leading to *Conversation Practice*. The second and third spreads develop reading or listening and teach more grammar and vocabulary connected with the topic.

8 writing units The two-page writing units on pp. 120–135 teach different types of writing for everyday life and exams. Each has a model text, *Grammar* or *Vocabulary*, *Keywords for writing* and *Practice*.

4 Review units Each review has a learner training discussion, two pages of games, tasks and pronunciation exercises to revise language and then a two-page test including a listening exercise.

Grammar Sixteen points of grammar are covered. Each *Grammar* section links to the previous text. An explanation or guided questions teach meaning. Exercises give controlled and freer practice. There's a link to the grammar reference if you need extra help.

Grammar reference This is on pp. 136–155 at the back of the book. Each section has an expanded explanation, further natural examples of usage and extra controlled practice exercises with a glossary.

Language patterns This is a short translation exercise into students' own language and back into English. It draws attention to other aspects of syntax and grammar based on a pattern seen in a text.

Vocabulary Vocabulary is carefully chosen to enable students to talk about the topic in the context of English as a lingua franca. Tasks generally move from meaning, to contextualised usage to personalised practice. Other sections focus on word-building.

***Outcomes* Vocabulary Builder (OVB)** The separate booklet allows students to look up meaning of new language which is key to learn, offering several examples of collocations and usage plus a page of revision practice.

Native speaker English Draws attention to common words or phrases that fluent speakers use, which students may hear or want to learn.

Keywords Most writing units have a focus on linking words and patterns, which help develop fluent, coherent writing. There's a link to the text, a short explanation and practice exercises.

Developing conversations These sections teach typical questions, responses and patterns common to conversation. An explanation clarifies the focus, while exercises give controlled practice.

Conversation practice A task lets students practise social and practical conversations based on their own experience or through role-play.

Speaking These sections give students the chance to exchange ideas. The final speaking task in each unit is a variety of longer tasks that draw the language and / or the themes of the unit together.

Listening These sections are introduced with a short description of the context. There is usually a pre-listening speaking task to generate interest or predict content, followed by tasks to guide students to understand the text and focus on vocabulary.

Reading These sections are introduced with a short description of the context. There is usually a pre-reading speaking task to generate interest or predict content, followed by tasks to guide students to understand the text and focus on vocabulary.

WHAT'S IN *OUTCOMES* TEACHER'S BOOK?

The Teacher's book is organised into three sections: Teacher's notes, Writing lessons and Communication activities.

TEACHER'S NOTES provide guidance on how to use the 16 units and four **REVIEWS** in the Student's book. Each unit opens with a brief **UNIT OVERVIEW** that allows you to understand the main elements of the lesson very quickly.

Under the same headings as in the Student's book, the notes give clear aims and simple steps to provide a very easy path through the material. Answer boxes and audioscripts embedded in the notes ensure you have everything you need at your fingertips. Suggestions throughout the notes help you with ways to set up activities, check and clarify meaning, monitor, conduct feedback, etc. An icon 👥 indicates where you might want to use a **COMMUNICATION ACTIVITY**. In addition, there's help through three mini features.

The **Tip** feature offers ideas on things such as:
- other ways to check meaning;
- how to adapt material for different groups such as mono- or multilingual classes;
- bringing extra material into lessons.

The **Alternatively** feature provides:
- a different way to stage an activity than the one suggested in the Student's book.

The **Optional activity** suggests:
- ways to extend an activity if students need to do more work.

The **Writing lessons** section opens with a two-page introduction on teaching writing. It explains the approach to writing and suggests ways you can provide feedback to students. The introduction is followed by **Teacher's notes** and the answer key for the eight writing lessons.

The **Communication activities** section contains simple instructions on how to use the 32 photocopiable activities. The activities are designed to revise key grammar and vocabulary from the Student's book in a fun and varied way. There are quizzes, word puzzles, questionnaires, games, information gaps and short role-plays. Each unit has two activities calculated to take 10–15 minutes of class time.

Other *Outcomes* components

***Outcomes* Workbook** The *Outcomes* Workbook thoroughly revises all the language areas that are in the Student's book. Each unit also has:
- a listening and a reading with tasks based on topics loosely connected to the theme of the unit and providing interest and extra challenges to students
- **Developing Writing** that focuses on types of text students might write in their academic, professional and personal lives and further work on relevant language.

The *Outcomes* Workbook also comes with:
- **Audio CD** of recordings of the listening and reading texts
- **Answer key** and **Audioscript** to aid self-study.

***Outcomes* ExamView®** Writing tests to check your students' progress takes a lot of time and work but the **ExamView®** CD allows you to create tests and exams in as little as five minutes. What's more:
- all the tests are closely based on the Student's book.
- the software also generates the answer key.
- it provides a variety of exercise types (True / False, multiple choice, Yes / No, matching, etc.)
- tests can be printed, computer-based, or on the Internet.
- you can easily edit the questions and add your own.
- you can save all tests for another time.
- it's easy to reorder questions to avoid cheating.

***MyOutcomes* online resource** Every copy of the *Outcomes* Student's Book has a unique code at the front of the book which provides access to **MyOutcomes** online resource where students will find additional work on all the elements of the Student's book. There are:
- over 230 activities practising the grammar, vocabulary, pronunciation and conversations in the 16 units
- additional listening, reading and speaking practice
- reviews every four units to test students' progress.

Teachers can also use the online resource if they apply for an access code. Go to **myelt.heinle.com** and request a MyELT instructor account. This will allow you to set specific work for all your students and then receive their results. You can then store these results through the **Grade book**, so both you and your students have a record of their marks and progress.

Outcomes advanced

In this introduction we try to answer these questions:
What are the goals of language students?
What is key language for students at Advanced level?
What is key for teachers to help them teach?

Key goals

The Common European Framework of reference (CEF) states that language learning and teaching overall goals should be:
1.1 *to deal with the business of everyday life in another country, and to help foreigners staying in their own country to do so;*
1.2 *to exchange information and ideas with young people and adults who speak a different language and to communicate their thoughts and feelings to them;*
1.3 *to achieve a wider and deeper understanding of the way of life and forms of thought of other peoples and of their cultural heritage.*
(Council of Europe, 2001, page 3)

These ideas underpin everything we do in the *Outcomes* series. At Advanced level, we look at can-do statements for C2 level as a guide to what students might want to achieve.

Business of everyday life You can see the communicative areas that are dealt with in the *how to* sections of the contents and title strip that heads each unit. *Outcomes* has a strong practical thread. For example, students at Advanced level learn the grammar and vocabulary to:
- talk about the nature of work and discuss terms and conditions of employment pp. 64–69
- present ideas and theories and ask for clarification pp. 84–85

For many students passing exams is also the business of everyday life, which is why *Outcomes* has a **Grammar reference** with exercises on all the grammar you'd expect. Similarly, **Writing** deals with both practical types of writing (writing a covering letter pp. 128–129) and exam-type writing (expressing your opinion pp. 122–123).

Communicating thoughts and feelings Practicalities are important, but just as important, and perhaps more motivating, is the ability to communicate in a way which reflects your personality, feelings and opinions. That's why most of the Developing conversations and Conversation practice work towards practising typical conversations we have to establish and maintain friendships:
- share and talk through problems pp. 24–25
- network and make small talk pp. 98–99

This is also why we constantly give students the chance to exchange their ideas, through Speaking, practice activities in Vocabulary and Grammar, the lead-ins to Reading and Listening and discussions about the texts.

Understanding other cultures Students will best understand other cultures by talking with other students, which the various speaking activities in *Outcomes* always encourage. However, many classrooms may not have people from a large mix of backgrounds, which is why we use texts with international contexts and reflecting other cultures throughout the world – including Britain. Students come to realise they share many of the same desires and concerns! Among others, you'll read and hear about:
- recent historical milestones in four different countries pp. 86–87
- the Electoral System Swiss style pp. 30–31

Native speaker notes also draw attention to ways fluent speakers express themselves, which may be different to the neutral international language that we generally present.

Key language

There were five guides to the input at Advanced level – the communicative outcomes (outlined in *Outcomes Goals*), the frequency of words, 'naturalness' of usage, student autonomy and teacher–student expectations or interest.

For example, in 'describing people' (pp. 20–21) students need to know a number of core adjectives which are presented and practised in Vocabulary. The practice gets them to think of language which might go with these words and the OVB provides further help in terms of collocations. Listening then gives a model conversation. Language patterns draws attention to the grammar around the word *he's / she's one of those people who...* . Developing conversations teaches expressions to give your impression. Grammar looks at using *would* to give opinions about people politely and provides a fuller context for the vocabulary.

This is typical of the way language input is focused on helping students achieve the stated communicative outcome, but not all language learning can be developed in this way. A lot of vocabulary may be very frequent but not specific to any one topic (e.g. *issue, unlike, refer*). The language highlighted through texts is largely of this nature. The exercises and OVB, then show a range of natural collocations. Similarly, some grammar may not be fundamental to a conversation in the way we saw with 'describing people'. Here, we make the choice based on what students and teachers expect to be covered at this level or have tested in exams. This may be 'exam grammar', but we try to give natural sounding examples.

Input is also decided on the basis that students need to learn outside the classroom. The *word families* strand in Vocabulary, the OVB language boxes and Reading shows students how words are formed. This helps them recognise and learn new words in their own studies. The same motives underlie Language patterns, but with a focus on grammar.

Finally, students and non-native speaker teachers often express an interest in colloquial language and idioms. The Native speaker note provides explanations and examples of this in contrast to the normal input, which can be freely used and understood in contexts where English is a lingua franca.

Key to learn

There are many ways to learn but it seems there are a few essentials:
- Students need to notice.
- Students need to understand.
- Students need to practise – spoken, written, receptive.
- Students need to make mistakes.
- Students need to repeat these steps a lot.

Noticing and understanding Obviously the exercises in Grammar and Vocabulary encourage students to notice and understand. Visuals and clear explanations of vocabulary and examples of collocations in the OVB reinforce meaning. The Language patterns exercise trains students to notice and consider how English compares with their own language.

Practice Students always have a chance to practise language. This goes from very controlled 'remember and test', and gap-fills to freer role-play and personalised speaking. Communication activities in this Teacher's book provide more practice.

Making mistakes Not all teaching and input can or should be provided by the coursebook. We all know from experience and research that people learn new language when they are struggling to express something and the 'correct' or better word is given. This is also why we have lots of speaking activities. They are not just opportunities for students to practise what they know; they are chances for them to try to say something new, stretch themselves and make mistakes, which you can then correct.

Repetition Seeing a word once is not enough! Some say you need to see and understand vocabulary ten times before you have learnt to use it! Maybe grammar takes even longer. Recycling and Revision is therefore a key part of the design of *Outcomes*. For example, the OVB, Workbook and *ExamView®* allow unit-by-unit revision, while Review after every four units ensures further revision at a later date.

With grammar, students can revise after the class by using the **Grammar reference** and exercises, the **Workbook** or **MyOutcomes**. Grammar structures are often looked at in several contexts over the course and at various levels. **Review** units test grammar and you can also create tests with **ExamView®**.

Apart from this revision we try to repeatedly re-use language from **Vocabulary** in **Listening** and **Reading**; in **Grammar** and **Grammar reference**; in **Developing conversations**; in workbook texts; in exercises and texts in other units of the Student's book and even in other levels of the series. And as we have seen, **Speaking** and **Conversation practice** allow students to re-use language they've learnt.

In terms of speaking, research suggests that students can improve performance with repetition. Within the first two pages of each unit there are often several opportunities to have conversations around the same topic as we saw with 'describing people' through **Vocabulary** or **Grammar** practice, **Developing conversations** and **Conversation practice**. The **Review** units also encourage students to look back and repeat speaking tasks.

Key to teach

Most teachers need or want material that:
- is quick and easy to prepare
- caters for mixed level classes
- motivates students

Quick and easy to prepare A coursebook is easy to use when the relation between input and outcomes is clear and we hope you already see that is the case with *Outcomes*. However, other aspects of the design should help you just pick up the book and teach:
- a limited number of sections appear in all units
- a regular structure to the units
- a variety of familiar tasks
- double-pages can exist as unique lessons but six-page units allow you to easily continue
- straightforward rubrics in Student's book fully explain tasks
- **Grammar** and **Vocabulary** have clear links to texts
- **OVB** follows the spreads of the book so you and your students can easily look up words in class.

Mixed level classes Students often start at different levels within a class and so the input in *Outcomes* Advanced revises and extends language encountered at Upper Intermediate. However, the exercises and design of *Outcomes* also works for multi-level classes.
- **OVB** The *Outcomes* Vocabulary Builder allows weaker students to easily look up new words, before, during and after class, because it follows the spreads of the book. Stronger students benefit from the **OVB** because it gives extra input through collocation lists, extra language boxes and practice exercises.
- **Grammar** The short explanations help weaker students with exercises in the units. The grammar reference helps weaker students with more examples, but stronger students will like the extra information that is always given.
- **Easy to difficult** Whether it is grammar or vocabulary, reading or listening, we usually move from easier to more difficult tasks in each section. For example, reading texts often allow language to be pre-taught, the first tasks are then based on general understanding and further tasks are more detailed.
- **Translation** Several exercises including **Language patterns** encourage students to translate. Translation is particularly important for weaker students who benefit from the support of their mother tongue and bilingual dictionaries. In monolingual classes, especially, it allows stronger students to help others in the class by providing the translations.
- **Test and remember** Tasks like this are comforting for weaker students, but they can also be made more challenging for stronger students by asking them to remember more.
- **Native speaker notes** and **Language patterns** These offer extra input for stronger students and classes. You might consider dropping them for weaker classes.
- **Teacher's notes** There are more ideas for dealing with multi-level classes in this book – particularly through the **Tip** and **Alternatively** features.

Motivating students As a teacher motivating students will be a major part of your job; however, we know a coursebook can often work against student motivation by having irrelevant or boring content, unclear, unrealistic or unfulfilled outcomes or simply by a dull design. *Outcomes* helps you motivate students by having:
- outcomes matching students, wants and needs
- a clear menu of input and outcomes at the start of each unit
- input and tasks that carefully match those outcomes
- a manageable number of keywords to learn in the **OVB**
- texts based on authentic sources that we think you'll find by turns informative, funny, even moving
- a range of speaking tasks that allow for play, humour and gossip, as well as serious discussion
- a fresh design with bright, interesting illustration

The CEF and Level There is not a direct correlation between publishers' levels and the CEF. Completing Upper Intermediate will not mean a student has reached B2 and completing Advanced is not equivalent to reaching C1. That's because the CEF descriptions of level or the ALTE can-do statements do *not* exactly describe content, but describe someone's *performance* in a language. We have used can-do statements from the C1 level at Advanced level as a guide to what tasks and outcomes students want to progress towards. However, at this level students' performance in *doing* any of the speaking, reading, listening or writing tasks may be assessed using CEF scales as being B2 (+), C1. If students are regularly outside the range of B2 (+), C1 (–), they are probably at the wrong level for this material.

01 CITIES

UNIT OVERVIEW
In this unit, students practise **describing different aspects of cities, urban problems and ways of dealing with them,** and **telling urban myths**. They learn how to **emphasise and reinforce what they say in different ways,** read articles about cities that have overcome problems and about urban myths, and listen to conversations about **different cities** and **disaster recovery,** and to a number of individuals talking about **urban myths**. The main grammar aim is **revision of perfect forms**.

Next class Make photocopies of **1A** p. 128.

SPEAKING

Aim
To get students thinking and talking about city life.

Step 1 Ask students whether they like living in a city and why / why not. Try to elicit some general advantages / disadvantages of city life. Put students in small groups to discuss the questions in A. Conduct brief feedback.

VOCABULARY City life

Aim
To introduce / revise adjectives associated with city life.

Step 1 Ask students to look at the adjectives in exercise A and match each with one of the sentences 1–9. Check in pairs. Then check with the whole group, paying attention to students' stress / pronunciation.

Answers
1 vibrant   4 polluted   7 congested
2 dangerous   5 affluent   8 sprawling
3 well-run   6 spotless   9 run-down

Step 2 Ask students to spend two minutes reading and memorising the adjectives in the box in A. They should then work in pairs and test each other. Student A should say four or five of the sentences in exercise A and Student B should respond with the correct adjective. Then swap.

Step 3 Ask students to look at the adjectives in exercise C and match them with their opposites in exercise A. Check in pairs, then check with the whole group.

Answers
1 filthy – spotless   4 chaotic – well-run
2 deprived – affluent   5 compact – sprawling
3 dull – vibrant   6 safe – dangerous

Step 4 Put students in groups and ask them to describe places they know, using the adjectives from A and C. Conduct brief feedback.

1A see Teacher's notes p. 120.

LISTENING

Aim
To hear the vocabulary in context and to extend it. To give practice in listening for detail and intensively.

Step 1 Tell students they are going to hear two conversations about cities. Ask them to listen and take notes on each of the cities. Play the recording.

🔊 1.1
Conversation 1
A = woman, B = man
A: How was your trip?
B: Great. <u>Really amazing</u>. Have you ever been there?
A: No. What's it like?
B: It's <u>really wild</u>. It took me by surprise, actually.
A: Yeah?
B: Yeah. I don't know what I expected, really. I just thought it'd be quieter, but the nightlife is <u>totally mad</u>.
A: Really?
B: Honestly. The people there party <u>like there's no tomorrow</u>. We went out with these people and we ended up in a place at about four in the morning and it was <u>absolutely packed</u>.
A: Yeah?
B: Seriously. You couldn't move. In fact, the whole city was still <u>buzzing</u>. You can still get stuck in traffic at that time of night.
A: Wow!
B: Actually, that was a bit of a downside, the congestion.
A: Really? Is it bad?
B: <u>Unbelievable</u>! You just spend <u>hours and hours</u> in your car <u>crawling</u> along, with everyone honking their horns. You'd be quicker walking really.
A: So did you?

8 OUTCOMES

> B: No, it's so <u>unbearably humid</u>, so you can't, really. Honestly, you only have to walk out of your hotel and you're <u>dripping in sweat</u>. It's just <u>like a thick wall of heat</u> that hits you.
> A: There must be a fair amount of pollution, then.
> B: That as well. There's this <u>appalling</u> cloud of smog that <u>constantly hangs over</u> the city. You sometimes really <u>choke</u> on the fumes when you're outside.
> A: Sounds pretty grim. Are you sure it's so great?
> B: Well, you know, it does have its drawbacks, but as I say it just has a <u>real buzz</u> – especially downtown with the <u>skyscrapers</u> and the neon lights flashing and the people and the noise. It's just a <u>very vibrant</u> place.
>
> **Conversation 2**
> **C = man, D = woman**
> C: What's your hometown like? It's supposed to be nice, isn't it?
> D: It is, if you like that sort of place.
> C: What do you mean?
> D: It's just <u>very conservative</u>. You know. It's <u>very affluent</u> – you see <u>loads and loads</u> of people in fur coats and posh cars, and the streets are <u>spotless</u>, but it's also just <u>incredibly dull</u>. There's not much going on.
> C: Right
> D: I know it's a bit more run down here, but at least it's more lively. There's more of a music scene, you know.
> C: Yeah, I know what you mean. So you wouldn't consider going back to live there?
> D: Maybe. I mean, don't get me wrong, it is a good place to live if you're bringing up kids – everything works <u>very smoothly</u> and as I say there's <u>not a speck</u> of litter on the streets. So if I were to settle down, I might move back. It's just not what I want right now.
> C: Fair enough.

Step 2 Put students in pairs and ask them to compare their notes and discuss which of the cities they think they would prefer to live in and why.

Step 3 Ask students to look at exercise C and try to complete the sentences with phrases from the recording. Play the recording. Check their answers and concept check the phrases by asking for other examples.

> **Answers**
> 1 a took me by surprise
>   b like there's no tomorrow
>   c a bit of a downside
>   d Sounds pretty grim
>   e have its drawbacks
> 2 a that sort of place
>   b more of a music scene
>   c wouldn't consider going back
>   d get me wrong
>   e were to settle down

Step 4 Put students in small groups and ask them to discuss the questions in D. Conduct brief feedback.

Developing conversations
Emphasising and reinforcing

Aim
To draw students' attention to ways of adding emphasis or reinforcing what they say.

Step 1 Read out the explanation, checking students understand as you read. Ask students to look at the audioscript on page 160 and underline examples of the different ways of emphasising / reinforcing. Check in pairs. Then check with the whole group. (Answers are underlined in the audioscript.)

Step 2 Ask students to add a reinforcing sentence for each sentence in B. Monitor and check students' sentences are appropriate.

Step 3 Ask students to look at the model conversation in exercise C. Model the conversation with a strong student, getting the student to use one of their examples to complete what A says. Then put students in pairs to have similar conversations. They should take turns to be A and use the sentences they have written.

Conversation practice

Aim
To give practice in the target language and round off this part of the unit.

Step 1 Ask students to think of two cities they know and make notes about the things in exercise A. Tell them to use as much language from this part of the unit as possible.

Step 2 Put students in pairs and ask them to have conversations beginning *Have you been to…?* Tell them to keep the conversations going by responding and asking further questions. Monitor and take notes on their use of language for a correction slot at the end.

> **pp. 10–11**
>
> **Next class** Make photocopies of **1B** p. 129.

Reading

Aim
To extend the topic and give practice in reading for specific information and exchanging information about similar texts.

Step 1 Ask students to look at the questions in exercise A and check they understand all the words / phrases. Then put them in small groups to discuss the questions.

01 CITIES

Step 2 Divide the class into three – As, Bs and Cs. Students A should turn to File 1 on page 152, Bs to File 12 on page 156 and Cs to File 18 on page 159. Draw their attention to the glossary in each case. Ask them to read their texts and answer the questions in B.

Step 3 Put students in same letter pairs to check their answers and discuss any vocabulary they're not sure about.

Step 4 Put students into threes with an A, a B and a C in each group. Ask them to tell each other about their cities, using the questions in B to help them. They should then decide together which they think is the most remarkable or interesting story and why. Ask them to report back to the rest of the class and try to encourage them to argue / discuss it all together.

Step 5 Ask each student to choose two new words / phrases from their text which they think are useful, and explain them to their partners. Check with the whole group and check the words / phrases they have chosen for meaning and pronunciation.

VOCABULARY Changes

Aim
To introduce verbs commonly used to talk about urban changes.

Step 1 Ask students to look at the sentences in exercise A and use the correct form of the correct verb from the box to complete each one. Do the first example with them. Check in pairs, then check with the whole group. Concept check by asking them for other examples.

> **Answers**
> 1 under<u>gone</u>   5 re<u>gen</u>erated
> 2 e<u>merged</u>   6 <u>tri</u>pled
> 3 over<u>come</u>   7 de<u>clined</u>
> 4 de<u>mol</u>ished   8 <u>flou</u>rishing

Step 2 Ask students to look at the questions in B and think about possible answers. Then put them in pairs or threes to discuss their ideas.

NATIVE SPEAKER ENGLISH *gentrified*

Read out the explanation in the box and check students understand. Ask them for examples of gentrification from cities they know. Ask them what they think are some advantages and disadvantages of gentrification.

GRAMMAR Perfect tenses

Aim
To revise, practise and consolidate perfect forms.

Step 1 Begin by asking students which perfect forms they know, with examples of each. Then read out the explanation in the box, or ask them to read it.

Step 2 Put students in pairs and ask them to discuss the sentences in A. They should decide whether one or both are correct and why. If both are correct, they should discuss the difference in meaning. Check with the whole group.

> **Answers**
> 1 *have been* – perfect infinitive after *may* – used with *for* + a period of time; something which started in the past and is still true now. *May always be* would refer to the future – not possible here.
> 2 *have fallen* – present perfect simple with a period of time which started in the past and continues now; *have dipped* – future perfect with *by* + point in time showing a time limit or deadline for the action or state. *Fall* would refer to present – not possible with *over the last 20 years. Dip* would be future simple. This is possible but future perfect more likely with *by*.
> 3 Both possible but past perfect emphasises change in 1976.
> 4 *having been* – because the process of rebuilding is complete. *Being* not possible with *since*.
> 5 *have contributed* – perfect infinitive – refers to an action or state which began in the past and has continued up to the present. *Contribute* not possible with *over the last twenty years*.
> 6 *was* – because it is a permanent state; *he'd been* would suggest he was no longer from Dortmund.

Step 3 Ask students in the same pairs to discuss which of the perfect forms in the sentences refer to finished actions or states and which to continuing states. Check as a group.

> **Answers**
> 1 continuing state   4 finished action
> 2 finished action   5 continuing action
> 3 finished state   6 continuing state

🎧🎧 **1B** see Teacher's notes p. 120.

LISTENING

Aim
To hear some of the perfect forms in context and to give practice in listening for gist and for specific information.

Step 1 Tell students they are going to hear an interview with Lloyd Jones, an expert on disaster recovery. Elicit some different kinds of natural disaster and check they understand *recovery*. Ask them to listen and decide what they think the main point of Lloyd Jones's answers is. Play the recording, then put students in pairs to compare their ideas. Check with the whole group.

01 CITIES

> **Answers**
> The main point is that different people define recovery in different ways. It is important that people's way of life survives after a disaster as well as rebuilding a city physically.

◊ 1.2
I = Interviewer, L = Lloyd Jones

I: Following the latest hurricane to hit the Caribbean we're here talking with Lloyd Jones, an expert on disaster recovery. Lloyd, this has been a particularly devastating storm. How long can we expect the city and region to take to overcome this crisis?

L: Well, in very basic terms – getting rubble cleared away, providing basic shelter, getting services up and running and so on – very quickly. Even with some of the logistical problems we've been seeing, I'd expect it to have happened in a matter of weeks, if not days, but, of course, real long-term recovery can take years.

I: Several politicians are already talking of this in terms of an opportunity – to rebuild a city which had suffered economic and social problems for years.

L: Hmmm, yes. I always slightly worry when I hear that.

I: Really?

L: Well, it very much depends what you mean by 'opportunity' and who the opportunity is for? For example, in a number of fishing villages struck by the Asian tsunami some years ago what emerged from the recovery was not a flourishing fishing industry, but rather hotels and tourism. This was seen by many as a positive step in developing the economy by those investing, but for the fishermen, it meant losing a way of life and control over their own income.

I: Right.

L: Unfortunately, throughout history it's often the rich who define recovery and the poor who lose out. For example, going back to the 19th century, most of the city of Chicago was devastated by fire. There was a huge push to reconstruct the city driven by an image of the future. Skyscrapers sprung up to replace what had been there, and you know what, during the construction more people died than in the fire itself!

I: So what should happen?

L: I think the best projects are those that fully involve the affected community – in fact, that are led by them. Where we're talking of very deprived areas with social problems, that can certainly be difficult, but outsiders often underestimate poor people's capabilities. People are resourceful.

I: Lloyd Jones, we have to leave it there. Thank you very much.

Step 2 Put students in pairs and ask them to look at the items in exercise B and discuss what Lloyd and the interviewer said about each of them. Then ask them to turn to page 160 and read the audioscript while they listen again to check. Play the recording. Check answers as a class.

> **Answers**
> 1 the hurricane = it was devastating
> 2 rubble and shelter = they are clearing rubble and providing shelter
> 3 an opportunity = some politicians say this is an opportunity to rebuild the city
> 4 fishing villages and the tsunami = they were largely replaced by hotels and tourism after the tsunami
> 5 Chicago = after the fire in the 19th century the city was rebuilt and a lot of people died in the reconstruction

Step 3 Ask students to look at the questions in exercise D and think about how they would answer them. Check they understand *heritage*. Then put them in pairs or threes to discuss their ideas. Conduct brief feedback.

SPEAKING

Aim
To extend the topic and give fluency practice.

Step 1 Tell students they are going to discuss ways of improving a city with problems. Read out the introduction, or ask students to read it. Check they understand *regeneration grant* = money from the government to help with improvements or rebuilding.

Step 2 Ask students to look at the list of items in A and think about how they would order them, according to importance or priority, and how much of the money they would allocate to each and why. Then put them in small groups to discuss their ideas. They should try to reach an agreement about how to spend the money. Monitor and make notes on their language use, especially target vocabulary, for a correction slot at the end.

Step 3 Ask each group to join another group to try to agree on one proposal between them. Ask the large groups to take turns to present their proposal to the rest of the class. Ask them to vote for the best proposal at the end. Finish with a correction slot.

Step 4 Put students in new pairs and ask them to discuss what they'd spend the money on if it was for their town / city. Conduct brief feedback.

pp. 12–13

READING

Aim
To familiarise students with academic texts and give practice in predicting, reading for detail and guessing meaning from context.

01 CITIES 11

01 CITIES

Step 1 Tell students they are going to read an academic text about urban myths. Check they understand *urban myth* and *academic text*. Then put students in pairs to discuss the questions in exercise A.

Step 2 Ask students to read the text and answer the questions in B. Tell them not to worry about the words in bold for the moment. Check in pairs, then as a group.

> **Answers**
> 1 Folklore is defined as stories which are often repeated many times and often gradually change or become more exaggerated with each re-telling.
> 2 Urban myths can be analysed structurally or from a literary point of view, culturally or psychologically.
> 3 Urban myths are usually about crime, accidents or death.
> 4 We create these stories to help us deal with our fear and anxieties about the world.
> 5 Popular myths spread quickly because of boredom, or because people want to express their anxieties, get attention, harm others or make small talk / entertain.

Step 3 Put students in pairs to discuss the meanings of the verbs in bold in the text. Then ask them to match each of the verbs with the sets of nouns in C. Check as a group.

> **Answers**
> 1 *offer* = give, provide
> 2 *undergo* = experience
> 3 *voice* = express
> 4 *explores* = analyses
> 5 *spread* = disseminate
> 6 *remains* = is still
> 7 *decode* = interpret
> 8 *emerge* = come out of

Step 4 Ask students, in the same pairs, to try to remember which word or phrase went with each of the verbs in bold in the text. Then ask them to look again at the text to check.

> **Answers**
> 1 remains meaningful
> 2 undergo variations
> 3 decode the meanings
> 4 explores historical, social and economic contexts
> 5 spread stories
> 6 emerge from deep rooted fears
> 7 offer lessons
> 8 voice personal worries

LANGUAGE PATTERNS

Aim
To draw attention to patterns using the phrase *out of*.

Step 1 Ask students to read the examples in the box and check they understand. Ask them to translate into their own language and notice any similarities / differences. In a monolingual class, ask students to compare their translation. In a multilingual class, ask students to work in pairs and tell each other if the sentences were easy to translate.

Step 2 Then ask them to close their books and translate the sentences back into their own language. At the end, they should open their books again and compare their translations with the original sentences. Ask them to discuss in pairs who had the least mistakes. What mistakes did they make? Why?

Alternatively If you prefer not to use translation, ask students to look at the sentences and tell you what pattern they notice: = *out of* meaning *because of* or *resulting from*. Try to elicit a few more examples.

LISTENING

Aim
To extend the topic of urban myths and give practice in listening and note-taking.

Step 1 Tell students they are going to hear three individuals talk about urban myths (without the end of each story) from their countries. Ask them to listen and take notes on what happened in each story. Play the recording.

Step 2 Put students in pairs and ask them to compare their ideas. They should try to use the words in exercise B to help them. Check with the whole group. If they have problems, play the recording again.

> ♪ 1.3
> **Speaker 1**
> A very terrible thing happened to a woman I used to work with. One day, she woke up and found her car had been stolen from outside her house, so she called the police and reported it, but when she got back home from the office that night, the car had been returned just in the driveway. It'd been completely cleaned and there was a note on the driver's seat apologising for taking it. Whoever had written the note said that his mum had been taken ill and he'd had to drive her to hospital. Next to the note there were a couple of tickets for a concert the following day. The woman, she was really thrilled you know – so happy – her car back, two free tickets – fantastic, so she called a friend and they both went to the concert and had a really fantastic time. Once she got home, though ...
>
> **Speaker 2**
> Someone told me a story about a guy from Tokyo who'd gone on a golfing holiday. On the third or fourth day, he suddenly collapsed and had to be rushed to hospital for treatment. Eventually, they diagnosed him as having been poisoned and they reported the incident to the police. The detective in charge of the case questioned the man, but he couldn't think of any reason why anybody would want to poison him. It was something really silly in the end. They worked out ...

12 OUTCOMES

> **Speaker 3**
> This mad thing happened to a guy that a friend of my brother's knows. Apparently, one day, he went to a supermarket to buy a few bits and pieces and as he was looking for the bread, he noticed this elderly woman just staring at him with these desperately sad eyes. He turned away, grabbed a loaf and went off in search of some milk. Once he'd found the milk, he turned round only to see the same woman there again – still just staring like mad at him. Anyway, he was getting a bit freaked out by this – as you would – so he rushed off to pay, but then he remembered that he'd had run out of toilet paper and so he went back to get some. When he got back to the cashier, there was the old woman again – in front of him in the queue and her trolley was almost full to the brim. This time she turns to him and she says: 'I'm really sorry for staring, but the thing is, you're the spitting image of my son who died last year.' She's wiping her eyes getting all tearful and she says: 'You've got the same eyes, the same hair. It's incredible.' As she was packing all her stuff away, she whispered to the guy and said: 'Could you do me a tiny little favour? Could you just say 'Goodbye Mum' when I leave? It'd mean the world to me' Well, what was he going to do? This little old lady and her tragic story trying to hold back the tears – so as she's leaving the store, struggling with all her shopping, he shouts out 'Goodbye Mum.'
>
> He felt like he'd done his good deed for the day, but then ...

Step 3 Ask students, in the same pairs, to discuss how they think each story ends. Then play the last part of each story for them to check. In the same pairs ask them to explain the stories to each other. Conduct brief feedback.

♪ 1.4

> **Speaker 1**
> Once she got home, though, she discovered she'd been burgled and all her valuables had been stolen. Then to top that, about a week later, the police called and told her that her car had been used as the vehicle to get away from a major bank robbery on the day that it had gone missing. That is so unlucky, no?
>
> **Speaker 2**
> It was something really silly in the end. They worked out that the man had actually poisoned himself by accident. Apparently, when he was playing golf he used to hold the tee – that plastic thing you put the golf ball on – between his teeth as he was walking round between the holes, but the golf course had been sprayed with pesticide, so he was basically just sucking in toxic pesticide.

> **Speaker 3**
> He felt like he'd done his good deed for the day, but then the cashier told him his bill was like 300 pounds. He said there must've been a mistake as he'd only bought a few things, but then the cashier explained things. She said, 'Yes, I know, but your mother said you'd pay for all of her shopping as well!'

Step 4 Put students in small groups to discuss the questions in exercise E. Conduct brief feedback.

VOCABULARY Binomials

Aim
To introduce / consolidate binomials (phrases consisting of noun + *and* / *or* + noun).

Step 1 Start by eliciting some binomials using prompts e.g. *fish and...?(chips), day and...? (night) do or....? (die)* etc. Ask for a definition of binomials. Then read out the explanation box.

Step 2 Put students in pairs. Ask them to check they understand the phrases in A and to identify the four which are in the wrong order. Check with the whole group.

> **Answers**
> 1 give or take, here and there, sick and tired, peace and quiet

Step 3 Ask students to look at the sentences in B and complete them with the correct phrase from A. Check in pairs, then check with the whole group.

> **Answers**
> 1 on and off
> 2 by and large
> 3 now and then
> 4 peace and quiet
> 5 long and hard
> 6 here and there
> 7 sick and tired
> 8 give or take

SPEAKING

Aim
To round off the unit and give fluency practice.

Step 1 Tell students they are going to tell each other urban myths. Put them in small groups and ask them to look at the pictures, each of which is from a famous urban myth. Ask them to discuss what they think happens in each story. Conduct brief feedback

Step 2 Ask students to individually choose one of the stories in exercise B or one they already know, and prepare to tell it. They could make a few notes if they wish. Then put students back in the same groups to take turns telling their stories. Conduct brief feedback by asking each group to tell the rest of the class which was the best / funniest / most surprising etc. story they heard.

02 CULTURE AND IDENTITY

UNIT OVERVIEW
In this unit students practise **talking about aspects of culture and society** and **their own personal and national identity, expressing opinions more forcefully, disagreeing politely** and **naming and describing useful objects**. They read texts about **foreign objects and national and individual identity**, and they listen to people talking about **society and culture in different countries**, and their feelings about **British culture**. The main grammar aim is the use of **emphatic structures**.

Next class Make photocopies of 2A p. 130.

VOCABULARY Society and culture

Aim
To lead in to the unit and introduce words and phrases commonly used to talk about society and culture.

Step 1 Begin by asking students to come up with one word or phrase to describe how they feel about their own country. Then put then in pairs or threes and ask them to discuss the questions in A. Check they understand *bureaucracy* = rules and regulations often involving a great deal of paperwork. Conduct brief feedback.

Tip In a multilingual group, try to mix the nationalities as much as possible for this – and similar – discussions.

Step 2 Ask students to match each of the sentences in B with one of the categories in A. Check in pairs. Then check with the whole group. Concept check all the words / phrases in bold by asking for other examples.

Answers
1 family / community life
2 religion
3 bureaucracy
4 crime
5 climate
6 crime
7 religion
8 bureaucracy
9 climate
10 cultural life
11 family / community life
12 cultural life

Step 3 Ask students which of the sentences in B describe positive things and which negative, and why they think this. Ask them what might be the causes and results of each scenario. Tell them there are not necessarily right and wrong answers and try to get some discussion going by eliciting examples from their own experience.

Answers
1 could be positive or negative
2 could be positive or negative
3 positive
4 positive
5 positive
6 negative
7 positive
8 negative
9 negative
10 positive
11 negative
12 negative

LISTENING

Aim
To give practice in listening and taking notes on the main ideas, and listening for specific information.

Step 1 Tell students they are going to hear two conversations about society and culture in two different places. Ask them to take notes on the main points about each place as they listen. Play the recording, then put students in pairs to compare their ideas. Conduct brief feedback.

🔊 **2.1**
Conversation 1
A = woman, B = man
A: So how long were you there for?
B: Just under a month, so long enough to get a feel for the place.
A: I really admire the fact you went there. It must've been fascinating, but also very challenging, I'd imagine.
B: Challenging in what way?
A: Well, I mean, it's a very male-dominated society, isn't it?
B: I don't know about that. It may have that reputation, but that wasn't really my experience of the place.
A: No?
B: No, not really. I mean, it's all very close-knit, but I didn't feel women there were any worse off than in many other places. In fact, the family we stayed with, the wife seemed to more or less run the show, to be honest.

14 OUTCOMES

A: Oh, OK. That's interesting. And how was the traffic? Do people really drive as badly as the stereotype has it?

B: Well, they're not the best drivers in the world, it must be said, and it does get quite congested, but to be honest, it wasn't that that really bothered me. It was more just the total lack of any decent public transport. There's no tube or anything and the buses were always so crowded that you end up driving yourself and then you become another part of the problem.

Conversation 2
C = man, D = woman

C: One thing that's surprised me here is the music scene. I've been to some amazing gigs – and people seem to really go for it! They're usually so formal and polite, but put them in front of a live band and they go absolutely crazy.

D: I know. Actually, I think the arts scene in general seems to be thriving. There are some great young film directors coming up as well.

C: Yeah, yeah. What amazed me was how much they get away with. I'd expected a lot more state control, because you hear about all the censorship before you arrive, but some of the topics they tackle are very politically sensitive.

D: Absolutely. I saw a film the other week that was basically dealing with corruption and the fact that people are always having to pay bribes.

C: Yeah? That sounds pretty close to the bone. Someone was telling me the other day, actually, that one thing making a big difference right now is the fact that the economy is doing so well. It just means there's a bit more money floating around, and so people are happy to invest in new projects, and all that's fuelling this freedom of expression.

Step 2 Ask students to look at the statements in B and decide if they are true or false. Then play the recording again for them to check. Ask them to justify their answers and correct the false sentences.

Answers
Conversation 1
1 F – also accept not given (NG) – she thinks it would be challenging
2 F – it's very close-knit
3 T – that wasn't my experience of the place (that it was a male-dominated society)
4 T – they're not the best drivers in the world
5 F – it wasn't that that bothered me

Conversation 2
6 F – they go absolutely crazy
7 T – the arts scene is thriving
8 F – I'd expected a lot more state control ... some of the topics are very politically sensitive
9 T – a film ... dealing with corruption and ... people always having to pay bribes
10 F – the economy is doing so well

Step 3 Put students in groups to discuss the questions in C. Conduct brief feedback.

Developing conversations
Disagreeing

Aim
To further exploit the listening and identify and practise ways of disagreeing politely.

Step 1 Try to elicit some ways of disagreeing politely as heard in *Listening* or from the students' own ideas. Then read out the explanation and ask them to look at exercise A and put the words in the correct order to form expressions. Then play the recording for them to check. Ask them to practise saying the expressions once they've heard them.

♫ 2.2 and answers
1 I'm not sure about that.
2 Isn't that a bit of an exaggeration?
3 I wouldn't go that far.
4 That's a bit over the top, isn't it?
5 Well, that's one way of looking at things.
6 That's a bit of an overstatement, isn't it?
7 I don't really see it like that myself.

Step 2 Put students in pairs and ask them to take turns giving the opinions in exercise C and responding, using one of the expressions from exercise A. Tell them to extend the conversation by explaining why they disagree. You could model with a strong student and in open pairs first. Check a few examples in open pairs at the end.

Grammar Emphatic structures

Aim
To introduce ways of expressing opinions more emphatically or showing that we have a different opinion.

Step 1 Read out the explanation and try to elicit more examples from students. Then ask them to look at the audioscript on page 161 and find an example of each of the three emphatic structures.

Answers
One thing that's surprised me here is the music scene.
What amazed me was how much they get away with.
One thing making a big difference right now is the economy doing so well.

Step 2 Ask students to look at the prompts in B and write complete sentences. Direct them to the grammar reference on page 137 if they need more help.

02 CULTURE AND IDENTITY 15

02 CULTURE AND IDENTITY

> **Answers**
> 1 The thing that disturbs me is that lack of democracy.
> 2 What worries me the most is the amount of censorship.
> 3 The thing that annoys me is the way the president talks to everyone.
> 4 One thing that drives me mad is the amount of traffic in the city.
> 5 The thing that scares me is the amount of money spent on weapons.
> 6 The thing / One thing that bothers me is the lack of investment in art and culture.
> 7 What concerns me is the power judges have.
> 8 One thing that gives me hope for the future is the fact that young people are so much more tolerant nowadays.

Step 3 Put students in pairs and ask them to check their ideas by taking turns saying their sentences to each other. If they agree with the idea, they should respond by saying *I know* and giving an example. If they disagree, they should say *Really? It's not that that... me. It's...* and explain their own ideas. You could model this with a strong student and in open pairs first. Check a few examples in open pairs at the end.

> 2A see Teacher's notes p. 120.

CONVERSATION PRACTICE

Aim
To give practice in the target language.

Step 1 Tell students they are going to have a conversation about the place they live now. Ask them to individually think about and make some notes on things they like and things which annoy them.

Step 2 Put students in small groups to explain their ideas and agree / disagree as appropriate. Remind them to use expressions from this part of the unit. Monitor and take notes on their use of language for a correction slot at the end.

pp. 16–17

> **Next class** Make photocopies of 2B p. 131.

SPEAKING

Aim
To extend the topic into the connection between household objects and culture, and to lead in to *Reading*.

Step 1 Begin by asking students if they can think of any objects which they associate with different cultures. Then put them in small groups to discuss the questions in A. Conduct brief feedback.

VOCABULARY Household objects

Aim
To introduce / revise objects commonly found in homes and verbs associated with each one.

Step 1 Ask students to look at the box and check they know the words. Put them in pairs to help each other with any words they are not sure about. Remind them they can check in the *Vocabulary builder* pp. 7-8. Concept check the more difficult words with the whole group e.g. *bucket, ladder, nail, pin, drill, needle*, by asking what each one is made of, is used for, etc.

Step 2 Put students in pairs or threes and ask them to decide which verbs in the box in B go with which object in A. There may be more than one possibility.

> **Answers**
> stick in = the oven, the dishwasher, a bucket – *put in* (informal)
> cover = the pan
> unblock = the sink, the toilet
> spread = glue
> thread = a needle
> knot = string
> heat = the pan, the oven
> flush = the toilet
> climb = up a ladder
> hit = a nail
> load = the dishwasher
> run = the tap
> cut = string, cloth
> turn off = the tap, the dishwasher, the oven
> plug in = a drill, the dishwasher
> wring out = a cloth

Step 3 Put students in pairs and ask them to 'test' each other by choosing one of the verb + noun phrases and either drawing or miming it. Their partner should guess the phrase. Then swap.

Step 4 Ask students to look at the pairs of objects in exercise D and decide what the difference is between them. Check in pairs then check with the whole group.

> **Answers**
> *rope* is thicker/ stronger than *string*
> *wire* is thinner than *cable*
> *cloth* is made of fabric and is thinner than a *sponge*
> a *bucket* is larger than a *bowl* and is used for cleaning / outdoors, you eat out of a bowl
> a *hammer* bangs nails into the wall and a *drill* makes small circular holes to put screws into
> a *mop* is used with water on the floor, a *brush* is used to sweep

16 OUTCOMES

02 CULTURE AND IDENTITY

> a *nail* is used with a hammer, a *screw* with a drill
> a *ladder* is something you can move around to climb on, *stairs* are permanent
> a *knee pad* is hard and protects your knee, a *bandage* is soft, used on wounds
> *soap* is usually small and hard, used for washing your hands, face etc. *washing up liquid* is used for washing the dishes

Step 5 Ask students to look at the list of items in E and decide whether they are problems or solutions. Check with the whole group. Ask them when these things might happen or when you might do these things.

> **Answers**
> *spill some water* – problem
> *rip your jeans* – problem (unless you do it deliberately!)
> *soak your jeans* – solution
> *stain a shirt* – problem
> *mend your shirt* – solution
> *protect yourself* – solution
> *sweep the floor* – solution
> *drop my glass* – problem
> *rinse my glass* – solution
> *wipe the table* – solution

Step 6 Put students in small groups. They should practise 'problems and solutions'. One student should think of an object they want, and give their partners a prompt e.g. *I've spilt my drink* or *I need to wipe the table*. Others should offer a suitable object e.g. *Would you like a cloth?* or *Shall I get you a mop and bucket?* until one student guesses the object correctly. Then they have a turn. Monitor and note down any mistakes in the target vocabulary, for a correction slot at the end.

> 2B see Teacher's notes p. 120.

READING

Aim
To give practice in reading for gist and for specific information, and in responding to text.

Step 1 Ask students to look at the title, *Foreign objects*, and guess what the text is about. Check they understand: *take something (or someone) for granted*. Direct them to the *Native Speaker English* box – it would make sense to use it at this stage in the lesson; *bemusement* = a feeling of slight confusion or puzzlement, not fully understanding something.

Step 2 Ask students to quickly read the introduction. Then put them in small groups to discuss the questions in A.

Step 3 Ask students to read the rest of the text and decide on the answers to the questions in B. Put them in pairs or threes to compare their ideas.

Tip In a multilingual class, it would be good to mix up the nationalities as much as possible here.

Step 4 Ask students to read the text again and answer the questions in C. Check in pairs, then check with the whole group.

> **Answers**
> 1 In-Ha = about not having a mixer tap
> 2 Ed = the rice cooker
> 3 Bob = with the waitresses
> 4 Maggie = to drinking *mate*
> 5 Sheila = drinking *mate*
> 6 Ed = no oven and a large meat cleaver in his flat
> 7 Ed = not having a cooker
> 8 Maggie = of her schooldays
> 9 Bob = with his friend about German toilets

Step 5 Round off this part of the lesson by asking students to look at the questions in D. Give them a moment to think about what they want to say. Then put them in groups to discuss. Conduct brief feedback.

NATIVE SPEAKER ENGLISH
take for granted

Read out the explanation in the box and check students understand. Ask them for examples of things we take for granted.

LANGUAGE PATTERNS

Aim
To draw students' attention to comparative structures with adverbs of degree.

Step 1 Ask students to read the examples in the box and check they understand. Ask them to translate into their own language and notice any similarities / differences. In a monolingual class, ask students to compare their translation. In a multilingual class, ask students to work in pairs and tell each other if the sentences were easy to translate.

Step 2 Then ask them to close their books and translate the sentences back into their own language. At the end, they should open their books again and compare their translations with the original sentences. Ask them to discuss in pairs who had the least mistakes. What mistakes did they make? Why?

Alternatively If you prefer not to use translation, ask students to look at the sentences and tell you what patterns they notice – comparative structures with *as ... as* or adjective + *er... than*, with an adverb or expression of degree.

> pp. 18–19

02 CULTURE AND IDENTITY

SPEAKING

Aim
To extend the topic and lead in to *Listening*.

Step 1 Ask students to think about how they would answer the questions in A. Put them in small groups to discuss the questions. Conduct brief feedback.

Alternatively As there is quite a heavy information load here, it might be useful to get students to do some research – either before the class or during it, if you have access to computers. You could 'jigsaw' the task, by asking each student to find out about 1–3 of the items, depending on numbers. They could then report back to the class.

> **Suggested Answers**
> How things are connected to British culture:
> *God Save the Queen* – national anthem
> *fish and chips* – typical 'British' food
> *curry* – most popular food in Britain
> *kilts* – Scottish people wear them
> *the Costa del Sol in Spain* – very popular holiday destination for Britons
> *ballet* – classical dance form that is still highly regarded in UK
> *hip-hop* – popular contemporary dance / music / culture / fashion, from the 1980s in UK
> *football* – very popular sport in UK
> *bowler hats* – old fashioned hats men used to wear in UK
> *Shakespeare* – very famous British writer, born in Stratford-on-Avon
> *Islam* – fastest growing religion in the UK
> *punk* – music / fashion / culture rebelling against authority, which emerged in UK in 1970s
> *cricket* – 'traditional' British sport
> *Harrods* – world-famous luxury department store in London
> *car boot sales* – popular, informal, form of market where people come together to sell their old things, mainly household / garden items and clothes
> *St George's Day* – day to celebrate England's national saint – not a public holiday
> *Easter* – one of the major Christian festivals of the year
> *Jamaica* – Jamaican population celebrates once a year at the Notting Hill Carnival in London

LISTENING

Aim
To give practice in listening for specific information and responding to text.

Step 1 Tell students they are going to hear three people talking about their feelings about British culture. Ask them to look at the box in *Speaking* and tick the things the speakers mention. They should also take brief notes on what they say about them.

> **Answers**
> 1 Vaughan: God save the Queen, St George's Day – he is Welsh and not English and prefers to be thought of as a republican i.e. is not keen on God Save The Queen or St George's Day.
> 2 Amir: fish and chips, Islam (Muslim), cricket, Costa del Sol – he is Muslim but runs a fish and chip shop. He sees himself as British but still supports Pakistan in the cricket (just as Brits on the Costa del Sol would support England in a football match against Spain).
> 3 Emily: bowler hats, Harrods, Shakespeare, curry, hip-hop – some people believe all English people wear bowler hats, shop at Harrods and recite Shakespeare, but in fact they might be into curry or hip-hop – everyone has their own idea of what British culture means.

> 🎧 2.3
> **Vaughan**
> What bugs me is the way people use British and English interchangeably. Wales is a separate country, with a distinct cultural heritage and language to the English. In fact, sometimes I think the English are jealous because they haven't maintained their own cultural traditions like us or the Scots. I mean, not many people celebrate St George's Day in England. I'd personally like the Welsh to gain even more autonomy from the UK. That's not because I'm very nationalistic or consider myself super-Welsh, because I'm not. I don't actually speak Welsh that well. Nor am I a big fan of flag-waving because I think that can lead to narrow-mindedness and can breed racism. No, I want independence for political reasons. Traditionally, the Welsh have been more left-wing but that's not really reflected in the British government. Also, I don't understand why we still have royalty. The only God Save The Queen I'll sing along to is an old anti-royalist punk song! In some ways, I'd like to be seen as a republican and citizen of the world first, then European, and Welsh, or even British – but never English!
>
> **Amir**
> I guess some people don't expect to see someone like me running a fish and chip shop, but for 99% of my customers, it's just not an issue. I was born here and my parents were born here and I'm as British as anyone else. I just happen to be Muslim as well, that's all. It's no big thing. I do get the occasional comment about it, but it doesn't bother me.
>
> The only time I ever feel vaguely conflicted about my identity is when England play Pakistan at cricket. I can't help it, but I always want Pakistan to do well. There's always a bit of banter about that with the local lads, but as I always say, I'm sure most English blokes living on the Costa del Sol still support England if they ever play Spain at football. It's human nature, isn't it?

18 OUTCOMES

02 CULTURE AND IDENTITY

Emily
Last week I went to a ceremony where a friend of mine, Nyasha, gained British citizenship. She's originally from Zimbabwe and came here as a refugee, so it was a big day for her. To become a British national, she had to pass a test, which meant learning things most British people don't even know about – like the year that eighteen-year-olds first got the vote!

I have to say, the more I thought about it, the harder it became to really say what being British means to me. You meet some foreigners who still believe we all wear bowler hats and shop at Harrods and can recite Shakespeare, and others who stereotype us as all being madly into football, drinking too much lager and eating curry or kebabs, but apart from liking curry I don't fit into either group!! I'm more into car boot sales and baking cakes. For my son it'd be hip-hop. I don't know ... I think everyone has their own idea of what British culture really means. For my son it'd be hip hop! It's a very personal thing.

Step 2 Ask students to look at the list in B and decide which speaker each one refers to. Play the recording again for them to check.

Answers
1 Vaughan   4 Emily
2 Emily   5 Amir
3 Amir   6 Vaughan

Step 3 Put students in pairs or threes and ask them to discuss the questions in C. Conduct brief feedback.

VOCABULARY Expressions with *thing*

Aim
To focus on expressions with *thing*.

Step 1 Read out the explanation in the box. Then ask students to look at the sentences in A and translate them into their own language, and notice any differences.

Alternatively If you prefer not to use translation, put students in pairs and ask them to think of a definition or another way of saying the phrases in italics. Check with the whole group and ask students to think of examples for each one.

Answers
1 It's no big thing – also *it's no big deal* – it's not very important
2 It's not the done thing – it's not appropriate behaviour
3 chance would be a fine thing – I would have to be very lucky to be able to do that
4 It's the furthest thing from my mind at the moment – I'm not even thinking about it
5 first thing in the morning – early, when I first wake up
6 It's the sort of thing – it's something
7 what with one thing and another – taking in to account a number of factors
8 just one thing led to another (often without *just*) – events naturally followed each other, were not planned

Step 2 Put students in pairs and ask them to discuss what 'it' could be in each case in A. Conduct brief feedback.

READING

Aim
To give practice in reading academic texts to identify the main ideas and summarise.

Step 1 Ask students to read the statements in A. Check they understand: *sociology, conflicted, diverse, founded on negatives*. Ask them to think about how far they agree with each of the statements. Then put them in small groups to discuss their ideas.

Step 2 Ask them to read the text and choose the four statements from A which best summarise what the writer says. Check in pairs then check with the whole group.

Answers
3, 4, 7, 8

Step 3 Ask students to individually write two or three sentences summarising the main ideas of the article. Then put them in small groups to compare their summaries and decide if they agree with the article or not, and why. Conduct brief feedback.

SPEAKING

Aim
To give fluency practice and round off the unit.

Step 1 Put students in groups of three and ask them to choose only one of the speaking activities in exercise A. Then ask them to work individually to prepare for the activity. They should each make their own list.

Step 2 When they are ready ask them to come together in their groups and present their lists to each other. They should comment or ask questions to find out more. Conduct brief feedback at the end.

Alternatively You could ask each group to decide on a joint list and present this to the rest of the class.

03 RELATIONSHIPS

UNIT OVERVIEW
In this unit students practise **talking about people they know** and **giving impressions of people they don't know well, expressing opinions more tentatively, sharing and talking through problems** and **discussing issues around divorce**. They read a text about **divorce,** and they listen to people talking about **other people and relationships**. The main grammar aim is different uses of **would**.

Speaking

Aim
To lead in to the topic and give personalised fluency practice.

Step 1 Lead in by telling students how you would describe yourself and how you think other people might describe you. Then ask students to work individually and list words that they feel describe their personality.

Step 2 Put students in pairs or small groups and ask them to compare their ideas. Then ask them to discuss the questions in B. If the class know each other well, they could ask their partner(s) if they see them as they expect or in different ways. Conduct brief feedback.

Vocabulary Describing people

Aim
To focus on adjectives – including compound adjectives – commonly used to describe people.

Step 1 Begin by asking students for some of the adjectives they used or heard in *Speaking*. Then put them in pairs or threes and ask them to look at the adjectives in exercise A and discuss whether they think they are usually positive or negative and why. Conduct brief feedback and concept check the words by asking for examples of this kind of behaviour.

Answers
in<u>com</u>petent = negative
<u>direct</u> = could be either depending on context / how it's said
a snob (not an adjective-adjective = <u>snob</u>bish) = negative
absent-<u>minded</u> = negative
quite hard work = negative
<u>bitch</u>y = negative
laid-<u>back</u> = positive (usually)
<u>principled</u> = positive
strong-<u>willed</u> = negative (usually)
thick-<u>skinned</u> = positive (usually)

Step 2 Ask students to match each of the sentences in exercise B with one of the words in exercise A. Check in pairs. Then check with the whole group.

Answers				
a 4	b 9	c 7	d 5	e 8
f 3	g 10	h 1	i 2	j 6

Step 3 Ask students to work in pairs and take turns to 'test' each other. Student A should close their books while B prompts them with any of the sentences a–j to try to elicit the correct descriptions in 1–10. Then swap.

Step 4 Put students in small groups to discuss the questions in D. Conduct brief feedback.

Listening

Aim
To give practice in listening for gist and specific information and listening intensively.

Step 1 Tell students they are going to hear three conversations about other people. Ask them to answer the questions in exercise A as they listen. Play the recording, then put students in pairs to compare their ideas. Conduct brief feedback.

Answers
Conversation 1
A colleague – incompetent, defensive, arrogant, full of himself, blames other people

Conversation 2
A famous musician – principled, decent, hardworking or fake, exploitative (depending on point of view)

Conversation 3
New neighbours – in a student house – guy next door – quiet (keeps himself to himself); girl – nice, bright, chatty but selfish; guy – pleasant but lazy (a slacker) and laid-back

20 OUTCOMES

🔊 **3.1**
Conversation 1
A = man, B = woman

A: So how's it all going? Any better?
B: I'd say things are worse if anything, to be honest. He doesn't seem to have a clue how the department should work or what's expected of him – and he's dragging the rest of the team down with him. I've tried to talk to him about it, but he always just gets really defensive and puts up this great big barrier. What really drives me mad, though, is the man's arrogance. He's so full of himself! He's one of those people who'll just never accept they've done anything wrong. He just blames it all on everyone else.
A: Sounds like an idiot to me! Maybe you need to go over his head and talk to someone else about it.
B: I would do, but our line manager isn't very approachable. And even when you do get to talk to him, he's not exactly the best listener in the world.

Conversation 2
C = woman, D = man

C: I can't stand him.
D: Really? I've always thought he comes across as a really decent guy.
C: You're joking, aren't you? He's so fake!
D: Do you think so? In what way?
C: All that rubbish about saving the world and helping the starving millions that he's always going on about.
D: What's wrong with that? I quite admire the fact he's prepared to stand up for what he believes in. He doesn't have to do all that charity work, does he? He could just keep his mouth shut and keep his millions and carry on making music.
C: Yeah, but it's all just self-promotion, really, isn't it? It's just to sell more CDs. If he was really bothered, he'd give all his money away and really help people. He just likes to be seen to be doing good.
D: I just think you've got him wrong. He's done a lot to raise awareness of various different causes and he works really hard to make a difference. You're just a cynic.
C: And you're just naive!

Conversation 3
E = man, F = woman

E: So what're they like? Are you getting on OK with them all?
F: Yeah, more or less. I haven't really seen much of the guy next door. I've passed him once or twice in the corridor, but he keeps himself to himself, really.
E: OK.
F: But the girl opposite is great. She seems really nice and bright and chatty. We hit it off straightaway.
E: That's good, then.
F: The only problem is she kind of hogs the bathroom. I mean, she's in there for hours every morning, doing her hair and her make-up. It's really annoying because we've only got the one bathroom.

E: Oh no! Really? That'd drive me mad, that would!
F: And the other guy, in the little room upstairs, seems pleasant enough, but he strikes me as a bit of a slacker. I mean, he's not working at the moment and he just seems ... well ... extremely laid-back about it.
E: To the point of horizontal, then, eh?

Step 2 Put students in pairs and ask them to look at the sentences in B and try to complete them with words / phrases (including phrasal verbs) from the recording. Then play the recording again for them to check.

Answers
1 a dragging	b gets, puts up	c go over
2 a comes across	b got	c raise
3 a hit (it) off	b hogs	c strikes

Step 3 Put students in groups to tell each other if the people described remind them of anyone they know. How?

LANGUAGE PATTERNS

Aim
To draw students' attention to patterns with *one of those people*.

Step 1 Ask students to read the examples in the box and check they understand. Ask them to translate into their own language and notice any similarities / differences. In a monolingual class, ask students to compare their translation. In a multilingual class, ask students to work in pairs and tell each other if the sentences were easy to translate.

Step 2 Then ask them to close their books and translate the sentences back into their own language. At the end, they should open their books again and compare their translations with the original sentences. Ask them to discuss in pairs who had the least mistakes. What mistakes did they make? Why?

Alternatively If you prefer not to use translation, ask students to look at the sentences and tell you what patterns they notice – patterns with *one of those people who* ... to describe someone in an informal, chatty way. Elicit a few more examples.

DEVELOPING CONVERSATIONS

Giving your impression

Aim
To practise ways of giving our impression about people.

Step 1 Try to elicit some ways of giving your impression of someone you don't know, as heard in *Listening* or from the students' own ideas. Then read out the explanation and elicit a few more examples by prompting students with the names of famous people.

03 RELATIONSHIPS

Step 2 Put students in pairs and ask them to think of five well-known people (in the public eye) and to then individually note down their impressions of them.

Step 3 Ask students to practise the target language by having conversations in their pairs. They should take turns to begin by asking *So what do you think of…?* or *What do you make of…?* or *What's your impression of…?* Conduct brief feedback.

GRAMMAR *would 1*

Aim
To introduce and practise different uses of *would* when expressing opinions.

Step 1 Read out the explanation and try to elicit more examples of tentative uses of *would*. Then ask students to look at the sentences in A and rewrite them, using the words in brackets to make them more direct. Do the first example with them. Check in pairs, then check with the whole group.

> **Answers**
> 1 They'll probably buy a new one.
> 2 It should arrive some time next week.
> 3 I think it was your own fault, to be honest.
> 4 I couldn't agree more with you on that.
> 5 Surely most people can see through the marketing.
> 6 It can't have been that hard to organise.

Step 2 Ask students to divide the sentences in B into four groups, depending on the use of *would* in each one. Then put them in pairs to compare and explain their ideas. Direct them to the grammar reference on page 138 if they have problems.

> **Answers**
> 1, 4 – requests (though 4 is a very sarcastic one); 2, 8 – to talk about past habits; 3, 5 – conditionals (second and third); 6, 7 – future in the past

CONVERSATION PRACTICE

Aim
To personalise the topic, give fluency practice and round off this part of the unit.

Step 1 Ask students to work on their own and, on a piece of paper, write the names of someone: they find a bit annoying; they don't get on well with; they get on really well with; quite unusual or eccentric; they admire. Check students understand *eccentric* = strange in an unusual and often interesting way.

Step 2 Put students in pairs and ask them to swap pieces of paper and ask and explain about the people on their lists. Conduct brief feedback.

---

pp. 22–23

> **Next class** Make photocopies of 3A p. 132.

VOCABULARY Divorce

Aim
To introduce / revise words and phrases used in the context of divorce.

Step 1 Ask students to look at the sentences and check they understand the words in bold. Put them in pairs to help each other with any words they are not sure about. Concept check the more difficult ones with the whole group.

> **Answers**
> pre-<u>nup</u>tial agreement = a legal contract signed before a wedding, usually about money
> <u>file</u> for di<u>vorce</u> = instruct a lawyer that you wish to divorce
> <u>cus</u>tody battle = fight about who the children will live with
> acri<u>mo</u>nious divorce = unfriendly, bitter
> <u>am</u>icable divorce = friendly, civilised
> go <u>through</u> (in this context) = become legal
> pay <u>main</u>tenance = money for childcare
> <u>grounds</u> for di<u>vorce</u> = legal reasons for divorce

Step 2 Put students in pairs or threes to discuss the questions in A. Conduct brief feedback.

READING

Aim
To give practice in reading for gist and for specific information and to respond to text.

Step 1 Tell students they are going to read an article about the history of divorce. Ask them to look at the items in A and note down why the writer mentions them as they read.

Step 2 Ask students to work in pairs. They should cover the article and look again at the items in A and try to remember what the author said about them. Conduct brief feedback.

> **Answers**
> 1 Sweden, Finland and Belarus = slightly more than one in two marriages there end in divorce
> 2 celebrity divorces and custody battles = these are often in the news nowadays
> 3 Mesopotamia, The Greek Empire and Cairo = these were examples of where divorces took place a long time ago
> 4 Emperor Charles V = he was the uncle of Catherine of Aragon, who was divorced by Henry the eighth
> 5 The Church of England = this was founded because of Henry and Catherine's divorce (which was not accepted by the Church of Rome)
> 6 1857 = the first time ordinary people in Britain were allowed to file for divorce

22 OUTCOMES

03 RELATIONSHIPS

7 TV, junk food, and Facebook have all been cited (given) as grounds for divorce

8 a heated argument at a wedding reception = this argument about cutting the cake ended in an annulment (similar to divorce) at a Polish wedding

Step 3 Ask students to look at the sentence starters in C and complete them individually. Then put them in pairs or threes to compare their responses to the article.

Step 4 Ask students to read the text again and underline the words which collocate with the words in bold. Check in pairs, then check with the whole group. Try to elicit other words that these items could collocate with.

Answers
share this dubious distinction; against a backdrop of ...; chronically high divorce rates; a male heir to the throne; divorces ... sanctioned by the Pope; comply with someone's wishes; cover a multitude of sins; follow such trends

Step 5 Ask students to look at the text again and find other words or phrases that collocate with *divorce*. Check in pairs. Then check with the whole group.

Answers
high-profile celebrity divorces; divorce was commonplace; to grant him his divorce; to file for divorce; .... divorces are instigated by women; divorce has now become too easy; divorces failed for ridiculous reasons; divorce cases

Step 6 Ask students to look at the questions in F and think about how they would answer them. Then put them in small groups to discuss their ideas.

GRAMMAR *would 2*

Aim
To introduce the use of *would* in the negative form, to talk about things people refused to do in the past.

Step 1 Read out the box. Check students understand and try to elicit a few more examples. Point out that this is also often used with inanimate objects e.g. *My computer wouldn't do anything this morning.*

Step 2 Ask students to look at the sentences in A and complete them, using *wouldn't* and the base form of one of the verbs in the box. Check in pairs, then check with the whole group. Direct them to the grammar reference on page 138 if you think they need more help.

Answers
1 wouldn't listen
2 wouldn't stop
3 wouldn't come
4 wouldn't let
5 wouldn't even put
6 wouldn't start
7 wouldn't hear
8 wouldn't leave

Step 3 Ask students to think of two things people (or objects!) they know refused to do. Then put them in pairs to tell each other, or ask them to tell the rest of the class.

3A see Teacher's notes p. 121.

pp. 24–25

Next class Make photocopies of 3B p. 133.

SPEAKING

Aim
To give fluency practice and lead in to *Listening*.

Step 1 Begin by eliciting different ways of expressing age e.g. *young, youngish, in her late twenties, forty-something*. Then ask for examples of different kinds of behaviour they associate with different age groups e.g. *tantrums = toddler, blushing = teenager*. Ask them to look at the list and check they understand all the phrases. They could use the *Vocabulary builder* on pp. 10–11 to help them here. Ask them to individually think about what age group (from the box) they associate each one with and why.

Step 2 Put students in pairs or threes and ask them to discuss their ideas. Conduct brief feedback at the end.

Answers
(other answers possible as long as students can justify them)
a toddler = wetting the bed, being very affectionate;
a teenager = feeling very self-conscious, being cheeky and answering back, fancying someone, going off the rails, having no commitments; *a thirty-something* = settling down, establishing a career; *a middle-aged person* = paying off the mortgage, going bald; *a pensioner* = being frail and unsteady on your feet; going into a home, losing your faculties

Step 3 Ask students in the same pairs / threes to discuss other behaviour or events they associate with each age group and which age they think is the best / most difficult and why. Get them to share their ideas at the end.

LISTENING

Aim
To give practice in listening for gist and specific information.

Step 1 Tell students they are going to hear five conversations about different relationships. Ask them to look at the relationships in exercise A and number them in the order in which they hear them being discussed. Check in pairs, then check with the whole group.

03 RELATIONSHIPS 23

03 RELATIONSHIPS

Answers
1 a neighbour
2 teacher and pupil
3 sisters
4 a couple
5 doctor and patient

3.2
Conversation 1
A = woman, B = man
A: It's a bit worrying actually. I haven't seen her around for a bit.
B: How old is she?
A: Well, she must <u>be getting on</u> because she mentioned going to university in the sixties and occupying the Chancellor's Office during a protest!
B: A bit of a radical then.
A: Oh yeah, and she's still very with it – she hasn't lost any of her faculties at all. She's one of these people who's always writing to their MP – calling them to account.
B: Maybe she's away visiting family.
A: I'm not sure she has any to speak of. I know she had a sister but she told me they'd had a major falling-out. I just would've thought she'd have mentioned going away, asked me to water her plants or something.

Conversation 2
C = woman, D = man
C: What's up?
D: It's Connor. He's got another detention. I actually had a phone call this time from Miss Jones.
C: You're joking.
D: She said he's just constantly answering back.
C: I think she just overreacts. I know he has a tendency to be a bit cheeky – let's face it, it's a bit of a family trait wanting to have the last word – but it's just harmless banter really: disagreeing for the sake of it.
D: It didn't sound like it.
C: She's just <u>singling him out</u> for punishment, if you ask me.
D: You should've heard what he said to her. He can be very hostile, you know.
C: He's <u>going through</u> a slightly more rebellious phase – but that's perfectly normal – she should be used to it – and this isn't going to help.
D: We should put our foot down with him or he's going to completely go off the rails.
C: Oh don't exaggerate. It'll all blow over.

Conversation 3
E = woman 1, F = woman 2
E: We've obviously both got a strong competitive streak, but I wouldn't call it sibling rivalry, would you?
F: No, not at all. I think it's all <u>channelled into</u> the tennis. We can both be pretty ruthless with each other. I mean, Sal showed no mercy when she thrashed me in the Open last year, but after the match – well, obviously I was disappointed – in bits, really – but Sal comforted me and once I got over the disappointment, I was really pleased for what she'd achieved – there was no jealousy or anything.
E: That's right. I think it's very much down to the way we were brought up, which was always very much share and share alike, and very loving
F: Absolutely.

Conversation 4
G = man, H = woman
G: Apparently, they were quite close at school, but nothing really <u>came of it</u> and then they just drifted apart and lost touch, as you do, you know, and then suddenly completely out of the blue he got this email and that's how they got back in touch. Like she'd been carrying this flame for him all this time.
H: Aww! That's so sweet.
G: The really amazing thing is that as it turns out she has a couple of kids already from a previous marriage.
H: No!
G: Yeah, but he seems to have taken it all in his stride and it seems to be really working out for them.
H: Oh I'm so delighted for him. He's such a lovely bloke.

Conversation 5
I = woman, J = man
I: I sometimes I feel we're just on a conveyor belt and she's just ticking boxes.
J: I know what you mean.
I: I mean I was feeling really under the weather, but she wouldn't listen, she just dismissed it as a slight bug.
J: I wouldn't <u>put up with it</u> – you should register with someone else. Why don't you try at my place? They're very good there. They're always very sympathetic if I need a sick note or to take time off work.

Step 2 Put students in pairs and ask them to look at the questions in B and try to answer them from memory. Then play the recording again for them to check.

Answers
1a because she hasn't seen her neighbour for a while
1b because she occupied the Chancellor's (at university) during the sixties
2a it's a family trait (characteristic), he's going through a rebellious phase
2b the man says they should be strict with him (*put our foot down*), the woman says they should wait for it to pass (*it'll blow over*)
3a they agree that they are both competitive
3b Sal beat her at tennis – mentioned to show she is not jealous
4a it was sweet that they got back in touch
4b it is amazing that she has been married before and has children
5a because the doctor didn't take her seriously
5b advises she try his doctor because they're always sympathetic

24 OUTCOMES

03 RELATIONSHIPS

Step 3 Ask students to look at the questions in C and think about how they would answer them. Then put them in pairs or small groups to discuss their ideas. Conduct brief feedback.

NATIVE SPEAKER ENGLISH *have a ... streak*

Write on the board the line from the audioscript: *We've both got a strong competitive streak*. Ask students what they think this means and try to elicit a few more examples. Then read out the box and check they understand.

VOCABULARY Phrasal verbs

Aim
To further exploit the *Listening* by focusing on some phrasal verbs from the conversations, including those used as part of an expression.

Step 1 Begin by asking students if they remember any phrasal verbs or expressions from the conversations. They could look at the audioscript on page 162 and find a few. Then read out the explanation and examples in the box.

Step 2 Ask the students to look at all the other underlined phrasal verbs in the audioscript and notice what they collocate with. Put them in pairs to discuss their findings. Check their answers and try to elicit other possible collocations for each.

> **Answers**
> she must be getting on (in age / a bit); single someone out – for punishment; going through – a phase; put our foot down; channelled into tennis; nothing really came of it; they got back in touch; I wouldn't put up with it

Step 3 Ask students to look at the sentences in B and complete them, using a phrasal verb from the conversations. Check in pairs. Then check with the whole group.

> **Answers**
> 1 came of
> 2 getting on
> 3 channelled her energy into
> 4 put up with
> 5 singled you out
> 6 go through

Step 4 Ask students to find six more phrasal verbs from the audioscript on page 162 and think of other examples of how to use them. They could write these down in their vocabulary notebooks. Check in pairs. Then check with the whole group.

> **Answers**
> to see someone around; to be with it; to call someone to account; to answer back; to blow over; to get over; to be down to; to bring up / be brought up; to take something in your stride; to be under the weather

DEVELOPING CONVERSATIONS
What's up?

Aim
To introduce short and natural ways of asking people what is wrong, and responding.

Step 1 Begin by asking students when we use *What's up?* or *What's the matter?* And what kind of answers you might give. Then read out the explanation in the box.

Step 2 Ask students to look at the sentences in A and complete them with a suitable problem. Check with the whole group.

> **Answers**
> 1 weather / rain
> 2 teacher / tutor
> 3 English (or any other subject)
> 4 flatmates / housemates / friends
> 5 ankle
> 6 baby

Step 3 Put students in pairs and get them to practise short conversations. They should begin by asking *What's up?* or *What's the matter?* and answer using their sentences from A.

SPEAKING

Aim
To give fluency practice and round off the unit.

Step 1 Tell students they are going to role-play conversations talking about problems and responding. Divide them into groups of three: A, B and C. As should look at File 2 on page 152, Bs at File 14 on page 157 and Cs at File 17 on page 158. They should choose one of the problems and prepare to talk about it as if it was actually happening to them. They should think about a few details they could add. They could make a few notes. Ask them also to look at the phrases in B which they can use to express sympathy.

Step 2 When they are ready ask them to come together in their groups and take turns. A should ask *What's up / the matter?* B should explain the problem and A and C should express sympathy. Then swap and repeat. When they have finished, they could start again with new problems, or talk about real or invented problems in a similar way. Ask a few groups to act out their conversations for the rest of the class at the end.

> 3B see Teacher's notes p. 121.

04 POLITICS

UNIT OVERVIEW
In this unit students practise **giving opinions about politics, talking about the consequences of political proposals** and **about voting and elections, and describing politicians and their qualities**. They also practise **telling jokes**. They read **texts about the effect of humour on politics** and **about the electoral system in Switzerland**, and they **listen to people telling jokes** and **talking about voting**. The main grammar aim is revision and extension of **conditionals**.

Next class Make photocopies of 4A p. 134.

Developing conversations

Giving opinions

Aim
To give practice in different ways of expressing opinions in the context of politics.

Step 1 Begin by asking students what they think about something current and controversial e.g. smoking in public places. Try to elicit different opinions. Then ask students to look at the sentences in exercise A and identify pairs of sentences with similar meanings. Check answers in pairs. Then check with the whole group.

Optional activity You could ask students to write the pairs on a scale – from strong disagreement to strong agreement, or you could do this on the board (answers included below).

Answers
1–12; 2–5; 3–10; 4–8; 6–9; 7–11
scale from strong disagreement to strong agreement:
3–10, 4–8, 2–5, 6–9, 7–11, 1–12

Tip For extra practice, 'test' students by giving a prompt of one of the sentences. Then ask them to say the equivalent sentence. Pay attention to stress and intonation. Continue this in pairs.

Step 2 Put students in small groups and ask them to discuss the topics in B, using the expressions they learnt in A. Check a few of their ideas at the end.

Listening

Aim
To hear the target language in context and give practice in listening for gist and intensively.

Step 1 Tell students they are going to hear two conversations about topics from *Developing conversations*. Ask them to listen and identify the topic in each case and the speakers' opinions about them. Play the recording.

Answers
Conversation 1: a maximum wage – speaker A thinks there should be a maximum salary for bankers etc. but speaker B thinks this may not be practical, although she agrees in principle

Conversation 2: hosting an international event (the Olympics) – speaker C is against having the Olympics in their city, but speaker D isn't sure because she doesn't know enough about it

4.1
Conversation 1
A: Personally, I'm in favour of curbing the salaries of people like bankers and executives.
B: How would you do that, though?
A: I don't know. I'm sure it's not without problems, but there must be a way. I just find some of these salaries are obscene – especially when they have people in the same company earning peanuts.
B: Hmm. I know what you mean.
A: And it twists everything else, because if they're earning that much, **it encourages other people to ask for more**, and it pushes up prices.
B: Curbing salaries may be OK in principle, but in practice? It's going to be unworkable, isn't it?
A: I don't see why. We have a minimum wage so why not a maximum one?
B: Well how are you going to decide the maximum? And **what would you include in pay**? What if they were given a boat or whatever, instead of money?
A: Well, **they'd just declare it as part of their income** in the normal way, no? And **it could be, say, ten times the lowest wage**.
B: Only ten? **I'm sure they'd be able to find ways round it.** And you don't think it'd discourage people from doing those jobs?

26 OUTCOMES

A: **Some maybe,** but I don't see that as a bad thing. I mean, maybe they'd think about doing other jobs that are more useful. Anyway, I thought you said it was a good idea in theory.
B: I did. I'm just playing devil's advocate. And, as I said, I do have major doubts about how it'd work.
A: Well, personally I think the benefits far outweigh the difficulties.

Conversation 2
C: Did you hear about this proposal to bid to hold the Olympics here?
D: Yeah. You don't sound happy about it.
C: No, absolutely not! I'm totally opposed to it. It's a complete waste of money. Aren't you against it?
D: I'm not sure where I stand really. **Won't the games make a lot of money** if we get them?
C: No. They always talk about them leaving a good legacy and boosting the economy, but it's all rubbish.
D: Really? I can't pass judgment. I don't know enough about it.
C: Have a look on the Internet. Apparently, in Montreal they're still paying taxes on the debt – and they held them in 1976!
D: Really?
C: I tell you, it's lucky we don't have a hope in hell, so **they'll only waste the money on the bid.** Imagine if we actually won it, though! **It'd be a recipe for disaster.** It'd probably bankrupt us

Step 2 Ask students to look at the sentences from the conversations in exercise B, and choose the correct word / phrase. Then play the recording again for them to check. Check answers in pairs. Then check with the group. Concept check by asking for other examples of when to use the words / phrases. Check differences between similar words e.g. *earn* and *make*.

Answers
1 a obscene   b pushes   c declare   d round   e advocate
2 a bid   b make   c legacy   d hell   e recipe

Step 3 Put students in pairs to discus the questions in exercise C. Conduct brief feedback.

GRAMMAR Conditionals 1

Aim
To practise different conditional forms and to contrast likely forms with unlikely forms.

Step 1 Ask students to match a sentence beginning 1–5 with the best ending a–e. Check in pairs. Then check with the whole group. Elicit what forms / tenses are used and the meaning in each case.

Answers
1d zero conditional, both verbs in present simple, to talk about what is always the case
2c first conditional to talk about a future possibility; *could* less definite here than *will*
3b a variation on first conditional with *going to*
4e second conditional to talk about a hypothetical situation; past simple in the *if* clause and *would* + base form in the main clause
5a second conditional for a hypothetical question

Step 2 Read out the explanation box and check students understand. Then ask them to look at the sentences in **bold** in the audioscript on page 163 and answer the questions in exercise B. Direct them to the grammar reference on page 139 if they need help.

Answers
1 a if they're earning that much
  b generally true   c likely
2 a if we had a maximum wage
  b unlikely   c unlikely
3 a if they were given a boat
  b unlikely   c unlikely
4 a if there were a maximum wage
  b unlikely   c likely
5 a if it were 10 times the lowest wage
  b unlikely   c likely
6 a if it were 10 times the lowest wage
  b likely   c likely
7 a if they get the games
  b likely   c likely
8 a if they make the bid
  b likely   c likely
9 a if they won the bid
  b unlikely   c unlikely

4A see Teacher's notes p. 121.

VOCABULARY Consequences

Aim
To introduce / revise verbs commonly found in the context of politics.

Step 1 Ask students to look at the box and complete the sentences in A with the correct verb. Check answers in pairs. Then check with the whole group. Concept check the more difficult ones with the whole group e.g. *compound a problem, trigger an election (or an event), undermine relations (or confidence), curb drug addiction*.

Answers
1 discourage   6 lead
2 compound   7 boost
3 benefit   8 undermine
4 trigger   9 curb
5 devastate   10 bankrupt

04 POLITICS

Step 2 Put students in pairs or threes and ask them to discuss possible conditions which might cause 1–10 in exercise A to happen. Check their ideas as a group.

Step 3 Ask students to rewrite five of the sentences from A using the verbs in C, so that they mean the opposite of the original. Point out that they will need to change more than just the verb.

> **Answers**
> (slight variations are possible).
> a It might encourage people to work.
> b It'll strengthen relations between the two countries.
> c It'll damage the economy and lead to a cut in jobs.
> d It's a good idea. If anything, it'll help to sort out the existing social problems.
> e It'll delay an election and make it later than they wanted.

Conversation practice

Aim
To give further practice in giving and responding to opinions, and conditionals.

Step 1 Tell students they are going to practise conversations similar to the ones they heard in *Listening*. Ask them to work individually and think of two proposals in areas such as health, education, housing, culture, transport etc. Tell them to choose one which they would like to see happen and one they have heard is happening (good or bad). Ask them to make notes on the possible consequences of each.

Step 2 Put students in pairs or small groups and ask them to have conversations, taking turns to begin *Personally, I'm in favour of...* or *Did you hear about this proposal to...?* Tell them to try to develop the conversations as much as possible by using conditional structures and expressing different opinions. Monitor and take notes for a correction slot at the end.

Tip You could ask students to prepare what they are going to say for homework, and conduct the discussion in the following lesson.

pp. 28–29

Vocabulary Politicians

Aim
To focus on nouns and adjectives of character.

Step 1 Begin by asking students what qualities they think a politician needs. Then ask them to look at the qualities in A and rank them in order of importance (1 = most important, 10 = least important) for a politician. Check they understand *charisma*, *ruthlessness*, *the ability to compromise*.

Step 2 Put students in pairs to explain and justify their rankings. Conduct brief feedback with the whole group.

Step 3 Put students in small groups and ask them to look at the adjectives and phrases in C and think of politicians they would describe using them. Conduct brief feedback.

Reading

Aim
To give practice in reading for specific information, and in responding to text.

Step 1 Tell students they are going to read an article about the effect of humour on politics and politicians. Ask them to look at the statements in A and mark them true or false as they read. Tell them to underline or highlight the part of the text that tells them the answer. Check in pairs, then check with the whole group.

Tip Ask them to correct the false statements.

> **Answers**
> 1 F – it means that being called names has no effect
> 2 T – they constantly ridicule all politicians
> 3 T – ...increases already widespread criticism, ... play into the public perception of politics
> 4 T – it's just a silly game and futile
> 5 T – an act of defiance against oppression
> 6 F – it was black humour
> 7 T – ... a release for people living in grim circumstances ...
> 8 F – telling of jokes was severely restricted

Step 2 Ask students to look at the questions in B and think about how they would answer them. Check they understand *satirical* = using humour to criticise something or someone real – often to do with politics. Then put them in pairs or threes to discuss the questions. Conduct brief feedback.

Listening

Aim
To give practice in listening for gist and intensive listening.

Step 1 Tell students they are going to hear three jokes. Ask them to listen and decide which book's argument each joke illustrates – Russell Peterson's or Ben Lewis's. Play the recording.

> **Answers**
> 1 Russell Peterson's
> 2 Russell Peterson's
> 2 Ben Lewis's

28 OUTCOMES

04 POLITICS

🔊 4.2
Joke 1
Two friends are strolling down the road when one turns to the other and asks 'So, what do you think of our president?' The other guy look around 'I can't tell you here. Follow me,' and he sneaks off down a side street. 'Now tell me what you think' he asks again. 'No, not here. It's not safe' and they tip-toe down the stairs of an old block of flats and into the deserted basement. Having checked that there was no-one around, the friend tries a third time: 'So, now you can tell me what you really think about our leader.' The other one glances around nervously 'Well,' he whispers, 'I actually really like him!'

Joke 2
A middle-aged couple have a son who's still living at home with them. They've started getting a bit worried because the boy seems quite unable to decide on a career, so they decide to do a little test. They take a 20-dollar bill, a Bible and a bottle of whisky and leave them on the kitchen table. They then hide, pretending they weren't at home.

The dad's theory was that if his son took the money, it meant he'd become a businessman; if he took the Bible, he'd become a priest and if he went for the whisky, he'd probably end up as a no-good drunk.

So anyway the parents hide away under the stairs and waited expectantly. After a while, the son arrives home and they peer out to watch him. First, he takes the money, holds it up to the light and then slips it into his pocket. Next, he picks up the Bible, flicks through it and then pockets that as well. Finally, he grabs the bottle, opens it and sniffs it, to check it is good quality, before sticking it into his bag. He then happily skips up the stairs to go for a nap.

'Oh no!' the father exclaims. 'Our son is going to be a politician!'

Joke 3
A man is walking down the street muttering to himself, cursing the government and the poverty that's ravaging the country. 'We have no food, no warm water, nothing!'

As it happens, a group of plain-clothes policemen come past in the opposite direction and overhear him. They all suddenly leap on him and drag him down to the station, where they throw him into the interrogation room. They make him sit on a chair and take a gun and fire blanks at him. The man's scared stiff and curls up in fear. The police, seeing him so terrified and, thinking he's learned his lesson, let him go.

As the guy trudges off home, he starts moaning to himself again: 'Stupid country! No food, no warm water. We haven't even got any bullets. Stupid!'

Step 2 Put students in pairs to compare their ideas and to discuss which joke(s) they found amusing and why. Conduct brief feedback.

Step 3 Draw students' attention to the explanation box. Then ask students to look at the lines in C and try to complete them with the correct word or phrase from the recording. Then play the recording again for them to check. Check the words by asking for synonyms or near-synonyms.

> **Answers**
> 1 a strolling
>   b sneaks
>   c tip toe down
>   d glances around, whispers
> 2 a peer
>   b slips
>   c flicks through
>   d grabs, sniffs
>   e skips
> 3 a muttering
>   b leap, drag
>   c curls up

Step 4 In small groups, ask students to take turns to say the sentences in C and act them out at the same time.

LANGUAGE PATTERNS

Aim
To focus on patterns with *unable to* + base form.

Step 1 Ask students to read the examples in the box and check they understand. Ask them to translate the sentences into their own language and notice any similarities / differences. In a monolingual class, ask students to compare their translation. In a multilingual class, ask students to work in pairs and tell each other if the sentences were easy to translate.

Step 2 Then ask them to close their books and translate the sentences back into their own language. At the end, they should open their books again and compare their translations with the original sentences. Ask them to discuss in pairs who had the least mistakes. What mistakes did they make? Why?

Alternatively If you prefer not to use translation, ask students to look at the sentences and tell you what patterns they notice (*unable to* + base form). Elicit a few more examples.

SPEAKING

Aim
To extend the topic and give practice in telling jokes.

Step 1 Tell students they are going to tell each other a joke. Put them in AB pairs. Student A should look at File 5 on page 153 and choose the joke they like best. Student B should look at File 7 on page 154 and do the same. They should read the joke and try to memorise it.

04 POLITICS

Step 2 When they are ready, ask students to work in their pairs and take turns telling each other their jokes from memory. Tell them they should use present tenses as this is normal in telling jokes or stories. Ask them to try to make the joke dramatic by miming certain actions and using different voices. Ask the pairs to choose the joke they prefer and explain why at the end.

Step 3 Ask students to read the questions in C and think about how they would answer them. Then put them in small groups to discuss their ideas. Conduct brief feedback.

pp. 30–31

Next class Make photocopies of 4B p. 135.

READING

Aim
To give practice in reading for gist and responding to text.

Step 1 Tell students they are going to read a text about the Swiss electoral system. Begin by asking them what they know / imagine about it and why.

Step 2 Tell students to read the text and put a tick in the margin for points they find positive and a cross for points they find negative. Tell them not to worry about the words in bold. Set a time limit of three to four minutes. Then put students in pairs to compare and explain their ideas. Conduct brief feedback.

Step 3 Ask students, in the same pairs, to look at the words in bold and discuss what they think they mean. Then ask them to find words based on *elect*, *normal*, *devolve* and *represent*.

Answers
1 devolves = passes power or responsibility down to a smaller or less powerful group
2 counterparts = people in equivalent positions in another country or organisation
3 petition = official request for change by a number of people
4 referendum = when everyone in the country can vote on a particular issue
5 polling station = place where people vote
6 bodies = organisations
7 irrespective = regardless
8 ballot papers = where people mark their vote
9 the party line = the view generally held by the party
10 lobby = try to persuade
11 turnout = total number of people who vote
2 elect = electorate; normal = the norm; devolve = devolution; represent = representatives

Step 4 Put students in small groups and ask them to discuss ways in which things are similar / different in their country.

Tip If you are in Switzerland, ask them to discuss ways in which things are different in other countries they know about.

VOCABULARY Elections and politics

Aim
To look at collocations related to elections and politics.

Step 1 Lead in by reminding students about collocation and eliciting some examples associated with politics and elections e.g. *a local MP*, *a right / left-wing party*, *a coalition government*. Then read out the explanation in the box.

Step 2 Ask students to look at the words in the box and match them with the sets of words / phrases in A. Ask them to look up any they are not sure about in the *Vocabulary builder* on pp. 15–16 and underline these.

Answers
1 figure   5 scandal
2 election   6 MP
3 poll   7 vote
4 consensus   8 victory
(*strike* and *party* are not used)

Step 3 Put students in pairs to compare the collocations they underlined and think of examples for each. Check meaning as a group by asking for examples and checking pronunciation / stress.

4B see Teacher's notes p. 121.

LISTENING

Aim
To give practice in listening for gist and detail.

Step 1 Tell students they are going to hear five people talking about their feelings about votes. In small groups, ask them to look at the box and answer the questions in A.

Answers
1 a local or general election; a referendum
2 the electorate – everyone in the area or in the country – though they may exercise their right not to vote
3 students' own answers
4 you might vote in a school or college election or as part of a committee or in a debate or meeting or for a talent show or similar
5 students' own answers

Step 2 Ask students to listen and decide which type of vote each speaker is talking about. Play the recording. Check answers in pairs, then with the whole group.

30 OUTCOMES

04 POLITICS

> **Answers**
> 1 a talent show vote
> 2 a strike ballot
> 3 a referendum
> 4 an opinion poll
> 5 election for student council

⟳ 4.3
Speaker 1
I used to like watching Star Quality, but since this scandal has erupted, I've lost interest in it. This story leaked out that they were encouraging people to phone in even though they'd already decided the result. They were manipulating things so that one guy didn't get voted off, because it helped the programme's ratings if they had a kind of hate figure. I might not have minded so much if the calls were free, but they're making a fortune on them.

Speaker 2
We only called a vote because negotiations were going absolutely nowhere and despite the massive support we've received from our members, the management is persisting with a derisory offer that will see wages fall in real terms next year. If it hadn't been for their intransigence, we would not be taking this action now. We understand the public's frustration – we share it – but the blame for this dispute should be laid firmly at the door of the train company.

Speaker 3
I'm totally in favour of a vote on the issue. The way the current system works, some parties get a seat with only 100,000 votes, while others who poll more than twice that don't get any. In the run-up to the election, the New Party had promised to hold one if they got into power, but in the event all that talk has faded away. I guess if they hadn't won a landslide victory, they'd be keener to bring about electoral reform, but I truly believe the vast majority of the electorate still wants to see a change and would vote yes, whatever their reservations.

Speaker 4
On another day I wouldn't have taken part, but I was at a bit of a loose end when the researcher called and she caught me off guard. It took about half an hour and I have to admit, I quite enjoyed it – moaning about the government. Mind you, when the results were published in the paper, I was a bit taken aback. It seems I'm in a small minority! People must be mad!

Speaker 5
I know in some places it's just tokenism with no real power, but that isn't the case here. In these days of voter apathy, it's important that kids learn democracy can give rise to positive change. Apart from deciding things like the end of term trips, pupil reps can decide on policy. It's unlikely we would've abolished uniforms if we didn't have a body like this. Voting isn't obligatory but nearly everyone does.

Step 3 In pairs, ask students to look at the items in C and decide which conversation each one refers to. Point out that one is extra. Play the recording for them to check. Get them to explain their choices in pairs, then check as a class.

> **Answers**
> a 3 – the New Party promised a referendum
> b 1 – the show had already decided the result
> c 5 – voter apathy
> d not mentioned
> e 4 – I'm in a small minority
> f 2 – we understand the public's frustration

GRAMMAR Conditionals 2

Aim
To give further practice in conditional forms.

Step 1 Read out the explanation box. Put students in pairs to complete the sentences from *Listening*. Play the recording again, if necessary.

Step 2 Ask students to check their answers with the audioscript on page 164. In pairs ask them to explain the verb forms to each other. Direct them to the grammar reference on page 139 if they need help. Check as a group.

> **Answers**
> 1 helped the programme's ratings (past simple in both parts to indicate something that was true)
> 2 the calls were free (second conditional = the calls aren't free)
> 3 we would not be taking this action now (*wouldn't* + continuous infinitive = we are taking the action now – mixed conditional)
> 4 they hadn't won a landslide victory (past perfect = they did win a landslide victory – mixed conditional)
> 5 wouldn't have taken part (*wouldn't* + perfect infinitive – hypothetical use (*if I'd been busier*)
> 6 would've abolished uniforms – as for 5 = we did abolish uniforms

Step 3 Ask students to write two conditional sentences about each item in C. Put them in small groups to compare their sentences. Elicit a few examples at the end.

NATIVE SPEAKER ENGLISH *Tokenism*

Ask students what they understand by *a token, a token gesture, tokenism*. Remind them of how this was used in the recording – *it's just tokenism, with no real power*. Read out the explanation, then try to elicit a few more examples.

SPEAKING

Aim
To give fluency practice and round off the unit.

Step 1 Ask students to discuss the questions in A in groups of three. Conduct brief feedback.

01 REVIEW

OVERALL AIMS
It is rarely enough for students to meet 'new' language and skills once. In reality, people learn these things by being exposed to them and activating them again and again. Therefore, each of the four review units are designed to revise material covered in the previous four units. The first pages are designed to revise the material in a fun, interactive way. The second two pages are more traditional listening, grammar and vocabulary exercises, which could be given as a progress test. In addition, these test pages expose students to exam-type questions they are likely to meet in common English exams.

TWO MINUTES

Overview
In this activity students decide for themselves which topic they want to give a short talk about. Each student performs this task individually in front of the group, who in turn have to give each other marks. Having an audience normally means students perform better. The rest of the group also has to listen carefully because they have the responsibility for marking their classmates. This whole process has the added advantage of promoting learner autonomy.

Aim
To provide fluency practice in the different topics practised so far and to raise students' awareness of their speaking ability by asking them to observe and assess each other.

Step 1 Put students into small groups and tell them they can refer to their notes to check language or the *Vocabulary builder* if they need to. They should take turns to present their talk and be observers. Each student should choose one of the topics, look back at the relevant part of the book and take five minutes to prepare what they want to say. One student gives a two-minute talk while other students listen and take notes on their strengths and weaknesses with use of language, interest and clarity. At the end, the observers each give the speaker a mark out of 10 and explain the mark using their notes as a guide (1 = poor, 10 = excellent). Repeat the activity with a different speaker until they've all given their talk. You can monitor / help where necessary. Conduct a brief correction slot at the end.

GAME

Overview
Games are valuable for language learners because as they become involved in the activity they become less self-conscious about speaking in a foreign language and less worried about making mistakes. In addition, games help develop classroom dynamics and they are fun – it's important to enjoy learning!

Aim
To recycle some of the language covered in the units in a fun, student-centred way.

Step 1 Put students in A / B pairs. Ask Student A to look at the questions in the green squares and Student B to look at the questions in the yellow squares. They should find the answers in the units and try to memorise them. They may need longer than five minutes for this.

Step 2 Tell students to play the game in pairs. They should take turns to throw a coin and move one of their squares for heads, and two of their squares for tails. They should answer the question on the square they land on. Their partner should check the answer in the relevant part of the book. If they get the answer right, they move forward one square (but don't answer the question on the new square until their next turn). If they get the answer wrong, their partner tells them the answer and they miss a turn – and use the coin again for their next turn. The first one to reach the last square is the winner. Students could then swap colours and play again.

Note In the next three activities, the students should work in groups of three and use the *Vocabulary builder* to help them if they want to.

32 OUTCOMES

Conversation practice

Overview
In this activity, students decide for themselves which conversation they want to repeat. Two students perform the task in front of a third, who acts as 'judge'. Having an audience normally means students perform better. The judge also has to listen carefully because they have the responsibility for marking their classmates. This whole process has the added advantage of promoting learner autonomy.

Aim
To give fluency practice and to raise students' awareness of their speaking ability by asking them to observe and assess each other.

Step 1 Put students in threes. They can refer to the *Vocabulary builder* if they wish. They should take turns to be a pair of speakers and an observer. Each pair should chose one of the topics, look back at the relevant part of the book and take a few minutes to prepare. They then conduct the conversation while the third student listens and takes notes. At the end, the observer should give each speaker a mark out of 10 and explain the mark (10 = excellent, 1 = poor). It would be useful if they could also use their notes to give more detailed feedback on strengths and weaknesses / errors. Then swap. Monitor and help / prompt where necessary and give some overall feedback at the end.

Act or draw

Overview
This is an enormously popular game amongst people the whole world over because it is so much fun. The gap between the actor / artist's performance and the 'guesser's' ideas leads to a lot of laughter and a lot of language use as well.

Aim
To revise vocabulary in a fun way.

Step 1 Put students in new groups of three and ask them to take turns to act or draw the words / phrases in the box, chosen at random. They should not speak while they are acting or drawing. Their partners should guess the word / phrase. Then they swap.

Quiz

Overview
This game is best played in teams of two or three in order to promote speaking. It's a good idea to give students a realistic time limit. The pressure also increases energy levels and makes the game more exciting. You could also conduct this as a race between teams.

Alternatively You could conduct this as a 'pub quiz' with you reading out the questions and groups of three or four students conferring quietly on the answers. Then in open class each group swaps their answers with another group. You read / elicit the answers and they mark each other's answers. Check with the whole group at the end. The winner is the group with the most correct answers.

Answers
1. An area with **crumbling** or **derelict buildings** is neglected and run down.
2. If you **rip** your shirt you need to mend or repair it.
3. If a situation is **grim** it is very bad.
4. When an economy is **thriving** it's doing well.
5. If you need to **clear rubble**, a building or part of it has collapsed.
6. If you're **thrilled** with something you feel very excited and pleased.
7. Houses or flats are **burgled** by a burglar.
8. An area might **go downhill** because it becomes poor, or people leave it or don't want to live there.
9. You might **single** someone **out** because they are especially good at something.
10. **Close-knit** describes a community.
11. Politicians try to **cover up** a scandal, e.g. their expenses.
12. If there's a **craze** everybody wants to be part of something e.g. Facebook, or wants to have something, e.g. iPhones.
13. If someone is **bitchy** they gossip in a nasty way about others.
14. Crime, or drug use, might be **cracked down on** by increasing the power of the police.
15. Four different **grounds** for divorce are: unfaithfulness, cruelty, neglect, irretrievable breakdown.

01 REVIEW

COLLOCATIONS

Overview
Collocations are words which usually go together such as *do me a favour*, and *a pressing problem*. Until relatively recently the concept of collocation was not an area that was covered in vocabulary teaching. However, computational linguistics has shown how important collocation is in language learning. This activity helps to develop students' awareness of the importance of collocation in natural language generation.

Aim
To revise and practise some common collocations from units 1–4 and to give students further learner training in using the *Vocabulary builder*.

Step 1 Put students in AB pairs and tell them to test each other on collocations from units 1–4. Student A looks at unit 1 of the *Vocabulary builder* and reads out a collocation, with a gap where there is '~'. They should say 'blah' for the gap and Student B should say the missing word. They could do 6–8 collocations and then swap.

IDIOMS

Overview

Aim
To revise, personalise and practise idioms from units 1–4.

Step 1 Put students in pairs / threes and ask them to discuss the meaning of the idioms 1–15. Remind them to use the *Vocabulary builder* if they need help. Ask them to individually think of a real example about themselves or someone they know. Then ask them to discuss this in their groups. Check the meaning of the idioms and check a selection of their examples as a group at the end.

> **Answers**
> 1 I'm putting across the opposite point of view to make for a more interesting discussion.
> 2 I've got nothing to do.
> 3 He's difficult to get on with.
> 4 She really wants it / wants to do it.
> 5 She said what she thought.
> 6 He betrayed me.
> 7 I accept things as they are without worrying unnecessarily.
> 8 You should insist on something.
> 9 We didn't get on when we met.
> 10 He does nothing to help with housework.
> 11 It was very unexpected.
> 12 It would be very lucky if that happened.
> 13 They are very rich.
> 14 It's not appropriate.
> 15 It spread very fast.

Note *Listening* and the rest of the review unit could be used as the basis for a progress test. The suggested scores are given below each exercise. Alternatively, these exercises could be done in pairs or individually and then checked in pairs, or you could conduct them as a quiz / competition, with students in teams. If students have problems with any of the exercises, refer them to the relevant pages in the grammar reference or the *Vocabulary builder*.

pp. 34–35

LISTENING

Aim
To give practice in listening for gist and detail. The audio is ♫ R1.1.

> **Exercise A answers**
> a Speaker 4
> b –
> c Speaker 3
> d Speaker 5
> e Speaker 2
> f Speaker 1
> g –
>
> **Exercise B answers**
> a –
> b Speaker 4
> c Speaker 5
> d Speaker 1
> e –
> f Speaker 3
> g Speaker 2

GRAMMAR

> **Exercise A answers**
> 1 that
> 2 had
> 3 would
> 4 having
> 5 would
> 6 lack
> 7 fact
> 8 be
>
> **Exercise B answers**
> 1 has tripled since
> 2 wouldn't have been so / got so
> 3 going to trigger an
> 4 drives / makes me mad is the amount
> 5 gone through
> 6 hadn't rigged the

01 REVIEW

LANGUAGE PATTERNS

Answers
1 She's one of those people **who's** always moaning.
2 It's nowhere **near** as complicated as it sounds.
3 correct
4 **He's** utterly unable to make up his mind.
5 correct
6 I read it three times out of **disbelief**.

PREPOSITIONS

Answers
1 to
2 of
3 on
4 in
5 with
6 against
7 as
8 in

OPPOSITES

Answers
1 sprawling
2 acrimonious
3 vibrant
4 secular
5 filthy
6 thriving
7 deprived
8 long-standing

MISSING WORDS

Answers
1 stand
2 figure
3 pocket
4 narrow
5 crawling

NOUNS

Answers
1 cloth
2 dishwasher / washing machine
3 toilet
4 drill
5 ladder
6 string / rope
7 nail
8 tap

WORD FAMILIES

Answers
1 assumption
2 underestimate
3 ridiculously
4 reservations
5 commitment
6 capability
7 wilful

VOCABULARY

Answers
1 B frail
2 A voices
3 C benefit
4 A by and large
5 C been through
6 A mixed up in
7 C run-up
8 A offering

05 NIGHT IN, NIGHT OUT

UNIT OVERVIEW
In this unit, students practise **talking about feelings** and **commenting on what they hear**. They learn how to **comment on books and guides** and how to **change the subject**. They read **a guide to entertainments** and **listen to people talking about a night out** and **about book clubs**. The main grammar aim is revision and consolidation of **noun phrases**.

VOCABULARY Feelings

Aim
To introduce expressions used to talk about a variety of feelings.

Step 1 Lead in by asking the students for any words or phrases they know to describe strong feelings – both emotional and physical. Then ask them to look at the sentences in A and guess the meaning of the words / phrases in bold, then translate them into their own language. Check in pairs, then check with the whole group.

Alternatively If you prefer not to use translation, ask students to think of a definition of the words / phrases. Concept check by asking for other examples.

> **Answers**
> 1 in stitches = very amused, couldn't stop laughing
> 2 yawning = opening mouth when tired or sleepy
> 3 in bits = very upset
> 4 stuffed = very full
> 5 tossing and turning = restless, unable to sleep
> 6 off his head = mad, drunk, incoherent
> 7 live up to the hype = fulfil (high) expectations
> 8 overwhelmed = unable to deal with strong emotions
> 9 rough = unwell, hung-over
> 10 mortified = very embarrassed

Step 2 Put students in pairs and ask them to look at the sentences in A again and invent reasons for each of the feelings, as in the example. Conduct brief feedback.

LISTENING

Aim
To give practice in listening for specific information and intensively.

Step 1 Tell students they are going to hear two conversations where people talk about a night out and something else. Ask them to look at the questions in exercise A and answer them as they listen. Check answers in pairs, then check with the whole group.

> **Answers**
> **Conversation 1**
> 1 went to a surprise party
> 2 dancing
> 3 bit rough; overwhelmed; in stitches; mortified
>
> **Conversation 2**
> 1 went out for dinner
> 2 a meeting / stress
> 3 tossing and turning; stuffed; off his head

> **5.1**
> **Conversation 1**
> A: Hey Maddy. You look a bit rough.
> B: I know. I'm exhausted. I didn't get to bed till 3.
> A: How come?
> B: Oh, this friend of mine, it was her 25th and we organised a surprise party.
> A: I bet she was pleased.
> B: Yeah, she was, she was, although she actually burst into tears when she first came in.
> A: Oh!
> B: Ah, she's been through a lot recently, which is partly why we planned the do.
> A: Cheer her up.
> B: Exactly. Anyway, she obviously found it a bit overwhelming at first, but she got over it pretty quickly.
> A: That's good. Where was it?
> B: In this bar. They'd hired a room and they had a band. I think they were friends of hers too.
> A: Any good?
> B: Yeah, brilliant. They played this old school rock and roll, but really well. Honestly, everyone was up dancing. Actually, it was hilarious – you know Finley, don't you?
> A: Vaguely – only really by sight.
> B: You've never seen him strutting his stuff then?

36 OUTCOMES

A: No, why?
B: He's awful. Honestly, he dances like a crippled chicken! We were in stitches watching him.
A: Poor bloke. He'll probably never dance again.
B: Nah. I mean I would've been mortified, but he's one of those people – he's so full of himself, I don't think he even registers when people are taking the mickey!
A: You won't be saying that when he comes and guns you all down in revenge!
B: Trust me, he's very thick-skinned. Anyway, talking of dancing, are you still going to those tango classes?
A: Yeah – on and off.
B: You must be getting quite good.
A: I wouldn't go that far. I'm still a bit prone to treading on toes.

Conversation 2
C: Hi, glad I caught you. Have you sorted everything for the big meeting?
D: Yeah, yeah, it's all in hand. I've also booked a table at Eugene's.
C: Excellent. I didn't mean to hassle you. I'm just stressing about it.
D: That's allright. I'm sure it'll be fine.
C: Yeah, it will. I could just do without it at the moment. Just too much on.
D: Tell me about it! I was tossing and turning all night! I just couldn't switch off.
C: I know. Perhaps you should take up meditation.
D: Yeah.
C: Anyway. Thanks for being so on top of things.
D No problem.
C: By the way, how was your meal the other night?
D: Oh, great. We went to this place, Porchetta?
C: Oh yeah. How was the food?
D: Gorgeous, but there was so much – you have six or seven courses. I lost count.
C: You must've been stuffed by the end.
D: I thought I'd burst – bit too much really. Actually, there was a bit of a scene while we were there. This guy just burst out shouting at a waiter – really ranting about something stupid, like there was a dirty fork or something.
C: It sounds like he was off his head.
D: I don't know. But they got him to leave.
C: Strange.

Step 2 Put students in pairs to compare answers. Ask them to discuss what each phrase they heard referred to in the conversations, and why the speakers used them. Then play the recording again for them to check.

Answers
Conversation 1 = *bit rough* – the second speaker: because she went to bed at three; *overwhelmed* – her friend: because it was a surprise party and she had been through a lot recently; *in stitches* – everybody watching the guy dance: because he was funny; *mortified* – she would have felt like this if she had danced so badly

Conversation 2 = *tossing and turning* – the second speaker: because he was worried about the meeting; the man; *stuffed* – the same man: because he ate so much; *off his head* – a strange man in the restaurant: because he was ranting about something very trivial

Step 3 Ask students to look at the sentences from the recording in exercise C and complete them with the correct preposition or adverb. Then ask them to look at the audioscript on page 164 to check their answers. Concept check with the whole group by asking for definitions or other examples.

Answers
1 into
2 through
3 over
4 of
5 of
6 to
7 in
8 off
9 about
10 on
11 by
12 out

Speaking

Aim
To further exploit the listening and give fluency practice.

Step 1 Ask students to look at the questions in A and think about how they would answer them. Then put them in small groups to discuss the questions. Conduct brief feedback.

Native speaker English
strut your stuff

Ask students what they think *strut your stuff* means from the conversation in *Listening*. *What were they talking about?* (Finley's dancing). *What did they think of it?* (not a lot). Read out the explanation in the box and try to elicit a few more examples.

05 NIGHT IN, NIGHT OUT

DEVELOPING CONVERSATIONS

I bet / imagine

Aim
To practise ways of commenting on what someone says, using *I bet / imagine ...* or *you must / must've ...* .

Step 1 Read out the explanation box. Ask students to look at the sentences in A and rewrite them using *must be / must've been*. Then play the recording for them to check. Ask them to notice the responses.

> **Answers**
> 1 That must've been pretty dull.
> 2 You must be glad you didn't go now.
> 3 He must've been a bit disappointed.
> 4 You must be feeling a bit rough now.
> 5 You must've been mortified.
> 6 She must've been quite upset.

> **5.2**
> 1 A: That must've been pretty dull.
>   B: Awful. I couldn't stop yawning.
>
> 2 A: You must be glad you didn't go now.
>   B: Absolutely. It obviously doesn't live up to the hype.
>
> 3 A: He must've been a bit disappointed.
>   B: Actually
>
> 4 A: You must be feeling a bit rough now.
>   B: Actually, I feel surprisingly fresh.
>
> 5 A: You must've been mortified.
>   B: I wouldn't go that far, but it was a bit embarrassing.
>
> 6 A: She must've been quite upset.
>   B: Oh she was in bits – just in floods of tears.

Step 2 Read out the next explanation box. Then put students in pairs to practise. They should take turns saying one of the sentences 1–6 in A and their partner should respond by agreeing or disagreeing. Model with a strong student, then in open pairs before continuing in closed pairs. Check a few examples in open pairs at the end.

CONVERSATION PRACTICE

Aim
To further exploit *Listening* and give fluency practice.

Step 1 Tell students they are going to practise similar conversations to the ones they heard in *Listening*. Ask them to think of a night which resulted in at least one of the feelings in *Vocabulary*, and prepare what they are going to say. They should try to use language from this part of the unit.

Step 2 Put students in pairs and ask them to take turns telling their partner about their night out and responding. Tell them to use as much language from pages 36–37 as they can. They should change the subject to something totally different half way through each conversation. When finished, they swap and repeat. Monitor and take notes for a correction slot at the end.

📖 **pp. 38–39**

Next class Make photocopies of 5A p. 136.

READING

Aim
To give practice in reading for gist and detail, and in responding to what you have read.

Step 1 Tell students they're going to read a *What's on* guide to London. Before they read, put them in small groups to discuss the questions in exercise A. Conduct brief feedback.

Step 2 Put students in pairs and ask them to read the online guide, ignoring the underlining. Ask them to comment on the items as they read, answering the questions in B and using some of the language suggested e.g. *it sounds too weird / gory / pretentious for my liking; it doesn't sound like my thing / my cup of tea; it sounds interesting / brilliant / dreadful; it sounds like a laugh / the kind of thing I'd like*, etc. You could read the first item and elicit responses from the whole group to demonstrate. Monitor and intervene / correct where necessary.

Step 3 Put students in small groups and ask them to choose together the three things they would all like to go to and discuss why. Then ask students to share and discuss their ideas with the rest of the class.

Step 4 Ask students to look at the list in D and decide which event each one refers to. Check in pairs. Then check with the whole group.

> **Answers**
> 1 Can-Can course, Rain Man
> 2 Rain Man, Blues Brothers
> 3 Douglas Bader
> 4 Blues Brothers, Odyssey UK, Richmond and Twickenham Jazz Club
> 5 Can-Can course, weight loss through Ayurveda
> 6 Cupcake decorating, Ayurveda
> 7 London treasure hunt
> 8 Ice Worlds
> 9 Art Bin
> 10 Douglas Bader

38 OUTCOMES

05 NIGHT IN, NIGHT OUT

LANGUAGE PATTERNS

Aim
To focus on patterns with *have + someone ...* .

Step 1 Ask students to read the examples in the box and check they understand. Ask them to translate the sentences into their own language and notice any similarities / differences. In a monolingual class, ask students to compare their translation. In a multilingual class, ask students to work in pairs and tell each other if the sentences were easy to translate.

Step 2 Then ask them to close their books and translate the sentences back into their own language. At the end, they should open their books again and compare their translations with the original sentences. Ask them to discuss in pairs who had the least mistakes. What mistakes did they make? Why?

Alternatively If you prefer not to use translation, ask them to look at the sentences and tell you what patterns they notice (*have someone* + adjective / adverb / adverbial phrase: similar in meaning to *make someone* + adjective / + base form + adjective). Try to elicit a few more examples.

SPEAKING

Aim
To exploit the reading and give personalised fluency practice.

Step 1 Ask students to look at the questions in A and think about how they would answer them. Put students in pairs or threes to discuss the questions. Conduct brief feedback.

VOCABULARY

Aim
To introduce phrases consisting of noun + *of* + noun.

Step 1 Read out the explanation in the box and try to elicit a few more examples. Ask students to look at the phrases in the explanation box and try to think of one more example for each. Put students in pairs to compare their ideas, then check with the whole group.

> **Suggested answers**
> *the secret of* success, the universe; *the format of* the lessons, the lecture, the course; *a wealth of* ideas, products; *the centenary of* her death, his first novel; *the loss of* his arms, his eyesight, his one true love; *the onset of* the recession, the disease; *the Battle of* the Somme, Waterloo, the sexes; *the existence of* this chemical, God; *a set of* ideas, priorities; *the disposal of* waste, sewage

Step 2 Ask students to look at exercise B and match a noun and *of* with the possible endings. Check in pairs. Then check with the whole group. Concept check by asking students when they would use the phrases.

> **Answers**
> 1 *a bundle of* fun / measures / wood / clothes
> 2 *a fraction of* the cost / an inch / a second
> 3 *a risk of* accidents / cancer / failure
> 4 *a flood of* enquires / complaints / people
> 5 *a sign of* life / weakness / things to come
> 6 *the supply of* water / drugs / blood to the brain
> 7 *the abolition of* slavery / the death penalty / VAT
> 8 *the tip of* my tongue / the island / the iceberg

GRAMMAR Noun phrases

Aim
To focus on noun phrases and give practice.

Step 1 Read out the explanation box. Then put students in pairs. Ask them to look at the questions in A and the underlined words in the article from *Reading, Where can we go*. Ask them to discuss the answers to the questions. Check with the whole group.

> **Answers**
> 1 *a barber surgeon*: noun phrase; *Rory McCreadie*; nine
> 2 *on Blues Brothers' classics*: prepositional phrase; *a twist*; six
> 3 *dance*: noun; *class*; four
> 4 *a wealth*: noun phrase; *hints and tips*; six
> 5 *marking the centenary of his birth*: participle clause; *display*; nine
> 6 *ice plays throughout the Solar System*: relative clause; *role*; six
> 7 *London*: noun; *most vibrant areas*; six
> 8 *six-week*: adjective; *exhibition*; three
> 9 *receiving four and five-star reviews across the board*: participle phrase; *sell-out show*; thirteen
> 10 *that follows the journey of Charlie Babbitt and his autistic brother Raymond across America*: relative clause; *film*; 17
> 11 *between the reflected and the real*: prepositional phrase; *the boundary*; eight
> 12 *and hosted by saxophonist Kelvin Christiane and vocalist Lesley Christiane*: participle phrase; *jazz club*; 23
> 13 *suitable*: adjective; *yoga and breathing exercises*; eight

Direct them to the grammar reference on page 140 if they need help.

05 NIGHT IN, NIGHT OUT

Step 2 Put students in pairs. Ask them to look at sentences 1–4 in exercise B and choose one each. They should add words to the subject and object and see who can write the longest sentence. Ask students to read out a few of their sentences to the whole class at the end.

> 5A see Teacher's notes p. 122.

pp. 40–41

> **Next class** Make photocopies of 5B p. 137.

SPEAKING

Aim
To lead in to *Listening* and give personalised practice.

Step 1 Lead in by asking students about book clubs: *What are they? Why do people join them? Are they popular in their area?* Then put students in small groups to discuss the questions in A. Conduct brief feedback.

LISTENING

Aim
To give practice in listening and summary writing.

Step 1 Tell students they are going to hear a radio programme about book clubs. Ask them to look at the summary in A and complete it as they listen. Tell them there may be various possible answers. Play the recording.

Answers
1 the reading habits of the nation / the publishing industry
2 different approaches to reading, celebrities discussing books, space for users
3 40,000 book clubs
4 Vegan Book Club, Socialist Feminist group
5 provide recommendations / act as filter
6 create a community
7 are really gossiping or dating clubs
8 sentimental autobiographical writing
9 the transformative effect of reading
10 to pass books on to others
11 community reading project designed to give everyone in an area the opportunity to read and then talk about one book
12 bookstore events, related arts / school events

5.3

When Oprah Winfrey added a book discussion club section to her phenomenally popular American talk show back in 1996, she could surely never have envisaged the impact she would have – not only on the reading habits of the nation, but also on the publishing industry itself. Winfrey personally chose all the books she endorsed and didn't benefit financially from any of her selections. In terms of sales, endorsement by Oprah is worth anywhere between 20 and 100 times the recommendation of any other public figure in the United States and has sufficient clout to fundamentally alter Amazon rankings, bestseller lists and author royalty payments. Her club now boasts over two million members and has a website that provides tips on different approaches to reading, celebrities discussing favourite pieces of literature and ample space for users to share their own thoughts on featured titles.

In the wake of all this highly visible public enthusiasm, book clubs have started springing up everywhere. In Britain alone, there are now an estimated 40,000 reading groups, with people meeting to discuss their latest literary loves in private homes or in cafés, in libraries and bookstores or simply online. This phenomenon has spawned such specialist gatherings as the Vegan Book Club and a Socialist Feminist group, as well as meetings specifically targeted at lovers of crime novels and even comics!

The remarkable surge in the popularity of book clubs seems to be down to a number of different factors. Cultural commentator, Rosalie Nicholson: 'We live in hectic times. As we all become ever busier and ever more bombarded with an overload of information, reading groups clearly represent a craving for trustworthy recommendations. They act as a kind of filter. In addition, book clubs seem to tap into some kind of desire for community in an age of increasing social fragmentation. Ironically, it seems that the solitary activity of reading can help provide a sense of shared experience.'

However, not everyone sees the trend in such a positive light. Here's critic Bryan Sewer:
'Let's face it, most reading groups are little more than gossiping circles or else simply a literary guise for dating clubs! And I know from my own observations that when they do finally get round to discussing books, the discourse is generally coarse and displays limited insight or intellect. I also fear that the whole nature of the set-up has created a tendency towards a certain kind of sentimental autobiographical writing, which one can only suppose must be easier for a mass audience.'

Bryan Sewer's opinion, though, seems to have little impact, and certainly hasn't halted the spread of

05 NIGHT IN, NIGHT OUT

communal reading. Indeed, one recent book club favourite, Reading Lolita in Tehran, by Azar Nafisi, details the transformational experience of reading and discussing frequently banned Western books in the Iranian capital in the 1990s. The appeal, it would seem, is universal.

On top of the multitude of reading groups now thriving, other innovative projects have also been conceived. Book Crossing is a free online book club that aims 'to make the whole world a library'. After having registered with the site, which connects users and attempts to track the movement of items donated, users are encouraged to leave books they've finished reading in public spaces, where they may then find new admirers.

Seattle, meanwhile, instigated the now globally popular idea of One City, One Book – a community reading project designed to give everyone within a specific geographical location the opportunity to read and then talk about one book at one particular time. As the idea has spread, different cities have added their own twists: bookstore talks by authors here, related arts programming there and sometimes even integration with school curricula. The city of Liverpool went so far as to celebrate its year as European Cultural Capital by funding 20,000 free copies of the year's chosen book, *The Savage* by David Almond.

Step 2 Put students in pairs and ask them to compare their summaries. Then ask them to look at C and match the verbs with the nouns. Ask them what each phrase refers to in the recording. Then play it again and let them read the audioscript on page 165 at the same time to check.

Answers
1f endorse a book = Oprah Winfrey endorses books on her show
2c boast over two million members = her book club boasts over two million members
3h share their thoughts = users of Oprah's website can share their thoughts about books
4a be down to a number of factors = the surge in popularity of book clubs is down to a number of factors
5e see the trend in a positive light = not everyone sees the trend in a positive light
6b halt the spread = negative opinions have not halted the spread of communal reading
7d track the movement of items = BookCrossing tracks the movement of items (books passed on from one reader to another)
8g fund free copies = the city of Liverpool funded free copies of one book as part of its year as European capital of culture (2009)

Step 3 Put students in small groups and ask them to discuss the questions in F. Conduct brief feedback.

VOCABULARY Describing books

Aim
To introduce words / phrases commonly used to describe books.

Step 1 Ask students to read the book reviews and choose the correct word / phrase to complete them. Check answers in pairs. Then check with the whole group.

Answers
1 1 centres   2 plot   3 protagonists 4 dialogue
2 1 based   2 bring   3 set   4 tale
3 1 traces   2 explores   3 Revolving   4 tackles
4 1 first   2 narrator   3 turns   4 insight
5 1 memoir   2 struggle   3 deals   4 recommend

Step 2 Ask students to look again at the reviews and underline any new adjective + noun collocations. Then put them in pairs to compare and discuss meanings. Check with the whole group.

Suggested answers
slim novel; loosely connected chapters; minimal dialogue; vivid portrayal; uplifting tale; gripping non-fiction work; domestic violence; civil rights movement; comic novel; hysterical effect; moving memoir; troubled relationship; abusive mother; heart-wrenching detail; a real page-turner

Step 3 Put students in small groups to discuss the questions in C. Conduct brief feedback.

SPEAKING

Aim
To give fluency practice and round off the unit.

Step 1 Ask students to imagine they are going to form a new book group. Ask them to work individually and think of a book they would like to read at the book group. They should prepare to describe it, making a few notes and using language from *Vocabulary* to help them.

Step 2 Put students in small groups. Ask them to take turns describing their book and trying to persuade their partners to choose it. They should vote on which book to read first.

Step 3 Ask each group to present their chosen book to the rest of the class.

Alternatively You could ask students to do this for homework and bring along their book recommendations to start the next class with.

5B see Teacher's notes p. 122.

05 NIGHT IN, NIGHT OUT 41

06 CONFLICT

UNIT OVERVIEW
In this unit students practise talking about **what people do during and after arguments**, and about **war and social conflict** and **peace and justice**. They learn how to give **negative / private information** and talk about **how they would like things to be different**. They read texts about **South Africa's recent history** and about the **Truth and Reconciliation Commission (in South Africa)** and listen to news items about **disputes**, and to people having arguments and **talking about the Truth and Reconciliation Commission**. The main grammar aim is *I wish*.

Next class Make photocopies of **6A** p. 138 and **6B** p. 139.

Speaking

Aim
To lead into the topic and give fluency practice.

Step 1 Begin by asking students how they usually behave during an argument. Then ask them to look at the sentences in A and check they understand the words / phrases in bold. Put them in pairs to check the meanings and to discuss which they sometimes do themselves. Concept check by asking for definitions or examples.

> **Answers**
> *storm off* = to leave in a temper; *slam* = shut violently; *sulk* = when you refuse to talk to someone in an aggressive way; *hold a grudge / bear a grudge* = when you refuse to forgive someone; *make up* = say sorry and forgive each other

Step 2 Ask students to look at the items in B, which people often argue about. Then put them in pairs and ask them to discuss what might cause arguments in these areas and which areas they think cause the worst arguments.

Step 3 Ask students in the same pairs to discuss which of the items in B they argue about most often; who with; and how these arguments usually end. Conduct brief feedback.

Listening

Aim
To give practice in listening for gist.

Step 1 Tell students they're going to hear two conversations in which conflicts occur. Ask them to answer the questions in A as they listen. Play the recording. Check in pairs, then check with the whole group.

> **Answers**
> **Conversation 1**
> 1 housemates
> 2 clearing up and paying the bills
> 3 the woman tells them to stop
>
> **Conversation 2**
> 1 colleagues or manager and employee
> 2 she gave a parcel to someone else to post and it hasn't arrived yet
> 3 he threatens to sack her but may not go through with it

> 🔊 **6.1**
> **Conversation 1**
> **A = woman, B = Ricardo, C = Owen**
> A: Ricardo! Ricardo!
> B: Yeah. What's up?
> A: Look! I wish you wouldn't do this! Really! It's not fair on the rest of us.
> B: Do what?
> A: Leave everything in such a state in here! Look at it. It looks like a bomb has exploded in here and it means I now have to tidy everything up.
> B: I'll give you a hand if you want.
> A: That's not the point! You used it last – you should've cleaned it up. That's the rule.
> B: OK, OK. There's no need to bite my head off about it. I just forgot. I'm sorry. I've just been really busy, all right?
> C: So busy you've not managed to clear all your debts yet!
> B: Meaning what?
> C: Meaning you still haven't paid Kathrin back the forty pounds she lent you for the gas bill three weeks ago.
> B: Not this again, Owen. I wish you'd stop going on about it. I've told her like a thousand times I'll sort it out when I get paid. That's on the 21st. Which is five days from now. OK?
> C: What is it with you? How come we never have a proper conversation? Why are you always so defensive all the time? And why do you always have to exaggerate everything?

42 OUTCOMES

> B: Who's the one exaggerating? You should listen to yourself – never, always, always, never.
> A: Can both of you just stop it? Please! Honestly, I wish I'd never mentioned it now! You're like a couple of kids.
>
> **Conversation 2**
> **C = man, D = Miriam**
> C: Miriam, Could I have a word?
> D: Can't it wait?
> C: Not really, no.
> D: It really is a rather awkward moment.
> C: Look, I don't think I would bother you like this if it was only something trivial. I do think it would be better if we sorted this out now.
> D: What do you mean? Sort what out?
> C: The small matter of the parcel for Milan… which they still haven't received yet.
> D: Have they not? That's weird.
> C: I thought I expressly asked you to send that parcel recorded delivery.
> C: I did! You can ask Kate if you don't believe me. She saw me hand it over to Shane.
> D: Woah! Stop right there. You did what?
> C: I gave it to Shane. He was on his way and he said he'd do it for me.
> D: Listen Miriam, I don't mean to be rude, but when I said I wanted YOU to send it, that's precisely what I meant. It's not someone else's responsibility, it's YOURS. Have you any idea what is riding on this deal? If we can't show we're capable of the most basic things, how on earth are they going to trust us with their account?
> C: I'm really sorry. Honestly, it won't happen again.
> D: It won't, because to be frank with you I'm really not sure there's a future for you here at all.
> C: No. I do understand I made a mistake.
> D: And not for the first time, I hasten to add.
> C: No, I know. It was stupid of me, really stupid. I don't know what I was thinking …
> D: That's as maybe, but it's a bit late for all that now.

NATIVE SPEAKER ENGLISH *I hasten to add*

Ask students to look at this phrase and tell you when / how they think it is used. Then read out the explanation in the box. Elicit how it was used in *Listening* (formally).

DEVELOPING CONVERSATIONS
Giving negative / private information

Aim
To practise giving negative or private information.

Step 1 Read out the explanation in the box and check students understand. Try to elicit a few more examples.

Step 2 Put students in pairs. Ask them to look at the sentences in A and complete them in their own way, imagining they are all said in an office over the space of a week. Their ideas can be serious or humorous. Monitor and check their sentences are accurate and appropriate.

Step 3 Ask each pair to join another pair and ask them to compare their sentences and choose the best ideas. Conduct brief feedback with the whole group.

GRAMMAR *I wish*

Aim
To revise *I wish* followed by various forms.

Step 1 Ask students to look at the sentences in A and divide them into three groups according to their grammatical pattern. Then put them in pairs to check their answers and discuss the form and meaning in each case. Direct them to the grammar reference on page 141 if they need help.

> **Answers**
> 1,3 = past simple to talk about wishes about the present, or things that are always true; 2,5 = past perfect to talk about wishes about the past; 4,6 = *would* + base form = to express irritation or annoyance, using *would* to talk about wishes you'd like people to do / stop doing

Step 2 Ask students to look at the sentences in C and complete them using the correct form of the right verb from the box. Check in pairs, then check with the group.

> **Answers**
> 1 had   3 wouldn't leave   5 would think
> 2 hadn't sent   4 could   6 had been

Step 3 Ask students to look at the sentence starters in D and complete them so that they are true for them. Monitor as they write and check their sentences are accurate. Then put them in pairs to share and explain their ideas. Conduct brief feedback.

6A see Teacher's notes p. 122.

VOCABULARY Adverbs

Aim
To focus on adverbs commonly used with certain verbs, or used at the beginning of sentences.

Step 1 Read out the explanation in the box. Then ask students to look at the sentences in A and complete them using the correct adverb from the box. Check in pairs. Then check with the whole group.

06 CONFLICT

Answers
1 expressly   3 strongly   5 vaguely   7 bitterly
2 freely   4 desperately   6 stupidly   8 dramatically

Step 2 Put students in pairs and ask them to think of other verbs that could go with each of the adverbs in A. Ask them to decide whether they change the meaning or whether the meaning is basically the same.

Suggested answers
1 bitterly – oppose, complain
2 freely – gave, told
3 desperately – wanted
4 strongly – advise
5 dramatically – declined
6 stupidly – told
7 expressly – warned, wanted
8 vaguely – recall, said

Step 3 Ask students to look at the sentences in C and choose the correct adverb to complete them. Check in pairs then check with the whole group.

Answers
1 both possible   3 Theoretically   5 Technically
2 Hopefully   4 Presumably   6 Frankly

CONVERSATION PRACTICE

Aim
To practise conversations similar to the ones in *Listening*.

Step 1 Tell students they are going to have conversations similar to those they heard in the recording. Put them in AB pairs. Student A should read File 3 on page 152 and prepare what they are going to say in both conversations. Student B should do the same with File 10 on page 156. They should try to use language from this part of the unit.

Step 2 When they are ready, ask pairs to role-play the conversations, taking turns to begin. Monitor and take notes for a correction slot at the end.

6B see Teacher's notes p. 122.

pp. 44–45

VOCABULARY War and peace

Aim
To extend the topic to more social conflict and to introduce vocabulary associated with war and peace.

Step 1 Begin by asking students for phrases related to war and peace used metaphorically e.g. *to conquer one's fears*. Check they understand *editorial* = an opinion piece in a newspaper, written by the editor. Ask them to read the editorial in exercise A and think about the questions. Then put them in pairs or threes to discuss the questions.

Step 2 Ask students to look at the sets of events in B and decide on the most likely chronological order, starting with the phrase in bold. Check in pairs, then check with the whole group. Point out that variations may be possible, as long as students can justify them.

Possible answers
1 tension rises – some fighting breaks out – conflict escalates – war rages – call a truce
2 take offence – have a row – fall out – get in touch – make amends
3 be invaded – defend yourself – lose ground – join forces (with an ally) – gain ground – defeat the enemy
4 declare a ceasefire – begin negotiations – talks break down – restart negotiations – reach a settlement – sign a peace agreement
5 plot to overthrow the president – stage a coup – seize control of the country – suffer sanctions – undermine the economic stability – return to democracy
6 be surrounded – be under siege for weeks – run out of food – surrender – become a prisoner of war
7 reports of human rights violation – seek a UN resolution – send in international troops – re-establish security – withdraw troops
8 plant a bomb – cause casualties and fatalities – claim responsibility – arrest – put on trial

Step 3 Tell students they are going to test each other on the phrases in exercise B. Ask them to individually look at the phrases again and try to memorise them. Then put them in pairs and ask them to take turns prompting their partner with one of the phrases in bold. Their partner should try to say the other phrases in the correct order. Then swap.

Step 4 Put students in small groups and ask them to try and think of real examples of the events in D and to discuss what happened and what they think the causes and results were. Conduct brief feedback.

LISTENING

Aim
To give practice in listening for gist, for specific information and intensively.

Step 1 Tell students they are going to hear four news stories about different issues, all using the vocabulary of war and peace. They should listen and decide which issue they think is the most serious and why. Point out that there is no right answer, but they need to be able to justify their choice.

Answers
1 industrial espionage – one drinks company on another
2 an affair / sexual harassment at work
3 full body scanners at airports
4 a protest about a statue

44 OUTCOMES

06 CONFLICT

6.2

A man working for a soft drink company is standing trial today accused of spying on its biggest rival. Dan Craddock is said to have infiltrated Jazz Drinks on behalf of its competitor Pit-Pots. Over recent years, the two companies have been engaged in a fierce battle to capture market share, pouring money into ever more extravagant advertising campaigns in an effort to outdo each other. Last year was Jazz Drinks' best ever and as Pit-Pots was losing ground, it is claimed they secretly recruited Mr Craddock, who held a high-level post in Jazz Drinks, to pass on information on marketing and pricing strategy for the coming year. Mr Craddock denies any wrongdoing. The case continues.

The TV presenter Jonas Bakeman is fighting to salvage his career following revelations of his affair with a researcher on his programme, *Justice Fight*. As reporters laid siege to his home, he released a statement expressing regret over the affair, but defended himself against allegations that he'd pursued and harassed the woman, Petra Campbell. He claimed it had been a case of mutual attraction and he had surrendered to weakness during a momentary lapse of judgment. However, Ms Campbell has made available evidence that she had been bombarded with text messages and emails of a personal nature and that the affair had been more than 'momentary'. Bosses of the TV company are to meet tomorrow to consider Mr Bakeman's future.

Campaigners have claimed victory in their battle against full body scanners in airports following a court decision supporting a woman who refused to accept a scan. A number of civil liberties groups had joined forces to back the woman in an attempt to defeat the government's proposals that everyone travelling by plane should have to pass through the machines. The campaigners say it is a gross invasion of privacy as the scanners can see through clothing. The government has said that it will not retreat in its policy and believe the scanners are an important part of its armoury in the war on terror. They plan to get the decision overturned.

And finally, peace has broken out in the village of Paulston. A dispute had been raging over a statue of St John of Bidshire, the multi-prize-winning pig of local farmer Tim Langford. The three-metre pink sculpture, which had been standing at the entrance of the village for over a year, had split the village into two camps, with half saying it was a hideous eyesore, while supporters of Mr Langford said it stood as a proud symbol of the local produce for which Paulston is famous. Protesters had marched onto Mr Langford's land, and sprayed the statue with paint. Reprisals against the vandals then followed. Now the local council has stepped in as peacemaker to broker an agreement between the two sides. The statue is to be relocated to a nearby sculpture gallery, but will be moved back to the village during the three-day summer festival.

Step 2 Put students in pairs or threes and ask them to explain their choices to each other. Conduct brief feedback.

Step 3 Ask students to look at the statements in C and decide whether they are true or false. Then play the recording again for them to check. Check answers in pairs. Then check with the whole group.

Tip Ask students to correct the false statements.

Answers
1 a F – accused of spying
b F – held a high level post for Jazz Drinks
c T
2 a T
b F – he defended himself against allegations that he'd harassed the woman
c T
3 a T
b F – a number of civil liberties groups backed her
c F – they plan to get it overturned
4 a T
b F – reprisals against the vandals followed
c F – the local council stepped in

Step 4 Ask students to look at the words / phrases in exercise D and match a word / phrase on the left with one on the right, to form phrases from *Listening*. Then ask them to look at the audioscript on page 166 to check.

Answers
1 e 2 a 3 h 4 f 5 b 6 g 7 d 8 c

Step 5 Put students in small groups and ask them to discuss any stories they have heard which are similar to those in *Listening*. Conduct brief feedback.

LANGUAGE PATTERNS

Aim
To draw students' attention to patterns with *ever*.

Step 1 Ask students to read the examples in the box and check they understand. Ask them to translate the sentences into their own language and notice any similarities / differences. In a monolingual class, ask students to compare their translation. In a multilingual class, ask students to work in pairs and tell each other if the sentences were easy to translate.

Step 2 Then ask them to close their books and translate the sentences back into their own language. At the end, they should open their books again and compare their translations with the original sentences. Ask them to discuss in pairs who had the least mistakes. What mistakes did they make? Why?

06 CONFLICT

Alternatively If you prefer not to use translation, ask students to look at the sentences and tell you what patterns they notice (different uses of *ever* = meaning *any time* or *always*). Elicit a few more examples.

SPEAKING

Aim
To give fluency practice in a debate format.

Step 1 Ask students to look at the items in A and choose two of them as a class. Then divide the class into groups of four or five. For one of the items, half the groups should agree with the statement and the other half should disagree, and vice versa for the other item.

Tip With a larger class, you could ask students to prepare four of the items, or divide the class into two halves. Try to plan it so that each group will have an opportunity to present.

Step 2 Ask each group to prepare what they are going to say either in support of or against the statements. They should discuss their ideas, including trying to anticipate what other groups will say and thinking of counter-arguments, and make notes. They should also elect a spokesperson. Give the groups about ten minutes for this.

Step 3 Choose a group in favour of the statement to start. Their representative should present their arguments for about two minutes. The rest of the class should listen and take notes. Then choose one of the groups against the statement to give the second presentation. Again, the class should take notes. After the presentation is finished, invite the rest of the class to make comments. They could vote for or against at the end. Then repeat with the second statement, making sure you use different groups. Monitor during the whole process, for a correction slot at the end.

pp. 46–47

SPEAKING

Aim
To lead in to *Reading* and give fluency practice.

Step 1 Put students in small groups and ask them to discuss what they know about South Africa. Conduct brief feedback, but be careful not to feed in too much as this is coming up in *Reading*.

VOCABULARY Social conflict

Aim
To look at vocabulary about social conflict used in *Reading*, give practice, and to predict the content of the text.

Step 1 Ask students to look at the nouns in the box in A and match them with the correct set of phrases 1–10. Check in pairs, then check with the whole group. Concept check by asking for definitions or examples.

> **Answers**
> 1 segregation   6 sanctions
> 2 boycott   7 march
> 3 massacre   8 dissent
> 4 condemnation   9 unrest
> 5 oppression   10 support

Step 2 Tell students they are going to test each other on the phrases. They should look at them again and try to memorise them. Then put them in pairs and ask them to take turns testing each other by prompting their partner with one of the words from the box. Their partner should try to remember as many of the collocates as possible. Then swap.

Step 3 Put students in pairs or threes and ask them to discuss how they think the nouns in the box in exercise A are connected with South Africa. Tell them to try to use some of the collocates in their discussion.

READING

Aim
To give practice in reading for gist and detail.

Step 1 Ask students to read the text about South Africa, ignoring the words in bold, and check if their predictions in *Vocabulary* exercise C were accurate. Conduct brief feedback.

Step 2 Put students in pairs and ask them to discuss how the nouns in bold are connected to South Africa's recent history. Check their understanding as a class.

Step 3 Ask students in the same pairs to look at the questions in C and discuss them in relation to the article. Conduct brief feedback, but don't tell students the answer to number 5, as this is coming up later.

> **Answers**
> 1 because it represented a huge change / achievement in 20 years
> 2 because he was leader of the banned African Congress and planned acts of sabotage
> 3 Apartheid began in the 1940s to help the white minority keep control of the country's riches.
> 4 It collapsed because it was costly and complicated to maintain and because of international and internal pressure.
> 5 Aim: to establish the truth about human rights violations, on both sides – but it focused mainly on the victims as a way of providing closure. Working methods: both sides could tell the truth about their actions, and request amnesty from prosecution.

46 OUTCOMES

06 CONFLICT

Step 4 Ask students to read the Wiki in D and check the answer to number 5 in exercise C. Conduct brief feedback.

Step 5 Ask students to look at the statements in E and decide whether they are true or false. Check in pairs and then check with the whole group. Get students to justify their answers by referring to evidence from the text.

Tip Ask students to correct the false statements.

> **Answers**
> 1 F – it aimed to establish the truth
> 2 T – it had no powers to prosecute
> 3 T – it could give amnesty from prosecution
> 4 F – they had to show their actions had been politically motivated and proportionate
> 5 T – compensation was offered in some cases

Step 6 Put students in small groups and ask them to discuss the questions in F. Conduct brief feedback.

Listening

Aim
To give practice in listening for gist and detail and to exploit the reading.

Step 1 Tell students they are going to hear three people discuss their experiences of The Truth and Reconciliation Commission. Ask them to listen and decide how each person feels and why. Play the recording.

> **Answers**
> **Speaker 1** = he thinks it was very important but flawed because it stirred up more bad feeling
> **Speaker 2** = she thinks it didn't solve any problems as it couldn't bring her son back, and she rejected the money she was offered
> **Speaker 3** = he thinks it has been a success as it has helped people to put the past behind them without seeking revenge

> **6.3**
> **Speaker 1**
> As a man of the church, I believe the Commission has been immensely important and has gone a long way towards healing a wounded, traumatised nation. It's only by learning about the wrongs of the past that we can ensure these mistakes will never be repeated.
>
> Obviously, though, it was not a perfect process. I was appalled at the evil that was uncovered. Bearing witness to such awful suffering takes its toll on you and more often than not, a day spent listening to testimony ended with tears and profound soul-searching questions about the Higher Purpose. I understand how these revelations stoked anger within the country, though I don't condone acts of vengeance against perpetrators.
>
> One thing that exacerbated the situation was the fact that perpetrators were given instant amnesty, whilst victims were required to wait before receiving compensation, payment which invariably failed to recognise the true degree of suffering experienced.
>
> **Speaker 2**
> I've tried to forgive and to forget, I truly have, but it's beyond me. My son was murdered by the police and I had to collect his bruised and bloodied body from the morgue. I went before the Commission to recount my experiences, yet rather than walk away healed, I left feeling worse than ever before. All I felt was that I was reliving his death all over again. That's why I rejected the sum that they offered me. It would've been like taking blood money! How can I put this behind me when I still don't know who did this to my boy or why it happened? I want justice.
>
> **Speaker 3**
> After years of being seen as a pariah state, as the lowest of the low, the Commission has at least shown the world we can draw a line under the past and move on in a civilised manner. In that respect, it's been a great success. When the old system collapsed, I was desperately worried there'd be a wave of revenge attacks, and although there's been a bit of that, by and large the transition has worked.
>
> The Commission has been key in shaping the national mood and moving people away from revenge and towards a place where we can all see the wrongs that were committed by both sides and the pain that was inflicted to all.

Step 2 Ask students to look at the items in B and match each one with one of the speakers. Then play the recording again for them to check. Check with the whole group.

> **Answers**
> 1 Speaker 3   6 Speaker 2
> 2 Speaker 2   7 Speaker 2
> 3 Speaker 1   8 Speaker 1
> 4 Speaker 3   9 Speaker 3
> 5 Speaker 2

Step 3 Put students in pairs or threes and ask them to discuss the questions in C. Conduct brief feedback.

Speaking

Aim
To give fluency practice and round off the unit.

Step 1 Ask students to look at the ideas about justice in A and think about their opinion of each one. Put them in small groups to discuss their ideas. Conduct brief feedback.

07 SCIENCE AND RESEARCH

UNIT OVERVIEW
In this unit students practise **explaining and discussing news stories** about **science and the uses and abuses of statistics**. They learn how to **express surprise and disbelief** and **talk about different kinds of science**. They **read texts about truth and statistics** and **about scientists,** and **listen to news stories about science** and to **scientists talking about their jobs**. The main grammar aim is revision of **passive forms**.

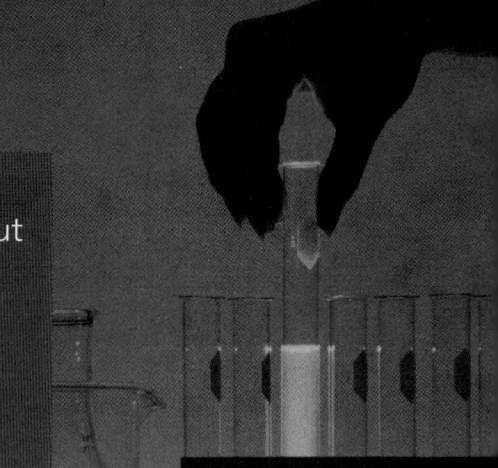

VOCABULARY Talking about science

Aim
To introduce words commonly used in the context of science.

Step 1 Begin by asking students how they feel about science and research. Try to elicit some words and phrases associated with the topic. Then ask them to look at the sentences in A and replace the words in italics with the correct form of the synonyms from the box. Do the first example with them. Put them in pairs to check their answers. Conduct brief feedback and concept check by asking how the pairs of words / phrases are different in each case. Read out the explanation in the box about synonyms / near synonyms.

Answers
1 breakthrough = step forward
2 root = underlying
3 diminished = impaired
4 stuck = inserted
5 thin end of the wedge = slippery slope
6 carried out = undertook
7 pave the way for = lead to
8 reproduce = duplicate
9 down to = due to
10 negative = adverse
11 condition = disorder
12 created = devised

Step 2 Put students in pairs to test each other. Student A should say one of the words / phrases from the box, and Student B should give the synonym. Then swap.

LISTENING

Aim
To give practice in predicting and note-taking.

Step 1 Tell students they are going to hear two conversations about science-based stories in the news. Put them in pairs and ask them to look at the headlines in A and discuss what they think each story is about and why.

Step 2 Tell students to listen and identify which headline each story goes with, and to take notes on the main points. Play the recording. Then put students in pairs to compare their ideas.

Answers
Conversation 1 = j
Conversation 2 = d

7.1
Conversation 1
A: Did you read that thing about transplanting the nose of mosquitoes?
B: What? Are you serious? I didn't think mosquitoes even had noses!
A: Yeah, well, it's obviously not a nose in the sense of our noses, but apparently it was like the smelling receptors on the antenna and what they do is they somehow get these receptors to grow on frog's eggs so that they can do tests on them.
B: How on earth do they do that?
A: To be perfectly honest, I'm not sure. They extract the DNA of the receptors or something and then inject it into the eggs. It's a bit beyond me really. I just thought it was amazing.
B: It sounds a bit dubious, if you ask me. I mean what's the point?
A: Well, apparently, they use them to see what smells trigger the receptors.
B: And?
A: Well, it's to stop the spread of malaria. Obviously, mosquitoes are strongly attracted to the smell of human sweat, but if they can find odours which create a bigger stimulus or which produce no trigger, then they could use those smells to manufacture traps to draw the mosquitoes away from humans or spray-on repellents to mask human smells.
B: OK. I suppose that makes sense. I have to say, though, I still find all that gene manipulation a bit disconcerting.
A: What do you mean?

48 OUTCOMES

B: Well, it's a slippery slope, isn't it? One moment it's mosquito noses, the next they'll be engineering babies.
A: Come off it! It's hardly the same thing!

Conversation 2
C: Did you read this thing about building a sun shield in space to prevent global warming?
D: No. It sounds a bit unlikely, though. I mean, how big would it have to be?
C: Apparently about 60,000 miles long!
D: 60,000! That's ridiculous! I mean, how on earth are they going to build something that big, let alone get it up there? They struggle to build a stadium here on time and on budget.
C: Well, that's it – the idea with this is it's not like one big structure, it's millions of little reflectors which form a massive cloud.
D: But how many would you need?
C: Trillions. They reckon if they deploy a stack of these things every five minutes it'd take ten years to make.
D: Hardly an instant solution then!
C: No.
D: And what about the cost?
C: I've no idea, to be honest, but they claim it's all quite feasible. Anyway, this guy's got a grant to look into it further.
D: You're joking! What a waste of money! Are you sure it isn't just a scam or some made-up story?
C: It was on a fairly reputable website.
D: Pah! Mind you, I sometimes wonder whether the whole climate change thing is a scam. It's all just about vested interests and people out to make a buck.
C: You're not serious, are you?
D: Yeah, why not?
C: Because the evidence is pretty incontrovertible.
D: Says who?

Step 3 Ask students to look at the statements in exercise B and decide if they are true or false as they listen again. Play the recording again.

Tip Ask them to correct the false statements.

Answers
1 F – to frogs' eggs
2 T – to prevent malaria
3 F – they are going to look for smells which attract mosquitoes
4 F – one is, one isn't
5 T – to prevent global warming
6 F – they want to build a sun shield in space
7 T – but hypothetically
8 F – he has funding to look into it further
9 T – all about vested interest and people out to make a buck

Step 4 Put students in pairs or threes and ask them to discuss the questions in D. Conduct brief feedback.

LANGUAGE PATTERNS

Aim
To draw students' attention to patterns with *hardly*.

Step 1 Ask students to read the examples in the box and check they understand. Ask them to translate the sentences into their own language and notice any similarities / differences. In a monolingual class, ask students to compare their translation. In a multilingual class, ask students to work in pairs and tell each other if the sentences were easy to translate.

Step 2 Then ask them to close their books and translate the sentences back into their own language. At the end, they should open their books again and compare their translations with the original sentences. Ask them to discuss in pairs who had the least mistakes. What mistakes did they make? Why?

Alternatively If you prefer not to use translation, ask students to look at the sentences and tell you what patterns they notice = *hardly* + noun phrase, adjective or verb in the affirmative, meaning *almost not*. Try to elicit a few more examples.

DEVELOPING CONVERSATIONS
Expressing surprise and disbelief

Aim
To look at ways of expressing surprise and disbelief using *on earth*.

Step 1 Read out the explanation box and check students understand the expression and why we use it (to express surprise, disbelief or sometimes frustration or anger; to emphasise what we are saying). Try to elicit a few more examples.

Step 2 Ask students to listen to the questions and repeat each one, paying attention to stress, linking and intonation.

🔊 7.2
1 What on earth for?
2 Why on earth would they want to do that?
3 What on earth's that?
4 Who on earth would buy something like that?
5 Where on earth are they going to get the money for that?
6 What on earth is he going on about?

07 SCIENCE AND RESEARCH 49

07 SCIENCE AND RESEARCH

Step 3 Ask students to look at the statements in B and write a question using *on earth* in response to each one. Do the first example with them first. Monitor as they write and check their sentences are appropriate.

> **Suggested answers**
> 1 What on earth is that?
> 2 How on earth …? / Why on earth …?
> 3 Where on earth is that?
> 4 How on earth …? / Why on earth …?
> 5 Why on earth …?
> 6 Who / Why / How …?

Step 4 Put students in pairs and ask them to practise. They should take turns saying one of the sentences in B and responding with their questions with *on earth*. They should then continue the conversation as long as they can. You could start in open pairs, paying particular attention to stress, linking and intonation, before continuing in closed pairs.

CONVERSATION PRACTICE

Aim
To give practice in responding to what you read.

Step 1 Tell students they are going to practise reading articles and responding to them. Divide them into groups of three: A, B and C. Student A should look at File 8 on page 155, Student B should look at File 15 on page 157 and Student C should look at File 19 on page 159. They should each read all the articles quickly and choose one to talk about. They should then read their chosen article in a little more depth and check they understand everything.

Step 2 When they are ready, ask students to come together in their threes and take turns telling each other about their articles, and responding. They should begin by asking *Did you read that thing about …?* and use language from this part of the unit. They should then discuss what they really think about each story.

Step 3 When they have finished one article each, ask them to choose another story they have read or one they have heard about and repeat the process. Conduct brief feedback at the end by asking what was the most surprising / strange / funny etc. story they heard.

pp. 50–51

Next class Make photocopies of **7A** p. 140.

VOCABULARY Statistics

Aim
To focus on phrases commonly used in the context of statistics.

Step 1 Ask students to look at the sentences in A and try to guess the meanings of the phrases in bold from the context. Ask them to translate them into their own language.

Tip With a monolingual class, put them in pairs to compare their translations. With a multilingual class, ask them to tell each other if the words / phrases were easy to translate. Ask them all to notice the grammar differences / similarities.

Alternatively If you prefer not to use translation, ask them to try to paraphrase the phrases. Check in pairs, then check with the whole group.

> **Answers**
> 1 a link, but where one figure is in opposition or in reverse of the other
> 2 distorted the figures (results / numbers) for their own benefit
> 3 it will be to their own advantage
> 4 are not really precise or accurate or they do not represent what they appear to
> 5 in contrast to what most people think
> 6 there are large problems with the research
> 7 to make a connection
> 8 an exception in the statistics
> 9 different bits of evidence which disagree with each other

Step 2 Put students in pairs and ask them to choose five of the words / phrases in bold from exercise A and think of real-life examples for each. Conduct brief feedback.

READING

Aim
To give practice in reading for gist and detail.

Step 1 Tell students they are going to read an article about statistics. Put them in pairs or threes and ask them to look at the questions and discuss why these questions would be important to ask about research.

Step 2 Ask students to read the article and find out why the questions in A are important in the context of deciding how valid a piece of research is. Check in pairs, then check with the whole group.

> **Answers**
> 1 because it will vary in how accurate it is
> 2 because it will affect its validity
> 3 because it will affect its validity
> 4 because numbers can be manipulated

07 SCIENCE AND RESEARCH

> 5 because sometimes the data and the conclusions are not really connected
> 6 because there may be self-interest involved

Step 3 Put students in pairs or threes and ask them to discuss the questions in C. Conduct brief feedback.

GRAMMAR Passives

Aim
To revise passive forms and give practice.

Step 1 Put students in pairs and ask them to look at the sentences from the stories they read earlier in *Conversation practice* and follow the instructions in A together. Direct them to the grammar reference on page 142 if they need help. Check with the whole group.

> **Answers**
> **Conversation 1** 1 which will be sold
> 2 scientists
> 3 which they will sell
> 4 because we are more interested in the frogs
> **Conversation 2** 1 getting killed
> 2 scientists, teachers
> 3 rather than killing them for dissection
> 4 because we are more interested in not killing the frogs
> **Conversation 3** 1 have cancerous cells inserted in their bodies
> 2 scientists
> 3 scientists insert cancerous cells into the bodies of the fish
> 4 because it is better stylistically and we are more interested in the fish
> **Conversation 4** 1 is thought to be
> 2 people in general
> 3 people think the so-called Love hormone is responsible
> 4 because it is better stylistically and the doer is general / unknown
> **Conversation 5** 1 a census undertaken (which was undertaken)
> 2 the department of Clinical Veterinary Science
> 3 which the CVS undertook
> 4 because the census is more important than the department and it is better stylistically
> **Conversation 6** 1 they were given
> 2 researchers
> 3 researchers gave them
> 4 because we are more interested in the penguins
> **Conversation 7** 1 is seen
> 2 people in general
> 3 people see the research

> 4 because the doer is unknown / general
> **Conversation 8** 1 has been extracted
> 2 scientists
> 3 scientists have extracted
> 4 because we are more interested in the DNA

Step 2 Ask students to look at the questions in B and think about how they would answer them. Then put them in small groups to discuss the questions. Conduct brief feedback.

Step 3 Ask students to look at the research reports in C and complete them using the correct active or passive form of the verbs in brackets. Check in pairs, then check with the whole group. Make sure students understand why the form is used in each case.

> **Answers**
> 1 had been reported   8 is defined
> 2 lead   9 were obliged
> 3 has dumped   10 treated
> 4 causing   11 involving
> 5 published   12 to be tightened
> 6 has found   13 has plunged
> 7 are kept

7A see Teacher's notes p. 123.

LISTENING

Aim
To give practice in listening for gist and detail.

Step 1 Tell students they are going to hear people commenting on each of the statistics in *Grammar* exercise C. Put students in small groups to discuss the questions in A.

Step 2 Ask students to listen and check their ideas from A. Play the recording. Check in pairs, then check with the class.

> 🔊 **7.3**
> 1 It's difficult to interpret this story without knowing the number of accidents per mile travelled. If there were twice as many journeys in fair weather then the snowstorm has indeed increased the accident rate. Furthermore, more evidence is needed over a period of time to establish a correlation. It could be that bad weather really does reduce incidents due to people driving more carefully.
> 2 The statistics themselves in this study were accurately collected and described. However, the lobby group who commissioned the study were so-called 'stay-at-home mums' and in the interpretation and the narrowness of the time frame for the study, there was a strong element of twisting the data to fit a conclusion they'd set out to find.

07 SCIENCE AND RESEARCH

The truth, which was excluded from analysis, is that aggression is a normal developmental stage, where children test boundaries. Not only is aggression normal, it doesn't usually last. The study failed to measure the stay-at-home toddlers' behaviour when they were mixed in groups, where the same levels of aggression can be observed. Indeed, a follow-up study by different researchers discovered that those kids who had been kept at home exhibited more aggression in school those who'd been in nursery i.e. it simply appeared at a later stage.

3 This statistic seems counter-intuitive, but only if you ignore other evidence. The statistic fails to mention that the number of fatalities plunged. As more survive accidents, more are treated for injury. Of course, the statistic also tells us nothing about the severity of the injuries.

4 The group are self-selecting, so we might imagine those strongly against animal testing will be more inclined to phone. Furthermore, the poll is biased because it followed a report on cruelty and mistreatment in one laboratory.

5 The base numbers are all true. However, the starting point that was chosen was the year when there had been a terrorist bombing in the city, which obviously inflated the figures. In previous years, the figures had actually been 94 and 98. Of course, whether that correlation can be attributed to government policy is another thing. There could be a number of underlying causes.

pp. 52–53

Next class Make photocopies of **7B** p. 141.

SPEAKING

Aim
To give fluency practice and lead in to *Listening*.

Step 1 Begin by asking students what their image of scientists is. *What stereotypes are there? Do they know any scientists? Are they really like that?* Then ask them to read the short text in A and think about their answers to the questions. Ask them to guess what they think *homogeneous* (all the same) and *hunched over* (bent over) mean from the context.

Step 2 Put students in small groups to discuss their ideas. Conduct brief feedback.

NATIVE SPEAKER ENGLISH *geeky*

Read out the explanation in the box and check students understand. Ask them whether these words are used positively or negatively (negatively). Concept check by asking them how they think geeks and nerds dress and behave.

LISTENING

Aim
To give practice in listening for gist and specific information.

Step 1 Put students in pairs or threes and ask them to discuss the questions in exercise A in relation to the different types of scientist in the box.

Step 2 Tell students they are going to hear five scientists talking about their jobs. They should decide which type of scientist from A each speaker is and note down what each job involves. Play the recording.

> **Answers**
> 1 astronomer – analysing visual data
> 2 agricultural scientist – research in lab or with animals in their habitat
> 3 military scientist – studying war and devising military strategies
> 4 hydrologist – studying water in the environment and assessing risk
> 5 anthropologist – studying different cultures

◎ 7.4
Speaker 1
There's a popular notion that we're a peculiarly nocturnal breed that stays up all night glued to our telescopes, but the reality is far more mundane. Most of the time, we work normal nine-to-five hours and are busy analysing visual data or working on computer programmes that'll help us process the abundance of information we receive. Where we differ from the vast majority of other scientists is in the fact that we do not have direct contact with our object of study. We are obviously unable to weigh, touch or dissect stars and so observation and reasoning skills become paramount.

Speaker 2
The job can involve anything from conservation to genetics, and you may end up being employed in museums or schools, by state or local governments or even by private companies. Broadly speaking, though, the profession splits into two main camps: there's the research side of things, based mainly in the lab, carrying out experiments to help determine the wellbeing of animals. Then there are those of us such as myself who work in situ. What we do is direct the activities that animals should go through, study behaviour patterns, advise on habitat and so on.

Speaker 3
As a rule, I don't discuss my own particular line work, though in essence the field I am involved in is one that remains vital for national security. We study the techniques, psychology and practice of war and other forms of armed conflict. We're responsible for developing new prototypes; we aim to increase the effectiveness of

52 OUTCOMES

07 SCIENCE AND RESEARCH

concepts and systems; we develop new training regimes, and we come up with strategies to enable us to maintain status in an ever-changing world. Obviously, this also means we play a very active role in advising central government on how best to ensure full capability.

Speaker 4
As with many other kinds of scientists, my work divides between fieldwork and office work. Generally speaking, what I do is I analyse, assess, forecast and report on the water environment. The work I do feeds directly into and helps underpin the work the Environmental Agency does. I mainly work with rainfall and river flow data – looking at the flood risk side of things, of course, but also looking at potential damage to the environment in low-flow areas and the like. It's incredibly rewarding knowing my endeavours may well lead to positive environmental outcomes.

Speaker 5
The stereotype is that we all spend our time in exotic locations around the globe, analysing mating rituals and spiritual beliefs, and there may once have been a grain of truth in those assumptions, but nowadays things are very different. Take me, for instance: I tend more towards the cultural side of things. I mean, my first research project was a study of reggae music around the world and I've also spent time in the UK studying pub etiquette. My partner, on the other hand, works freelance as a personal trainer, assisting business people with transitions from one culture to another during relocations on a global scale.

Step 3 Ask students to look at the statements in exercise C and decide which speaker does each one. Then play the recording again for them to check.

Answers
1 the hydrologist
2 the agricultural scientist
3 the military scientist
4 the hydrologist
5 the astronomer
6 the anthropologist
7 the agricultural scientist
8 the anthropologist
9 the astronomer (in that they have no direct contact with stars – the object of their research)
10 the military scientist

Step 4 Put students in small groups to discuss the questions in D. Conduct brief feedback.

VOCABULARY Forming words

Aim
To focus on ways of forming nouns, and give practice.

Step 1 Ask students to look at the sentences in A and complete them with a noun formed from the adjective in brackets. Check in pairs, then check with the whole group. Check the stress on each of the nouns.

Answers
1 exploration
2 variables
3 diversity
4 capability
5 manipulation
6 aggression
7 prevention
8 cynicism
9 abundance
10 fatalities
11 probability
12 implications

Step 2 Ask students to look again at the adjectives in A and decide which six can be made into verbs and what the verbs are in each case. Check in pairs, then check with the whole group.

Answers
1 explore
2 vary
3 manipulate
4 prevent
5 abound
6 imply

Step 3 Put students in small groups and ask them to look back at the statements and decide which ones they agree with and why / why not. Conduct brief feedback.

7B see Teacher's notes p. 123.

SPEAKING

Aim
To give fluency practice and round off the unit.

Step 1 Put students in groups of four or five. Tell them they are going to do some research into different kinds of scientists and report their findings. Ask them to look back at the scientists in the box in *Listening* exercise A and each choose a different one, which was not featured in the recording. Ask them to work individually and find out as much as they can about the job, qualifications required, career opportunities etc. from the Internet.

Tip If you have access to computers, this can be done in class time. If not, the research can be done for homework and brought along to start the next lesson with.

Step 2 Ask students to come together in their groups and report their findings to each other. At the end, ask each group to vote for the best-sounding job. Conduct brief feedback with the whole group.

Step 3 Ask students to look at the questions in 2 and think about how they would answer them. Then put them back in the same groups to discuss their ideas. Conduct brief feedback at the end.

Alternatively If short of time, you could ask each group to choose two of the questions each and discuss them. Then report back to the rest of the class on their ideas.

08 NATURE

UNIT OVERVIEW
In this unit students practise describing natural landscapes, **animals**, their **habits** and their **habitats**, and learn how to use **tags to emphasise their opinions** and how to **describe different ways of talking**. They **read texts** about natural history programmes and about **differences between men and women**, and **listen to people talking about two different landscapes** and about **animal habitats and features**, and to a **lecture about gender and language**. The main grammar aim is revision of different uses of **auxiliaries**.

Next class Make photocopies of 8A p. 142.

VOCABULARY Describing scenery

Aim
To lead in to the unit and focus on ways of describing landscapes.

Step 1 Begin by asking students what kind of landscapes they like. Then ask them to label the pictures with words from the box. Check in pairs, then with the whole group.

Answers
1 a mountain range
2 plains
3 a peak
4 a crater
5 the mouth of the river
6 a glacier
7 wetland
8 a stream
9 cliffs
10 a bay
11 a gorge
12 woodland

Step 2 Put students in pairs and ask them to look at the sentences in A and decide whether both or only one of the words in italics is possible. If both are correct, they should discuss the differences. Check with the whole group. Ask them to explain differences between similar words and explain why the incorrect ones are incorrect.

Answers
1 rolling hills, winding streams, thick or dense woodland
2 arid, edge or fringes, dunes
3 countryside or landscape, fertile
4 track or road, rugged, gorges
5 breathtaking or stunning, sandy or rocky, crystal clear

Step 3 Ask students to look at the questions in C and think about how they would answer them. Then put them in pairs or threes to discuss the questions. Conduct brief feedback.

Tip In a multilingual class, try to mix nationalities as much as possible. In a monolingual class, get them to try and agree on the answers to the questions.

5B see Teacher's notes p. 123.

LISTENING

Aim
To give practice in listening for gist and detail.

Step 1 Tell students they are going to hear two conversations in which people talk about the scenery in places they have visited. Ask them to look at the questions in A and answer them as they listen. Play the recording.

Answers
Conversation 1
1 Jura in France
2 on holiday
3 mountainous with gorges and valleys, winding rivers – rugged

Conversation 2
1 Venezuela – to a big glacier
2 working, doing research
3 breathtaking, dense woodland with ice and mountains

8.1
Conversation 1
A: So how was your holiday? Did you have a good time?
B: Yeah, it was amazing, it really was.
A: Where were you again? France somewhere, wasn't it?

54 OUTCOMES

B: Yeah, Jura, right near the Swiss border. It's an amazing bit of the country. We started off in the southeast, where it's really mountainous, with all these gorges dropping down into the valleys and these winding rivers, and then we slowly worked our way northwards, to where all the vineyards are, because it's a big wine-making region up there.
A: Wow! It sounds great. So were you driving, then?
B: No, we weren't, actually. We were hiking.
A: Seriously?
B: Yeah, it was a group thing. We booked it over the Internet.
A: It must've been pretty strenuous.
B: To be honest, it wasn't that bad. I mean, it's pretty rugged in places, but you soon get into the swing of it. It was great exercise, I can tell you! I haven't felt this fit in years.
A: I bet! And what were the other people on the tour like? Did you all get on OK?
B: Yeah, they were all great. What was weird, though, was that there was a couple there from my hometown.
A: Yeah? That's a bit spooky.
B: Yeah. Look. That's them there in the photo. Marcin and Edyta.
A: Oh, OK. They look nice – and that's an amazing view behind them!
B: Yeah, stunning, isn't it? That's Mont Blanc you can see in the background.

Conversation 2
C: So what is it that you do, then?
D: I'm a geologist.
C: Oh, OK. And where are you based?
D: I work all over the place, really, but the last six months, I've been in Venezuela. I actually only got back the other day, so I'm still getting back into the swing of things a bit.
C: I imagine it must take a while. So what were you doing there? I mean, what was your project?
D: Oh, I was doing some research on a big glacier there, Glacier Los Perros, seeing what kind of impact global warming has had on it.
C: That sounds amazing, it really does.
D: Yeah, it was wonderful. It's a breathtaking place, Venezuela. Have you been there?
C: No, never, no.
D: Where we had our HQ was right on the edge of all this dense woodland, looking out over the ice, with these snow-capped mountains off in the background, and every morning when I got up, my heart just leapt to see it all. It was something else.
C: And what're its prospects? I mean, how did it come out after the research?
D: Well, nothing's conclusive as yet, but it does seem that there's definitely some melting going on, unfortunately.

Step 2 Put students in pairs. Ask them to look at the items in B and try to remember what the speakers said about them. Then play the recording again for them to check.

Answers
Conversation 1
a Jura is near the Swiss border
b there were vineyards to the north – where they hiked to
c the woman booked the holiday on the Internet
d the holiday made her feel very fit
e there was a couple from her hometown on the holiday

Conversation 2
f he works all over the place
g he only got back the other day
h he was doing research into global warming
i he had a view of snow-capped mountains
j the results of the research were inconclusive but there seemed to be evidence of global warming

Step 3 Put students in pairs or threes to discuss the questions in exercise D. Conduct brief feedback.

Language patterns

Aim
To draw students' attention to patterns with *this*, *that*, *these* and *those*.

Step 1 Ask students to read the examples in the box and check they understand. Ask them to translate the sentences into their own language and notice any similarities / differences. In a monolingual class, ask students to compare their translation. In a multilingual class, ask students to work in pairs and tell each other if the sentences were easy to translate.

Step 2 Then ask them to close their books and translate the sentences back into their own language. At the end, they should open their books again and compare their translations with the original sentences. Ask them to discuss in pairs who had the least mistakes. What mistakes did they make? Why?

Alternatively If you prefer not to use translation, ask students to look at the sentences and tell you what patterns they notice = *this, that, these, those* used informally / in a chatty way. Try to elicit a few more examples.

08 NATURE

DEVELOPING CONVERSATIONS
Emphatic tags

Aim
To practise ways of adding a tag to emphasise opinions.

Step 1 Read out the explanation in the box and check students understand. Try to elicit a few more examples.

Step 2 Ask students to look at the sentences in A and add an emphatic tag to give it more emphasis. Then play the recording for them to check their answers.

> **8.2 and answers**
> 1. I wouldn't drive it if I were you, I really wouldn't.
> 2. The views were just stunning, they really were.
> 3. The scenery takes your breath away, it really does.
> 4. I just love it there, I really do.
> 5. It made no difference whatsoever, it really didn't.
> 6. He'll never change, he really won't.
> 7. I've never been anywhere like it, I really haven't.
> 8. That sounds amazing, it really does.

Step 3 Ask students to repeat the sentences with the tag, paying attention to intonation and putting the stress on *really*.

CONVERSATION PRACTICE

Aim
To practise conversations similar to the ones heard in *Listening*.

Step 1 Tell students they are going to have conversations similar to those they heard in the audio recording.
Ask them to work individually and think of two places they know that have different and interesting scenery. They should imagine they went there, what they were doing there, how they travelled around and what the place was like. They could make a few notes.

Step 2 Put students in small groups and ask them to take turns telling each other about their places. They should try to emphasise their opinions by adding tags, and use language from this part of the unit. Tell them to pretend they've been to the place their partner tells them about. Tell them to choose the best place they heard about and why. Monitor and take notes for a correction slot at the end.

pp. 56–57

Next class Make photocopies of 8B p. 143.

SPEAKING

Aim
To give fluency practice and lead in to the next *Listening*.

Step 1 Begin by asking students what they know about *Men are from Mars, Women are from Venus* by John Gray. If they know nothing or very little, ask them what they can guess from the title. Then ask them to read the short text.

Step 2 Put students in small groups and ask them to discuss the questions. Conduct brief feedback but don't give 'answers' as these are coming up in *Listening*.

LISTENING

Aim
To give practice in listening for main ideas and detail, and summary writing.

Step 1 Tell students they are going to hear a lecture about gender and language. They should complete the summary notes as they listen. Tell them slight variations are possible. Play the recording. Check answers in pairs, then check with the whole class.

> **Answers**
> (slight variations are possible)
> 1. retreating into their cave
> 2. communicate with others / reach out
> 3. these myths / the myth of difference
> 4. a negative effect on our culture
> 5. based on scientific research
> 6. both sexes talk equally
> 7. 16,000 words
> 8. power / positions of power
> 9. stereotypes we already have
> 10. occasions which back up the evidence
> 11. gender roles
> 12. swear / express their anger by swearing

> **8.3**
> It's common knowledge that men and women do things differently, isn't it? The male of the species, we're told, retreats into a cave to brood at the slightest sign of stress, whilst the female reaches out and shares her feelings. After all, women are better communicators, aren't they? Well, aren't they?
>
> That's certainly how we've been conditioned to see things over the last twenty years or so. The glut of self-help books that have followed in the wake of *Men are from Mars, Women are from Venus* have served to perpetuate the myth of difference and, I would argue, have had a profoundly negative effect on our culture.

56 OUTCOMES

It's easy to assume these books must be based on valid scientific research, but in reality very few are. Indeed, even a cursory inspection of the literature of the field reveals that in fact men and women communicate in remarkably similar ways. Take the notion that women talk more – and use more words to do so. Despite being widely reported as fact, research actually shows that both sexes tend to talk equally as much and use as many words per day while doing so – around 16,000.

Then there's the belief that men interrupt more. Evidence actually suggests that women interrupt at least as much as men. Whilst some men do interrupt far more than the vast majority of women, this is atypical, and such actions are often tied in to a position of power. Ultimately, when and how people interrupt has far more to do with social status and power than it does with genetic make-up and 'nature'. Linguistic studies have shown there's an overlap of more than 95% in the way the sexes communicate. Yet still myths of Venus and Mars prevail. Given this, it's surely worth asking why!

Well, firstly, such sweeping generalisations as 'Women are more in touch with their feelings' appeal because they match the stereotypes we already have. As such, we recall occasions on which evidence backed up this idea up – and forget examples that might contradict it!

A more significant reason for the continuing appeal of such theories, though, may well lie in the fact that gender roles have changed dramatically over recent years. Both women and men now frequently aspire to an education, a career, a decent income – and both often act, talk and maybe even dress in similar ways. For many people, these changes have happened too quickly and are deeply unsettling. What better way to comfort yourself than a return to the traditional gender roles and stereotypes of the past?

Should you require any further proof that difference is rooted in nurture far more than nature, consider the village of Gapun in Papua New Guinea, where the men pride themselves on their ability to speak indirectly and never say what they mean, whilst the women frequently give voice to their anger by launching into lengthy swearing sessions. Does this prove that sometimes it is women that are from Mars? I suspect not. Personally, I see this as proof that we are all from earth and need to start dealing with this fact rather better than we have been!

Step 2 Ask students to look at the words in C and match an adjective with the correct noun phrase, as they were used in the recording. Then put students in pairs to check and to discuss what the lecturer said about each of the adjective + noun collocations.

Answers
1g common knowledge = it is common knowledge that men and women do things differently
2e a negative effect = books like this have a negative effect on our culture
3b valid scientific research = these books are not based on this
4a a cursory inspection = a cursory inspection of the literature on the subject shows men and women communicate in similar ways
5c sweeping generalisations = these books are full of sweeping generalisations about men and women
6h the continuing appeal = the continuing appeal of these theories lies in people's fear of change
7d unsettling changes = changes in gender roles can be found unsettling
8f traditional gender roles = people take comfort in clinging to traditional gender roles

Step 3 Ask students to listen again and read the audioscript on page 168 as they listen to check their answers to the questions in exercise C. Play the recording again.

Step 4 Put students in small groups and ask them to discuss the questions in F. Conduct brief feedback.

NATIVE SPEAKER ENGLISH *the slightest*

Read out the box and check students understand the use of *the slightest* to mean *any at all*. Try to elicit a few more examples with *the slightest*.

GRAMMAR Auxiliaries

Aim
To revise various uses of auxiliaries and give practice.

Step 1 Ask students to look at the sentences in A and complete them using the correct auxiliary.

Answers
1	a isn't	b aren't
2	a are	b doing
3	a do	b does
4	a Does	b Did
5	a do	b have

Step 2 Put students in pairs to compare their answers and to identify the five different uses of auxiliaries represented by each pair of sentences. Ask them to think of other examples of each use. Direct them to the grammar reference on page 143 if they need help.

08 NATURE

08 NATURE

> **Answers**
> 1 question tags
> 2 substitution – to avoid repeating a whole phrase
> 3 emphasis
> 4 as a response
> 5 with *so* or *neither / nor* – another type of substitution

> 🗣 🗣 **8B** see Teacher's notes p. 123.

VOCABULARY Communicating

Aim
To introduce and have practice in pairs of words commonly used in the context of communication.

Step 1 Ask students to look at the sentences in A and complete each one with the correct pair of words from the box. Check in pairs. Then check with the whole group. Concept check by asking for other examples or definitions.

> **Answers**
> 1 gossip + rumours
> 2 mince + blunt
> 3 shuts up + word
> 4 twisting + words
> 5 manners + butting into
> 6 listener + shoulder
> 7 articulate + struggle
> 8 bush + point

Step 2 Put students in pairs to discuss the question in B. Conduct brief feedback.

SPEAKING

Aim
To give freer practice of the vocabulary and personalise the topic.

Step 1 Ask students to look at the questions in A and think about how they would answer them. Check they understand *defy gender stereotypes* = behave in a different way from what is expected according to the stereotype, and its opposite = *conform to traditional gender stereotypes*. Elicit a few examples of each.

Step 2 Put students in small groups to discuss their answers to the questions in A. Conduct brief feedback.

📖 **pp. 58–58**

READING 1

Aim
To give practice in reading for gist and detail.

Step 1 Tell students they are going to read an article about natural history programmes. Check they understand *natural history* = *nature*. Put them in pairs or threes and ask them to discuss the questions in A. Conduct brief feedback.

Step 2 Ask students to read the article, ignoring the words in bold, and make a list of the reasons the writer gives for watching natural history programmes. Check in pairs, then check with the whole group.

> **Answers**
> 1 he marvels at the ingenuity of the human race
> 2 he is interested in other forms of life and it makes him feel humbled
> 3 he enjoys the details of animals' lives – it is like watching six films rolled into one
> 4 it reminds him that we are part of nature too

Step 3 Put students in pairs and ask them to discuss the questions in C. Conduct brief feedback.

Step 4 Ask students to look at the sentences in D and complete them with the correct form of the words in bold in the article. Check in pairs, then check with the whole class.

> **Answers**
> 1 predators   5 food chain
> 2 prey   6 flock
> 3 mate   7 herd
> 4 foraging   8 rear

VOCABULARY Animals

Aim
To extend the topic and introduce words associated with animals.

Step 1 Ask students to look at the photos and label them with words from the box in exercise A. Check in pairs, then check with the whole group.

> **Answers**
> 1 legs, fur, feelers, nostrils, a claw
> 2 a tail, legs, fur, nostrils
> 3 legs, a claw, a beak, a wing, a breast, a tail, a toe
> 4 a tail, a beak, a breast
> 5 legs, nostrils, a hump
> 6 scales, teeth
> 7 a beak
> 8 a hoof, legs, a horn

08 NATURE

Step 2 Ask students to listen to the recording and identify the animals being described. Ask them to make notes on what the different parts of their body are for. Check in pairs. Then check with the whole group.

> **Answers**
> 1 **mole:** claws for digging, tail for storing fat; feelers for 'seeing'; star-shaped nose to smell its prey
> 2 **sparrow hawk:** wings and tail to fly fast; markings to camouflage it; long legs to kill mid-flight; long slender middle toe to grip and hold prey; beak for plucking and tearing flesh

8.4

1
Unusually for this species, it can swim underwater as well as burrow underground, which is handy, as it inhabits low wetland areas. Its long claws are adapted for digging through the earth and its water-resistant fur allows it to remain submerged in water. The long thick tail is thought to store extra fat to draw upon during the mating season. The mole is functionally blind, which is why it has developed the distinctive star-shaped set of feelers that give it its name.

The feelers are incredibly sensitive to movement. Uniquely, the mole can also smell underwater. It does this by blowing out tiny bubbles through its nose in order to capture scents that are sucked back in. These adaptations are highly efficient and the star-nosed mole is apparently the fastest eater in the animal kingdom, being able to identify, snatch and consume its prey all in a matter of milliseconds.

2
The sparrow hawk is most commonly found in woodland. Its short, broad wings and long tail allow it to manoeuvre quickly through the trees. The light striped markings on its breast and its darker upper parts help it to blend into the background, which allows it to lie in wait for its prey before shooting out. It has relatively long legs that enable it to kill in mid-flight and the long slender central toe is adapted to grasp with a small protuberance on the underside enabling it to grip and hold on to its prey. Its small hooked beak is used for plucking and tearing flesh rather than killing. It also sometimes hunts on foot through vegetation. In recent years, it has encroached more and more into cities where it has no predators and where it is often seen as a pest damaging garden bird populations.

Step 3 Ask students to match 1–10 in exercise C with the correct endings. Check in pairs, then check with the whole group.

> **Answers**
> 1 e   6 j
> 2 g   7 d
> 3 a   8 h
> 4 f   9 c
> 5 i   10 b

Step 4 Put students in pairs or threes. Ask them to look at the photos again and discuss the questions in exercise D. Conduct brief feedback.

READING 2

Aim
To give practice in reading for detail and exchanging information.

Step 1 Tell students they are going to read about different animals and exchange their information. Divide the class into two halves – A and B. Ask Group A to look at File 6 on page 154 and Group B to look at File 11 on page 156. Ask them individually to read their texts and make notes on the areas in B.

Step 2 Put students in same letter pairs. Ask them to check their answers and help each other with any vocabulary they are not sure about. Remind them to use the *Vocabulary builder* for help.

Step 3 Put students in AB pairs and get them to take turns telling each other about their animals. They should then choose the animal they prefer and say why. Conduct brief feedback.

SPEAKING

Aim
To give fluency practice and round off the unit.

Step 1 Put students in pairs and ask them to choose either question 1 or 2 in exercise A. They should then work individually to prepare.

Step 2 Ask pairs to come together and discuss their ideas / findings. Conduct brief feedback at the end.

Alternatively Ask all students to follow the procedure for *Speaking* question 1. Then set the preparation part of question 2 for homework, and get students to report their findings in the following lesson.

02 REVIEW

Two minutes, game, conversation practice & act or draw

For aims and suggested procedure, see Review 01, pages 32–35.

Quiz

Answers
1 You might feel **rough** because you are tired, ill or hungover.
2 If you were **mortified** you would feel very embarrassed.
3 Authors, musicians and artists are all paid **royalties**.
4 If someone holds a **grudge**, they feel bitter about something done against them in the past, and possibly seek revenge.
5 A murder or violent crime might be described as **cold-blooded**.
6 If fighting **escalates**, it increases and gets more violent.
7 A politician might **seize power** by staging a coup.
8 If something is **prevalent**, there is a lot of it.
9 You could **devise** a plan, a scheme, a set of rules etc.
10 A political party or country with financial interests in the country at war might have a **vested interest** in a war continuing.
11 Examples: there is **a negative correlation** between income and birth rate: the richer the country, the lower the birth rate. A **positive correlation** might be: there is a positive correlation between people graduating from university and getting good jobs.
12 You could **manipulate** figures, statistics or a person to prove a point or get what you want.
13 A mountainous and rocky landscape is **rugged**.
14 Someone might **butt in** (interrupt) when you are having a conversation with someone else and you might feel annoyed.
15 Rodents (e.g. mice, rats, hamsters) **gnaw**.

Collocations

For aims and suggested procedure, see Review 01, pages 32–35.

Idioms

Answers
1 He was mad, drunk or under the influence of drugs.
2 I couldn't sleep.
3 We couldn't stop laughing.
4 He was very upset.
5 We need to forgive and forget.
6 You can see signs of something – usually bad – about to happen
7 We are at risk of things deteriorating in the future.
8 The research is flawed.
9 You're being inaccurate about what I said.
10 I didn't get a chance to speak.
11 Don't drop hints – speak directly.
12 Can you say what your main point is?
13 I got used to it.
14 He was teasing someone.
15 It was incredible.

pp. 62–63

Listening

For aims and suggested procedure for the rest of the review, see Review 01, pages 32–35. The audio is R2.1.

Answers
1 *Predators and Prey*
2 overwhelming
3 photo journalism
4 make new connections and get insights
5 taking photos of construction projects
6 was threatening wetland
7 vested interests
8 of relaxing
9 lion
10 people's protests

60 OUTCOMES

Grammar

Exercise A answers
1 I **did** go to several shops, but they weren't on sale anywhere.
2 It's an adventure story, **based** on his travel experiences.
3 I occasionally wish **I did** something else, but generally I like my job.
4 The disease is believed **to have** a genetic component.
5 We won't be gone that long, **will** we?
6 They're building a thirty-five-**storey** office block which is due to open next year.
7 I wish I'd said something, but I **didn't**.
8 The device can withstand high temperatures after **being** treated with the special paint.

Exercise B answers
1 ended up being thrown out
2 If only I hadn't sold
3 so am I
4 I didn't live
5 have two teeth taken out
6 prize-winning economist

Language patterns

Answers
1 usual
2 hardly
3 all
4 As
5 that
6 had

Prepositions

Answers
1 into
2 around
3 out
4 from
5 of
6 on
7 for
8 to

Opposites

Answers
1 fertile
2 sparse
3 fierce
4 flawed
5 stuffed
6 arid
7 adverse
8 elaborate

Missing words

Answers
1 called
2 issue
3 plot
4 murmurs
5 track

Verbs

Answers
1 establish
2 express
3 draw
4 gain
5 claim
6 carry out
7 diminish
8 grasp

Forming words

Answers
1 fatalities
2 frantically
3 exploratory
4 settlement
5 resolutions
6 underlying
7 harassment

Vocabulary

Answers
1 C boasted
2 A traces
3 B insight
4 A endorse
5 A freely
6 A down
7 C memoir
8 B appeal

09 WORK

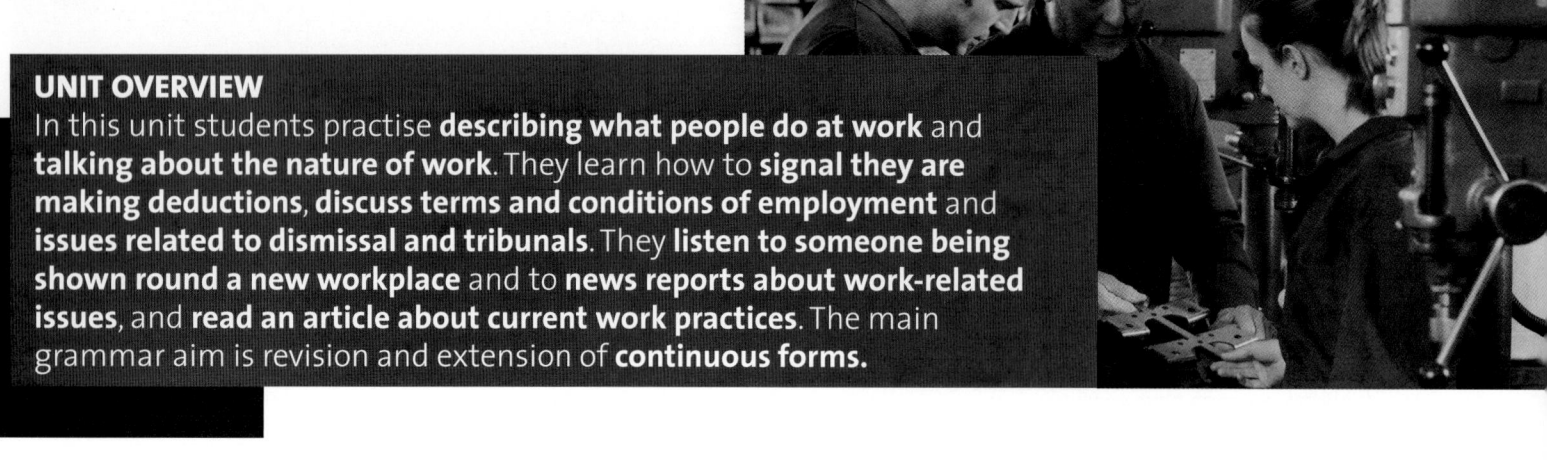

UNIT OVERVIEW
In this unit students practise **describing what people do at work** and **talking about the nature of work**. They learn how to **signal they are making deductions, discuss terms and conditions of employment** and **issues related to dismissal and tribunals**. They **listen to someone being shown round a new workplace** and to **news reports about work-related issues**, and **read an article about current work practices**. The main grammar aim is revision and extension of **continuous forms**.

Next class Make photocopies of 9A p. 144.

VOCABULARY Company jobs and tasks

Aim
To revise verbs commonly found in the context of work.

Step 1 Ask students what job they do, or would like to do and what that job entails. Then put them in small groups to discuss the questions in A and to answer the questions in B. Conduct brief feedback and check the answers to B.

Answers
a rep = a representative – usually a sales rep; a CEO = a Chief Executive Officer; a PA = a Personal Assistant; in HR = in Human Resources; in R & D = in Research and Development; in admin = in administration

Step 2 Ask students to look at the box and complete the sentences in C with the correct form of the verb. Check in pairs, then check with the whole group. Concept check the more difficult ones with the whole group e.g. *troubleshoot* = find solutions to problems as they arise.

Answers
1 input
2 troubleshoot
3 schedule
4 liaise
5 place
6 process
7 draw up
8 network
9 oversee
10 come up with

Step 3 Put students in pairs or threes to discuss the questions in D. Conduct brief feedback.

LISTENING

Aim
To give practice in listening for detail and intensively.

Step 1 Tell students they are going to hear a conversation with someone being shown around on their first day at work. Begin by asking how that person might feel, what they might want to know about etc. Ask them make notes on each of the items in A as they listen. Play the recording. Put students in pairs to compare their ideas. Conduct brief feedback.

Answers
Tasneem = will be working with Harry on project, liaises with external service providers; *Harry* = first day in job, has just moved to Redditch; *Bianca* = main admin assistant, deals with travel and bookings; *the photocopier* = a bit temperamental, tends to jam; *Mary* = managing director, seems down to earth; here most days; *the company* = very busy, three or four new staff, a lot of changes

🔊 9.1
H = Harry, T = Tasneem, B = Bianca
H: Hi, I'm looking for Tasneem.
T: That's me. You must be Harry.
H: That's right.
T: Nice to meet you. Did you find us OK?
H: Yeah, yeah. Well, I came here before for my interview.
T: Right. So where do you live? Does it take you long to get here?
H: I've just moved to Redditch, but it was quicker than I expected. I've actually been hanging around in the coffee bar over the road for the last hour.
T: Really? You were eager to get here, then.
H: Well, I didn't want to be late and, you know, first day nerves and all that.
T: Sure. Anyway, I'm sure you'll settle in quickly. We're a pretty good bunch. Nobody bites. Well, almost nobody!
H: Right.
T: So, raring to go, then?
H: Absolutely.
T: OK, well, just dump your stuff down here for the moment and I'll show you the ropes.
H: OK.
T: I should've said, we'll be working alongside each other on this new project. I liaise with our external service providers. I was just emailing one of them

62 OUTCOMES

to schedule a time for us all to meet when you arrived. Anyway, as you can see, the office is mainly open-plan. We'll sort you out with a spot later.
H: Right.
T: It's a bit chaotic at the moment with all the changes. We've been rushed off our feet so it'll be good to have more people.
H: I'm not the only one who's being taken on now, then.
T: No. Three or four more are supposed to be joining in the next couple of weeks.
H: That's good. There'll be some others in the same boat.
T: Yeah. This is Bianca. She's our main admin assistant. She'll sort out any travel or bookings and other stuff. Bianca, this is Harry.
B: Hiya. Nice to meet you. Hope Taz is treating you well. She's a real slave driver, you know.
H: Really?
B: Oh yeah, she's probably being all kind and helpful now, but wait till you get started.
H: That sounds ominous.
T: Take no notice. She's just pulling your leg. You need to watch her!
B: Don't know what you mean! Actually, Harry. Can I just take a quick photo while you're here? I'm just sorting out your entry card and setting up your email.
H: Sure.
B: OK. ... Say cheese. ... Lovely – very handsome. That's it. Anything you need or you're not sure about, don't hesitate to ask.
H: Thanks. I'll get the card later, then.
B: If that's OK.
T: OK, let's move on. OK. That lot over the far side are the sales team. We won't disturb them now. I can introduce you later. To be honest, you won't be having that much to do with them in your day-to-day dealings.
H: OK. What about these rooms? Are they offices?
T: Um, the last two are the boardrooms for meetings. The near one is Mary's office. She's the managing director.
H: OK. What she's like?
T: She's OK. She comes across as being quite down-to-earth ... the few times we've talked.
H: She's not in the office that much, then.
T: No, she's here most days, but as I said, I guess we've all been so busy that everybody just sticks to their own tasks. Anyway, just going back to the rooms – that one with the door open is the photocopier room. I'd better show you how it works. It's a bit temperamental. It has a tendency to jam if you don't treat it with loving care.
H: OK.
T: So how come you moved to Redditch? It's not that close to here.
H: No, but I'd been thinking about moving out there for a while and I happened to get the house just before I got this job.

Step 2 Ask students to listen again and write down four new phrases. Play the recording again. Put students in pairs and ask them to compare their phrases and help each other with meaning and pronunciation. Tell them to check with the audioscript on page 170. Check with the whole group and concept check the phrases by asking for synonyms or near-synonyms.

> **Suggested answers**
> *hanging around* = waiting; *nobody bites* = everyone is friendly; *raring to go* = keen to get started; *dump your stuff* = put your things down; *show you the ropes* = introduce you to everything; *sort you out with a spot* = find you a place; *rushed off our feet* = extremely busy; *in the same boat* = in the same situation; *a real slave driver* = someone who makes others work hard; *pulling your leg* = teasing you; *day-to-day dealings* = everyday tasks; *down-to-earth* = practical and realistic; *how come* = why, how did it happen that ...?

Step 3 Put students in pairs or small groups ask them to discuss the questions in D. Conduct brief feedback.

NATIVE SPEAKER ENGLISH *raring to go*

This may well have been covered in exercise C. If not, ask students what they think it means and when someone would use it. Then read out the explanation in the box. Elicit a few personalised examples from students.

DEVELOPING CONVERSATIONS
Deductions

Aim
To introduce a way of making deductions.

Step 1 Ask students to look at the audioscript on page 170 and find examples of comments ending in *then*. Use the examples to try to elicit the information in the box about meaning (deduction) and pronunciation (rising intonation). Then read out the explanation in the box. Ask students why the speakers made these deductions and what the replies were in each case. Tell them to look again at the audioscript to check.

> **Answers**
> 1 Because he had arrived early – *Well, I didn't want to be late.*
> 2 Because they have taken on more people – *No. Three or four more are supposed to be joining.*
> 3 Because she says 'the few times we've talked' – *No, she's here most days.*

Step 2 Put students in pairs. Tell them to take turns saying a sentence in B and replying with a deduction, ending in *then*. Their partner should then give a response. Remind students to use rising intonation on the deductions. Monitor and check their responses are appropriate.

09 WORK

GRAMMAR Continuous forms

Aim
To revise various continuous forms.

Step 1 Elicit some continuous forms, put them on the board and ask about form and meaning. Then read out the explanation box. Ask what the continuous aspect suggests (an ongoing action or event; a temporary state, sometimes unfinished).

Step 2 Ask students to look at the questions in A and complete them with the correct continuous form. Then play the recording for them to check their answers.

> **Answers**
> 1 've (actually) been hanging around – present perfect continuous to indicate an action that went on for some time and is just finished (in this case)
> 2 'll be working – future continuous for an action or situation which will go on for some time in the future
> 3 was (just) emailing – past continuous – informal use, to show a recent past action
> 4 's being taken on – present continuous passive, for something happening now or around now
> 5 are supposed to be joining – *supposed to* + continuous infinitive, with a future meaning
> 6 's (probably) being – present continuous, for something happening now (unusual use of *be*, which is usually stative and therefore not found in continuous form; here it means *acting* or *behaving*)
> 7 won't be having – negative of future continuous, indicates an ongoing situation
> 8 'd been thinking – past perfect continuous, an action which went on for some time before another action or event in the past (I found a house)

Step 3 Put students in pairs and ask them to discuss why the continuous form is used in each case (answers above). Direct them to the grammar reference on page 144 if they need help.

> **🔊 9.2**
> 1 I've actually been hanging around in the coffee bar over the road for the last hour.
> 2 I should've said, we'll be working alongside each other.
> 3 I was just emailing one of them to schedule a time for us all to meet when you arrived.
> 4 I'm not the only one who's being taken on now, then.
> 5 Three or four more are supposed to be joining in the next couple of weeks.
> 6 She's probably being all kind and helpful now, but wait till you get started.
> 7 To be honest, you won't be having that much to do with them in your day-to-day dealings.
> 8 I'd been thinking about moving out there for a while and I happened to get the house just before I got this job.

CONVERSATION PRACTICE

Aim
To practise conversations similar to *Listening*.

Step 1 Tell students they are going to practise similar conversations to the one they heard in *Listening*. First, ask them to draw a rough map of where they work / study. Then ask them to look at the items in A and think about how to answer them. Put students in pairs and ask them to take turns to explain the items in A. Conduct brief feedback.

Step 2 Tell students they are going to work in groups to welcome each other and show each other round their place. Ask them to think of things they can say to welcome them / show them around and questions they might ask when being shown around. Then ask each pair to join another pair and take turns playing different roles. Student A should be in charge of the guided tour and Student B should play the parts of other people who work / study there. C and D should be new to the company. Then swap. Monitor and take notes for a correction slot at the end.

> 9A see Teacher's notes p. 124.

pp. 66–67

VOCABULARY

Adverb–adjective collocations

Aim
To focus on common adverb–adjective collocations.

Step 1 Ask students to look at the sentences in A and choose the alternative in italics that is most true for them. Point out that they are all possible but they should choose the one which best fits them.

Step 2 Put students in pairs and ask them to compare their answers and discuss any differences in meaning. Then ask them to look again at the sentences in A and choose one of the adverbs and connected adjective to tell each other about things they have done or something they believe. Conduct brief feedback.

READING

Aim
To give practice in reading for specific information.

Step 1 Tell students they are going to read a true story from a book on management called *The Living Dead*. Put them in pairs or threes and ask them to discuss what the title means and what they think the article is about. Do not conduct feedback but ask them to read the first part of the article and answer the questions in B together. Then ask

64 OUTCOMES

them to read the second part and answer the questions in C together. Check with the whole group.

> **Answers**
> **B**
> 1 He has been allowed to stay at home and work from home but he has nothing to do.
> 2 His friend is envious.
> 3 He thinks the system has cheated him because he feels underemployed and unhappy about the situation.
> 4 He probably started off working from home some of the time and the situation has now continued and been extended.
>
> **C**
> 1 There was not much to do at work, so he took a year off to do an MBA, after which he went back to find nothing had changed.
> 2 He was made redundant.
> 3 'The living dead' are the people who have nothing or little to do at work.

Step 2 Ask students to look at the words and phrases in D and match the correct halves together, as used in the article. Check in pairs, then check with the whole group.

> **Answers**
> 1 my vitality drained away
> 2 acquire new skills
> 3 sponsor me
> 4 spark my interest
> 5 get the most out of its investment
> 6 his mind was drifting off
> 7 set the wheels in motion
> 8 pass this on to someone else
> 9 which begs the question
> 10 make me redundant

Step 3 Put students in pairs and ask them to re-tell the story using the phrases in exercise D and their own words.

Step 4 Put students in pairs or threes. Ask them to discuss the questions in exercise F. Conduct brief feedback.

Listening

Aim
To give practice in listening for gist and detail.

Step 1 Tell students they are going to hear a brief summary of the lessons Bolchover has learnt from his experience (described in *Reading*). Ask them to look again at the questions in exercise F and answer them as they listen. Play the recording.

> **Answers**
> 1 No, not according to the speaker.
> 2 The company for not using his skills and keeping quiet about the situation.
> 3 Large companies should be broken up into smaller companies, where this is less likely to happen. Workers should speak up if they feel underemployed.

9.3
Is David Bolchover's experience a freak occurrence? Well maybe, but only in the sense that he was allowed to stay at home to not work. Bolchover argues that much of the workforce in many big companies is badly under-employed at work and backs up his arguments with a barrage of statistics; one in three of all mid-week visitors to a UK theme park had phoned in sick. In one year, there were nine million dubious requests for sick notes from the doctor. That's about a third of the working population! Two-thirds of young professionals have called in sick because of a hangover, and on it goes.

Once at work things don't improve: on average, employees spend 8.3 hours a week accessing non work-related websites and 14.6% of all so-called 'working' Americans say they surf the net constantly. 18.7% send up to 20 personal emails a day and 24% said they had fallen asleep at their desk, in a toilet or at a meeting.

Bolchover argues that there's a conspiracy of silence over this workplace slacking. Workers have no vested interest in saying they do nothing, while businesses want to maintain their image of being highly efficient.

Underemployment happens, he suggests, because workers feel a disconnection with big companies. Unlike with small companies, employees don't see how their small contributions fit into the whole picture. Furthermore, managers typically fail to develop or motivate workers because, he claims, in large corporations people progress not by looking down, but by looking up. Instead of managing effectively and getting the most of those under you, the way to get ahead is by advertising yourself and networking with those above you. People below you don't give promotions.

With smaller companies, slacking happens less because workers see how failure to pull your weight can directly impact on colleagues and the company. Bolchover suggests the solution, therefore, is to break up large companies into smaller competitive units. From a worker's view, he suggests doing nothing might seem fun at first, but in the end it's soul-destroying and a waste of talent.

Step 2 Ask students to look at the numbers in B and note down what statistics they are connected to from the recording. Play the recording again for them to check.

09 WORK

> **Answers**
> 1 1 *one in three* of all mid-week visitors to a theme park were 'off sick'
>   2 *nine million* workers made dubious requests for a sick note in one year
>   3 *two-thirds* of young professionals have called in sick because of a hangover
>   4 *8.3 hours per week* are spent by each employee on average each week accessing non-work related websites
>   5 *14.6%* of working Americans surf the net constantly
>   6 *18.7 %* of working Americans send up to twenty personal emails a day
>   7 *24%* of working Americans said they had fallen asleep at their desk, in the toilet or in a meeting
> 2 because they are better at controlling what employees do and employees feel more responsible

Step 3 Put students in small groups to discuss the questions in C. Conduct brief feedback.

pp. 68–69

> **Next class** Make photocopies of 9B p. 145.

SPEAKING

Aim
To extend the topic and give fluency practice.

Step 1 Ask students to look at the questions in exercise A and think about them as they read the *Fact File*. Check they understand *stationery* = paper, pens and related items; *maternity leave* = time off for a woman after she has a baby; *GDP* = gross domestic product; *forced labour* = where people are made to work whether they like it or not. Put students in small groups to discuss the questions. Conduct brief feedback.

VOCABULARY The world of work

Aim
To introduce collocations commonly used in the context of work.

Step 1 Begin by asking students to think of some common collocations about work. They could find some in the *Reading* text and tell you. Then ask them to look at the sentences in A and complete them with the correct pair of words from the box. Point out that they may need to change the order of the words. Check in pairs, then check with the class.

> **Answers**
> 1 quit + notice
> 2 subsidised + perk
> 3 compassionate leave + grateful
> 4 crèche + childcare
> 5 early retirement + pension
> 6 absenteeism + crackdown
> 7 tribunal + dismissal
> 8 raise + opposition
> 9 cuts + voluntary redundancy
> 10 union + collective bargaining

Step 2 Put students in pairs and ask them to take turns testing each other. One should say a noun phrase from exercise B and the other, with exercise A covered, should try to remember the verb that went with it. Then swap. Ask them to look back at the sentences to check their ideas and find any other new collocations. (Possible answers: afford to do something; live on; demand sick notes; award compensation; on the grounds of; facing a lot of; in the end; pay rises).

> **Answers**
> 1 give a week's notice
> 2 take early retirement
> 3 launch a crackdown
> 4 be awarded compensation
> 5 face a lot of opposition
> 6 be granted compassionate leave
> 7 live on the state pension
> 8 take someone to a tribunal
> 9 raise the legal minimum wage
> 10 take voluntary redundancy

Step 3 Put students in small groups to discuss the questions in D. Conduct brief feedback.

> **9B** see Teacher's notes p. 124.

LISTENING

Aim
To give practice in listening for gist and detail.

Step 1 Tell students they are going to hear five news reports related to work. Ask them to look at the statements in A and write the number of the news item which goes with each as they listen. Play the recording.

> **Answers**
> 1 e   2 a   3 f   4 d   5 b
> c is not used

> **9.4**
> 1 A 27-year-old man has been arrested and fined for stealing biscuits from a colleague's desk. While working a night shift in a call centre, Michael Campbell thought no-one would mind if he helped

66 OUTCOMES

himself to the remains of a biscuit tin abandoned in a corner. The following day, however, a co-worker returned to find her £7 gift selection gone – and decided to trawl CCTV footage to find the culprit. Campbell was then arrested and hauled in front of a magistrate, who ordered him to repay the cost of the biscuits as well as £150 court costs. He was also dismissed from his job as a result of the incident and is currently retraining as a bar manager.

2 A postman who was sacked after taking a week off work to mourn the death of a pet has won over ten thousand pounds' compensation. David Portman had a history of taking numerous weeks off work because of unfortunate 'accidents', and was absent for a total of 137 days in just five years, an employment tribunal heard. In his defence, Mr Portman claimed the majority of his injuries were incurred during the course of his duties at work! However, when he took further leave following the demise of his dog, his bosses decided enough was enough. The tribunal felt this was a step too far and they insisted he be awarded compensation, especially as management had failed to tell the postman he could have applied for compassionate leave!

3 A new study released this week shows that paternity leave schemes in Iceland are now one of the most generous in the world – and suggest that this is to the immense benefit of society. Last year, nearly all new Icelandic fathers took their full entitlement of three months of work at 80% of their salaries. Since legislation to ensure such leave in 2002, gender roles have been transformed and the divorce rate has dropped sharply – while the birth rate has risen. The director of one of the country's biggest firms recently went on record to state he wanted all fathers on his staff to take their full 12 weeks leave on full pay as they provided positive role models which could benefit both company and country in the long run.

4 Budget airline Ryanair is cutting costs ever further by banning its staff from charging their mobile phones at work. Passengers with the no-frills firm do not get pre-assigned seats and all food and drink is charged for, while cabin crew have to pay upwards of a thousand pounds for initial training and are then expected to buy their own uniforms. Now, however, the company has decided that any use of mobile phone chargers at work is unacceptable, and amounts to theft of the company's electricity. A spokesperson claimed yesterday that all savings will go towards lowering fares for European consumers.

5 A new research project has begun in New Zealand to explore whether the country's rapidly ageing one million plus generation of over-65s is planning to slip awkwardly into its golden years as a burden on the state or whether there will be a reinvention of the way society views older people and the workforce. Many signs seem to suggest the latter is the most likely option. All the indications are that many of this generation are not eagerly anticipating retirement. Instead, they plan to work, contribute to social causes and continue to influence society, as they have all their lives. However, they want to do so on their own terms and with more time for leisure, travel and their families. This could revolutionise the workforce as employers begin to offer sabbaticals, part-time work, flexible hours and other incentives to retain experienced staff.

Step 2 Put students in pairs and ask them to re-tell the story, using the words / phrases in C. Then ask them to look at the audioscript on page 171 to check their ideas.

Step 3 Put students in small groups to discuss the questions in E. Conduct brief feedback.

LANGUAGE PATTERNS

Aim
To focus on patterns with reporting verbs + subjunctive.

Step 1 Ask students to read the examples in the box and check they understand. Ask them to translate the sentences into their own language and notice any similarities / differences. In a monolingual class, ask students to compare their translation. In a multilingual class, ask students to work in pairs and tell each other if the sentences were easy to translate.

Step 2 Then ask them to close their books and translate the sentences back into their own language. At the end, they should open their books again and compare their translations with the original sentences. Ask them to discuss in pairs who had the least mistakes. What mistakes did they make? Why?

Alternatively If you prefer not to use translation, ask students to look at the sentences and tell you what patterns they notice: (reporting verb + subjunctive (base form).

SPEAKING

Aim
To extend the topic and give fluency practice.

Step 1 Tell students they are going to read and discuss three employment tribunal cases. Ask them to read the three cases in A and decide what they think should be done in each.

Step 2 Put students in small groups to discuss their ideas. They should try to reach a unanimous decision (one decision between the group). Ask students to share their ideas with the rest of the group. Still in their groups, ask them to discuss the questions in C. Conduct brief feedback.

10 HEALTH AND ILLNESS

UNIT OVERVIEW
In this unit, students practise **describing different surgical and medical procedures, conditions and symptoms, explaining and understanding body actions, making comments about past and present situations** and **showing they are not being exact when describing things**. They read about **Eastern and Western medicine** and **different medical conditions**, and listen to a **mindfulness exercise,** conversations about **surgical procedures** and a news story about **a miracle cure**. The main grammar aim is revision of **modal verbs**.

SPEAKING

Aim
To lead in and get students thinking and talking about surgical procedures.

Step 1 Begin by asking students what different kinds of surgery they can think of. Then ask them to look at the first set of questions in exercise A and try to answer them. Check in pairs. Then check with the whole class.

Answers
reconstructive surgery = rebuilding parts of the body after an accident or fire. Might involve taking a skin graft from another part of the body and attaching it to the part to be repaired.
cosmetic surgery = changing the shape of parts of the body for aesthetic reasons. Might involve removing fat or adding some kind of filler e.g. silicone.
experimental surgery = surgery done usually on animals for the purposes of scientific research.
exploratory surgery = when surgery is used to find out about something rather than to treat or cure.
keyhole surgery = surgery which uses only small incisions (cuts) rather than large, invasive ones.
laser surgery = using a laser rather than cutting to 'zap' a part of the body – can be used to correct eyesight or treat cancer.

Step 2 Put students in pairs / threes to discuss the other two questions in A. Conduct brief feedback.

LISTENING

Aim
To give practice in listening for specific information.

Step 1 Tell students they are going to hear two conversations about surgical procedures. Ask them to look at the questions in A and answer them as they listen. Play the recording.

Answers
Conversation 1
1 laser surgery
2 numbing the eyes and slicing a flap in front of each eye
3 return visits for after-care
Conversation 2
1 dental surgery
2 having a hole drilled at the back and a temporary filling
3 having the temporary filling replaced by a permanent one

♫ 10.1
Conversation 1
A: You look so different without your glasses on. I almost didn't recognise you there.
B: The glasses have gone! They're a thing of the past. I had my eyes done the other day, with laser surgery.
A: Really? That's brave of you. Didn't it hurt? I've always imagined it must do.
B: No, not really, but it is quite scary because what they do is they numb your eyes and then they kind of clamp them open so they can slice this tiny little flap in the front of the eye – and you kind of have to watch as the whole thing happens.
A: Sounds horrendous! How do they administer the anaesthetic? Is it an injection or something?
B: No, they just pour in a bucketful of these eye drops and they do the job. Oh, and they dosed me up with a couple of Xanax as well, just to calm me down.
A: And how long does the whole thing take?
B: It's over in a matter of minutes. After they cut the eye open, you have to stare at this laser for a minute or two and that reshapes the inside of your eye – and then you're done.
A: And how long does it take to recover from?
B: To be honest, the next day I woke up and I pretty much had perfect vision. They're still a bit sore, and I have to go back a few times for the after-care, but it's all very quick. I should've got it done years ago, really!
A: Right. Wow! I still think I'll stick with contact lenses for the time being, though, personally.

Conversation 2

C: So why did you have to rush off to the dentist's the other day, then?
D: Oh, haven't I told you? Well, about a week or so ago, I got this excruciating pain in my upper jaw and I went along to get it looked at and he told me that one of my teeth had died somehow and that I'd need a root canal.
C: Died? How did that happen?
D: He said I must've taken a knock. I'm not sure, but I think it might've been my daughter, actually, thrashing her arms and legs around while I was changing her nappy one day.
C: Kids, eh! All that work and that's the kind of thanks you get.
D: Yeah (laughs). And then today I went in and he drilled a hole in the back, cleaned everything up and then stuck some kind of temporary filling in, to prevent any bacteria or anything getting in.
C: That can't have been much fun! Did it hurt at all?
D: No, not really. I mean, I was conscious of what he was doing, but I couldn't feel anything.
C: Do you have to go back again sometime?
D: Yeah, next week. They'll remove the temporary filling and put a more permanent thing in, but then I'm done.
C: How much is all that going to set you back, then? It must be quite expensive.
D: It's not that bad, but it's not cheap either. I won't see much change from five hundred pounds.

Step 2 Ask students to try to decide if the statements in B are true or false. Play the recording again for them to check.

Tip Ask them to correct the false sentences.

Answers
Conversation 1
1 T
2 F – they gave him eye drops
3 T
4 F – they're a bit sore
5 T
Conversation 2
6 T
7 F – it might have been her daughter
8 T
9 F – I was conscious of what he was doing
10 F – I won't have much change from £500

Step 3 Ask students to complete each phrase in C with the correct verb from the box. Then ask them to look at the audioscript on page 171 to check their answers.

Answers
1 drill	3 change	5 recover	7 slice
2 take	4 numb	6 thrash	8 administer

Step 4 Put students in pairs or threes to discuss the questions in exercise D. Conduct brief feedback.

NATIVE SPEAKER ENGLISH
in a matter of

Ask students what they think the speaker meant by *it's over in a matter of minutes* = *it's over very quickly*. Read out the explanation in the box. Try to elicit a few more examples.

VOCABULARY Operations

Aim
To introduce phrases about operations.

Step 1 Ask students to look at the sets of phrases in A and put them in the most likely chronological order, starting with the phrase in bold. Check in pairs, then check as a class.

Answers
1 suffered third degree burns – was rushed to hospital – was put on a drip – had a skin graft – had to wait for the scarring to heal
2 had to fast for twelve hours – was given an anaesthetic – had my wisdom teeth removed – gums bled a lot and cheeks swelled – had stitches removed
3 was diagnosed with kidney disease – was put on a waiting list – finally found a donor – had a transplant – took part in a rehabilitation programme
4 severed three fingers – lost a lot of blood – had the fingers sewn back on – underwent extensive physiotherapy – regained feeling in the fingers
5 broke his leg in three places – had an operation to insert metal pins – got an infection – had part of the leg amputated – got a prosthetic limb
6 found a lump – had it diagnosed as malignant – had an operation to have it removed – had chemotherapy – the cancer went into remission – had a relapse

Step 2 Ask students to look again at the phrases and try to memorise them. Then ask them to take turns testing each other. Student A should say a phrase in bold and Student B – with the phrases covered – should try to say the rest of the phrases in the correct order. Then swap.

Step 3 Put students in pairs to discuss the questions in exercise C. Conduct brief feedback.

DEVELOPING CONVERSATIONS
Vague language

Aim
To draw students' attention to vague language.

Step 1 Read out the explanation, checking students understand as you read. Elicit a few examples of each type. Then ask students to look at the sentences in A and rewrite them using vague language. Check in pairs, then check with the whole group.

10 HEALTH AND ILLNESS 69

10 HEALTH AND ILLNESS

Answers
(slight variations are possible)
1 I asked for a second opinion, but they just kind of ignored me.
2 He used some kind of bleach solution on my teeth.
3 It should cost about a hundred euros or so.
4 They told me that some kind of build-up was damaging blood vessels in my brain.
5 He somehow managed to slice the end off one of his fingers!
6 They use a kind of tiny little knife to make the incision.
7 It was quite a traumatic birth, but they somehow managed to deliver her after about an hour
8 They just glued the skin back together again using some kind of clear plastic tape.

Step 2 Put students in pairs and ask them to discuss what they know about the items in exercise B, using vague language. Demonstrate with a strong student first. Monitor and correct where necessary.

CONVERSATION PRACTICE

Aim
To give further practice of the target language.

Step 1 Ask students to think of a medical or surgical experience they, or people they know, have had. Ask them to prepare what they can say about them. Tell them to try to use language from this part of the unit. Put students in small groups to discuss their experiences. Monitor and take notes on their language use for a correction slot at the end.

pp. 72–73

Next class Make photocopies of **10A** p. 146.

SPEAKING

Aim
To extend the topic and lead in to *Reading*.

Step 1 Put students in pairs to take turns asking and answering the questions in A. They can choose one of the alternatives given or make up their own answers. Tell them to think of one more question to ask each other. Check words like: *grumpy, moan, demeanour, mood swings, blow up, dwell on, shrug off, belly, supple, crouch down* before they start. Conduct brief feedback.

READING

Aim
To give practice in reading for gist and responding to text.

Step 1 Tell students they are going to read an article about 'Eastern' and 'Western' medicine. Begin by asking them what they think some of the main differences are. Then put them in small groups to discuss the questions in A. Tell them not to worry if they don't know. Do not conduct feedback as they are going to find out by reading.

Step 2 Ask students to read the text and compare their ideas about the items in A and what the text says. Check in pairs. Then check with the whole group.

Answers
1 *Mindfulness and meditation* – mindfulness = meditation therapy; gaining in popularity; used to treat depression and anxiety and maybe strengthen immune system; involves noticing negative patterns of thought and fully experiencing the moment; comes from Eastern Buddhist philosophy
2 *Depression* – negative moods often go with negative thoughts; usually disappears when depression passes or with medication; small things can bring depression back again
3 *Life expectancy and well-being* – life expectancy doubled in developed countries in the 20th century; we are living longer in sickness rather than health
4 *The worried well* – people who are actually healthy but are anxious about low-level complaints – hypochondriacs
5 *Traditional Chinese Medicine* – more focused on maintaining good health; more successful at treating certain common conditions; believes in harmony between mind, body and the environment

Step 3 Ask students to look at the sentence starters in C and complete them so that they are true for them. Ask them to compare their ideas in pairs. Conduct brief feedback.

LANGUAGE PATTERNS

Aim
To draw attention to patterns using *the more...the more*.

Step 1 Ask students to read the examples in the box and check they understand. Ask them to translate the sentences into their own language and notice any similarities / differences. In a monolingual class, ask students to compare their translation. In a multilingual class, ask students to work in pairs and tell each other if the sentences were easy to translate.

Step 2 Then ask them to close their books and translate the sentences back into their own language. At the end, they should open their books again and compare their translations with the original sentences. Ask them to discuss in pairs who had the least mistakes. What mistakes did they make? Why?

Alternatively If you prefer not to use translation, ask students to look at the sentences and tell you what pattern

70 OUTCOMES

10 HEALTH AND ILLNESS

they notice = *the* + comparative form, to show cause and effect. Try to elicit a few more examples.

VOCABULARY Body actions

Aim
To introduce verbs commonly used to talk about physical actions or reactions.

Step 1 Ask students to look at the phrases in A and think about why these actions / reactions would be done or would happen. Put them in pairs to discuss their ideas.

> **Suggested answers**
> *your mind drifts or wanders* when you are distracted or bored; *your belly rises and falls* when you are breathing deeply; *your heart beats fast* when you are anxious or afraid; *your body shudders* when you see / hear something horrible; you *wipe your forehead* when you are hot and sweaty; *you raise your eyebrows* when you are surprised or sceptical; *you raise your hand* when you want to say something; *you clutch your chest* when you have a pain; *you click your fingers* to get someone's attention; *you drop your head* when you are tired or depressed; *you shrug your shoulders* when you don't know or don't care; *you clench your fist* when you are angry or want to threaten someone; *you support your back* when you have backache; *you stretch your legs* when you are tired or when you have been sitting for a long time; *you flutter your eyelashes* when you want to flirt with someone

Step 2 Ask students to look at the verbs in B and discuss in pairs which part of the body is used in each case. Check as a class.

> **Answers**
> *kick* = foot; *stroke* = hand; *clap* = hands; *pat* = hand; *scratch* = finger nails; *sniff* = nose; *blink* = eyes; *hug* = arms; *spit* = mouth; *crouch* = whole body but mainly legs; *glare* = eyes; *frown* = face but mainly mouth and eyebrows; *grin* = mouth; *nod* = head; *punch* = fist (hand)

Step 3 Ask students in the same pairs to test each other. They should take turns miming an action from exercise B and their partner should guess what it is.

> 10A see Teacher's notes p. 124.

LISTENING

Aim
To practise responding physically to instructions and to experience an exercise in mindfulness.

Step 1 Tell students they are going to hear a mindfulness exercise. They should listen and do what the speaker tells them to do. Play the recording.

🔊 10.2
... Coming to sit now. We'll be sitting for a while so make yourself comfortable on your chair, but also moving forward so your back is not leaning against the chair, but is supporting itself and your back, neck and head are in line in an erect posture, but not stiff. Let your shoulders drop and relax so your posture embodies a sense of dignity, a sense of taking a stand, of being awake, aware, in touch with this moment. And letting your eyes close, relaxing your facial muscles, not frowning or feeling tension there and now we're coming to focus on our breathing.

Focusing on wherever you notice the breath moving most distinctly in and out of your body. And this might be at the tip of your nose, at the back of the throat, or in your chest or belly. Noticing how it rises with the in breath and falls on the out breath. And noticing precisely the sensations that accompany each in-breath and each out-breath. Each breath is unique with its own sensations and simply tuning in to each one in its own time, giving each one its own attention. This breath coming in ... this breath going out .... Allowing the breath to anchor you in the present moment. And whenever you notice your mind wandering, bring it gently back to your breath, back to the present moment. And the mind may wander many times. Sometimes it may wander for a short time, sometimes a longer time, and you may find yourself judging and criticising yourself for the wandering mind but that's what minds do. If you have a mind, it will wander. So the task of meditation is not to still the mind or banish thoughts and feelings, but simply to notice its patterns, to be aware of what it's doing and then as soon as you notice that it's wandered, to acknowledge where it's wandered to and then gently bringing it back. So if it happens many times, bring it back many times. Beginning over and over again with the next in breath ... or the next out breath. And then using the stretches of silence to carry on this work by yourself.

... And now at a certain point expanding your awareness around the breath so that you're aware of the whole body as you sit here. Aware of the space that your body takes up and the space around the body and the boundary between these two spaces, the skin. Aware of sensations in your body. And if there are any intense sensations then breathing into them directing the breath to the edge of that intensity and into the centre to explore what's here, right now. Allowing yourself to be open, to soften around the intensity instead of tightening or clenching as we so often do. Opening yourself up to experience the sensations you're feeling here right now, in this moment ... and in this moment ... and in this moment. And now letting go of any intention to focus on anything – the breath or the body and allowing yourself to sit here, resting in awareness itself. Whatever comes up.

And taking this sensation of spaciousness, of awareness of this present moment into your day and remembering that this moment of presence is always available to you at any time by simply reconnecting, through your breath, to your mind and body.

Step 2 Put students in small groups to discuss the questions in exercise B. Conduct brief feedback.

10 HEALTH AND ILLNESS

pp. 74–75

Next class Make photocopies of 10B p. 147.

SPEAKING

Aim
To give fluency practice and lead in to *Reading*.

Step 1 Tell students they are going to read a text about different physical or mental disorders. Put them in small groups to discuss what they know about the conditions or disorders in A. Check their ideas, but not for *vitiligo* and *Tourette's* as they are going to find out about those by reading.

> **Answers**
> *autism* = disorder in which sufferers have problems with social interaction, often clever at maths and related subjects; various levels of severity
> *diabetes* = disorder related to level of sugar in blood; treated by diet and insulin; Type A and Type B (less severe)
> *narcolepsy* = disorder in which sufferers fall asleep frequently
> *post-traumatic stress* = stress suffered after a shock or trauma; can be delayed and can take many forms
> *migraines* = really bad headaches and visual effects; often triggered by certain foods e.g. chocolate
> *gluten intolerance* = disorder in which body rejects food including wheat or gluten and is therefore undernourished; treated by cutting gluten out of diet
> *leprosy* = skin disease, not common nowadays; sufferers used to be isolated as it is very contagious; has negative connotations
> *asthma* = breathing disorder by which it sometimes becomes very hard for sufferers to breathe; becoming more common; treated with inhalers
> *bulimia nervosa* = eating disorder in which sufferers binge eat (eat a lot) and then deliberately throw up (vomit) so as not to put on weight
> *eczema* = skin disease which causes red marks on body; treated with ointment or alternative medicine

READING

Aim
To practise reading for gist and exchanging information.

Step 1 Tell students they are going to read different texts about one of the disorders. Divide the class into two groups: A and B. Ask the As to read the text on the page and the Bs to read the text in File 13 on page 157. They should all answer the questions in B as they read.

Step 2 Put students in same letter pairs to check their ideas and discuss any words / phrases they are not sure about.

> **Answers**
> *Vitiligo*: **symptoms** – white patches on skin; **problems** – psychological – sufferers can see themselves as unattractive, unhealthy or disabled; **affects** 1% of the population; **causes** – not clear but classified as auto-immune disorder when body mistakenly attacks healthy cells; **treatment** – light therapy, oral medication, strong sunscreen, skin grafts and psychotherapy
> *Tourette's syndrome*: **symptoms** – a variety of tics, sometimes obsessive-compulsive behaviour, sleep disorders and learning disabilities; **problems** – can cause stress and psychological damage; **affects** 1%, mostly boys; **causes** – an inherited neurological disorder; **treatment** – therapy or drugs

Step 3 Put students in AB pairs. Ask them to use the items in B to help them tell each other about their disorder. Ask them to decide which condition they think is worse and why.

Step 4 Ask students each to choose two words from their own text which they think are useful to learn / remember. In pairs, ask them to explain their choices to each other.

VOCABULARY Medical conditions

Aim
To introduce words associated with medical conditions.

Step 1 Ask students to look at the sentences in A and replace the words in italics with the correct word from the box. Check in pairs, then as a class. Check concept / collocation by asking for other examples and about differences between the pairs of words.

> **Answers**
> 1 fail
> 2 exacerbated
> 3 long-term
> 4 tiredness
> 5 relieved
> 6 passed on
> 7 genetic
> 8 stick to
> 9 triggered
> 10 shortage
> 11 swollen
> 12 block up

Step 2 Put students in pairs to discuss what conditions might cause the symptoms in A. Check as a class.

> **Suggested answers**
> 1 motor neurone disease
> 2 RSI (repetitive strain injury)
> 3 sciatica
> 4 underactive thyroid
> 5 insomnia
> 6 measles or mumps
> 7 some cancers, autism
> 8 coeliac disease, diabetes
> 9 eczema, psoriasis
> 10 anaemia
> 11 indigestion
> 12 smoking

LISTENING

Aim
To give practice in listening for gist and intensively.

Step 1 Tell students they are going to hear a news extract about a child with a rare medical condition. Ask them

72 OUTCOMES

10 HEALTH AND ILLNESS

to answer the questions in A as they listen. Play the recording.

Answers
1. headaches, low red blood cell count, weak immune system, asthma, eczema, fatigue, problems with speech, weak heart, arrested development
2. They said there was nothing they could do.
3. They searched the net for alternative remedies.
4. They found a doctor who recommended a special diet.
5. Dexter will probably be able to lead a full life and it could help other sufferers from this disease and from cancer.

10.3

The dedicated parents of an eight-year-old boy who had been suffering from a blood disorder so rare that it does not even have a name have amazed doctors by finding a cure for him.

Dexter Austen-Brown's illness had been likened to living with a permanent hangover, but after a period of painstaking research, his parents Stephen and Anne discovered that the condition could be relieved with the aid of ordinary dietary protein supplements. Incredibly, doctors now believe that the treatment could also prove to be a breakthrough for sufferers of cancer and other diseases and have commissioned official research.

Before being treated, Dexter had required regular painful blood transfusions because of his low red blood cell count. As he was growing up, his immune system was so weak that he often suffered from ailments such as asthma and eczema. He was weak, frequently fatigued and struggled with speech. In terms of his all-round development, he was at least a year and a half behind other children. His heart was having to work much harder to compensate, leaving him vulnerable to heart attacks.

After countless tests, his parents were informed that there was nothing doctors could do to help their son. This did not deter them, however, and they turned to the Internet in a hunt for alternative therapies. They toyed with the idea of acupuncture before coming across nutritional consultant Richard Wright.

Mr Wright discovered Dexter suffered from a shortage of vital proteins in his body. He was thus put on a special diet of additional dietary supplements, which cost around £10,000 a year. The new diet has been incredibly successful. His last blood count revealed an average number of red cells and his height has shot up. Mr Austen-Smith, a teacher, said, 'We're obviously delighted about the result of all our hard work, though I have to say it's no thanks to many in the medical profession. The doctors can't have considered Dexter's condition as thoroughly as they should've done and they clearly should've looked into other options themselves, but having said that, I also wish we'd started our research earlier. We could've come to our own conclusions sooner and that way, Dexter wouldn't have had to go through all this trauma.'

Step 2 In pairs, ask students to look at the adjectives in B and try to remember which nouns they were used with in the news extract. Play the recording for them to check.

Answers
1 parents	7 heart attack
2 blood disorder	8 tests
3 hangover	9 therapies
4 research	10 proteins
5 blood transfusions	11 the new diet
6 immune system	12 number of red blood cells

Step 3 Put students in pairs or threes to discuss the questions in C. Conduct brief feedback.

GRAMMAR Modal verbs

Aim
To revise modal verbs to talk about the past.

Step 1 Begin by eliciting some modal verbs and common meanings. Try to elicit some examples of past forms. Then read out the explanation box. Ask students to look at the sentences in A and choose the best alternative. Check answers in pairs, then play the recording.

Answers
1 should've	5 can't have, should've
2 must've	6 should've
3 might've	7 could've, wouldn't
4 can't	

Step 2 Put students in pairs to discuss the differences in meanings of the pairs of sentences in C. Direct them to the grammar reference on page 145 if they need help. Check as a class.

Answers
1. *must've been* = I'm sure it was; *can't have been* = the opposite
2. *must've been* = I'm sure it was; *might've been* = maybe it was
3. a I was unable to do anything about it
   b I don't think they tried very hard
4. a It was wrong to drive off
   b It was wrong to be driving so fast (continuous action)
5. a I'm sure he was in pain for some time before
   b I'm sure it hurt when he had his teeth out
6. a I'm sure (I deduce) she picked up the infection (but I could be wrong); b statement of fact
7. a refers to the past; b refers to the present

10B see Teacher's notes p. 124.

SPEAKING

Aim
To round off the unit and give fluency practice.

Step 1 Put students in small groups to discuss the questions in A. Conduct brief feedback.

11 PLAY

UNIT OVERVIEW
In this unit, students practise **talking about sports and games and explaining how to play them**. They practise **recognising and using playful language and irony**, and **metaphors about sports and games**. They **read an article about word and language play**, and **listen to conversations about success and failure in sport and childhood games**, and to a **lecture about playing cards**. The main grammar aim is **linking words**.

Speaking

Aim
To lead in to the topic and get students thinking and talking about sports and games.

Step 1 Ask students whether they like sports and games and why / why not. Then put students in small groups to discuss the questions in exercise A. Conduct brief feedback with the whole class.

Vocabulary Doing and watching sport

Aim
To introduce and revise some words / phrases associated with sport, and give practice.

Step 1 Ask students to try to work out what the words / phrases in **bold** in exercise A mean. Then put them in groups to help each other with meanings and discuss their answers to the questions. Check with the whole group.

Answers
1 A **crowd** (the spectators) would **go wild** if they were pleased e.g. if their team scored. They would **boo** if they were displeased with a player, team or referee.
2 A team **gets knocked out** of a tournament when it loses and is no longer in it.
3 The referee **sends someone off** when they commit a foul (usually in football).
4 **suspended** = not allowed to play for a period of time, as a punishment (several matches); **substituted** = swapped for another player during a match; **dropped** = no longer part of the team because of ability
5 Football and hockey have a **keeper** (goal keeper).
6 If someone makes a **reckless** (careless) **tackle**, they may be given a yellow card or a red card (punishments) or there could be a free kick or a penalty.
7 The **underdog** is the team less likely to win; opposite = stronger team.
8 A **tight** game is close; an **open** game has a lot of passing and long balls from both teams; a **dirty** game has a lot of fouls or cheating e.g. diving.
9 If a player **challenges a decision**, they hope it will be **overturned** (reversed) rather than **upheld** (maintained).
10 If you **blow your chances**, you come close to winning or being promoted and lose at the last minute.
11 You could **cheat** by diving or pretending to be more injured than you are (in football), by 'throwing' the result (e.g. deliberately making the team lose), by taking performance enhancing drugs (any sport, athletics), by stepping over the line when serving or by taking unnecessary breaks (tennis).
12 You might begin to **fade** if you were tired.
13 If a player or team gets **thrashed**, they get severely beaten.
14 **relegated** – opposite = pro<u>mot</u>ed.
15 If you **scraped through** you would just win; or you might draw but just win overall (e.g. if there are two games in total).

Step 2 Ask students to choose five of the items in bold in A and think about how they could apply to themselves, as in the example. Elicit a few more examples to get them started. Then put them in groups to tell each other about their experiences. Conduct brief feedback.

Listening

Aim
To extend the topic and give practice in listening for detail and intensively.

Step 1 Tell students they are going to hear three conversations about sporting activities: one about a tennis match, one about a mountain walk and one about a football game. Ask them to decide which four words in exercise A go with each activity. Then ask them to listen to check and to decide how good each activity was for the main speaker and why. Play the recording. Check answers in pairs, then check with the whole group.

74 OUTCOMES

Answers
Conversation 1: a tennis game = *double fault, rallies, deuce, fade*; quite good = pretty tight.
Conversation 2: a mountain walk = *trudge, clouds broke, hypothermia, stunning*; bad but good in the end.
Conversation 3: a football match = *draw, penalty, the crossbar, the return game*; good = an amazing game, very open.

◐ 11.1
Conversation 1
A: How was the tennis?
B: Good.
A: Who won?
B: Mena, but it was pretty tight actually.
A: What was the score?
B: 6–3, 6–2, I think.
A: Hmm, right. Very close!
B: No, honestly, it was! I mean, most of the games were quite even – lots of deuces. She just did some great shots at the crucial moments.
A: She's quite good, then.
B: Well, neither of us are exactly pros. I mean, we both have a tendency to serve double faults, and if anything I probably actually have a better technique, but she's just fitter and stronger. I tend to fade towards the end.
A: Oh, right.
B: We're both getting better though. We had some pretty long rallies. A couple of shots down the line, you know.
A: So I'll be expecting to see you at Wimbledon soon.
B: Not quite!

Conversation 2
D: How was the weekend?
C: Don't ask?
D: Oh dear. What happened?
C: Well, Hannah took us for a little 'stroll' which involved trudging up some 2000-metre mountain in the pouring rain.
D: Hmm, sounds very relaxing!
C: Honestly, I could've killed her at one point, because she was so enthusiastic and jolly and I was like 'This is just awful. I'm exhausted, I'm soaked and I'm close to getting hypothermia' – and we couldn't see a thing because it was shrouded in mist from about 1000 metres. I felt like bursting into tears, not grinning like an idiot!
D: Oh dear. So what happened?
C: Well, in the end, I just bit my tongue and we continued to the top. And funnily enough, when we got there, the clouds suddenly broke, the sun came out and we got this amazing view. I mean, it only lasted for about five minutes, but it was stunning!
D: It made it all worthwhile, then.
C: Well, I wouldn't quite go that far. I won't exactly be raring to go if she suggests something like that again.

Conversation 3
E: How was the game last night? I missed it.
F: Incredible. Arsenal were lucky to draw. Honestly, it could've been about five-nil after the first 20 minutes. The Arsenal keeper made some great saves and then Manu missed a ridiculously easy goal. He managed to kick the ball over the crossbar when he was literally only a metre from the line.
E: Ah, Manu ... he's so overrated. There's no way he's worth 60 million or however much he cost. He's rubbish.
F: You're right. He's totally useless ... that's why he scored those two fantastic goals after that!
E: OK. OK. He IS good, just not THAT good!
F: No, I do know what you mean – and actually for his first goal the Arsenal keeper made a right cock-up to let them score.
E: Right. So, how did Arsenal manage to get back in the game then?
F: Well, they made some substitutions and brought on Wallace, who made a huge difference.
E: Really?
F: Yeah, really. He scored a great goal, which got the whole team going. Then Arsenal got a slightly dubious penalty and a Barça defender got sent off.
E: It wasn't a penalty, then.
F: Well, it wasn't exactly the strongest tackle I've ever seen, let's put it that way. Anyway, it was an amazing game. Really open.
E: Sounds it. I'll have to watch the return game next month. We'll thrash them at home!
F: I don't know. Two of your defenders are suspended, and you have a couple of other people injured. And Arsenal will be the underdogs so they won't have any pressure on them. Honestly, I wouldn't be surprised if Barça got knocked out.
E: By Arsenal? Not a chance.

Step 2 Put students in pairs. Ask them to re-tell each conversation using the words in A. Play the recording again if necessary. Conduct brief feedback.

Step 3 Put students in pairs or threes to discuss the questions in D. Conduct brief feedback.

NATIVE SPEAKER ENGLISH *a cock-up*

Read out the explanation in the box and check students understand. Ask them for other examples. Check they understand that the expression could be considered quite rude / taboo in certain circles and they should be very careful about using it.

11 PLAY 75

11 PLAY

DEVELOPING CONVERSATIONS
Irony and humour

Aim
To draw students' attention to ways of being ironic and adding humour.

Step 1 Read out the explanation, checking students understand as you read.

Step 2 Ask students to look at the underlined examples in the audioscript on page 172 and answer the questions in exercise A about them. Check in pairs, then check with the whole group.

> **Answers**
> 1 *He managed to kick the ball over the crossbar* – ironic because this is not clever. Draw students' attention to the explanation about this here.
> 2 *He's totally useless* – more sarcastic than ironic – in fact he's really good
> 3 *made a huge difference* – actually means the opposite of what it appears to be saying
> 4 *it wasn't exactly the strongest tackle I've ever seen* – ironic way of saying, in fact, it was a pretty weak tackle

Step 3 Ask students to look at sentences 1–5 in exercise B and match them with an ironic comment a–e. Check answers in pairs, then check with the whole class.

> **Answers**
> 1 c   2 d   3 a   4 e   5 b

Step 4 Ask students to look at the sentence beginnings in C, and complete them in two different ironic ways which are true for them. Point out the use of *manage to*. Monitor and check their sentences are correct and appropriate.

Step 5 Put students in pairs to tell each other their sentences. Ask them to try and continue the conversations further. Elicit a few examples from the whole class at the end.

CONVERSATION PRACTICE

Aim
To give practice in the target language.

Step 1 Ask students to think of two sporting events or experiences they saw or were involved in – one successful and one a failure – and make some notes about them. They should also write two questions to start a conversation about their own events / experiences, as in the examples.

Step 2 Put students in pairs. Ask them to have conversations beginning with the lead-in questions. They should give each other their questions and take turns to ask and answer. Tell them to keep the conversations going by responding and asking questions. They should try to use irony / humour where appropriate. Monitor and take notes on their language use for a correction slot at the end.

pp. 78–79

> **Next class** Make photocopies of **11A** p. 148.

SPEAKING

Aim
To give fluency practice and lead in to the next part of the unit.

Step 1 Check students understand all the games in the box. (*The Sims* and *Call of Duty* are both computer games.) Then put them in small groups to discuss the questions in exercise A. Conduct brief feedback.

VOCABULARY Games

Aim
To introduce words commonly used in association with games.

Step 1 Ask students to look at the sentences in exercise A and decide whether they refer to a card game, a board game or a computer game. Check in pairs, then check with the whole group.

> **Answers**
> 1 cards   7 board
> 2 board   8 computer
> 3 board   9 cards
> 4 computer 10 computer
> 5 cards   11 cards
> 6 computer 12 board

Step 2 Put students in pairs to 'test' each other. They should take turns to explain (without using the word) mime or draw one of the words from A and their partner should guess the word.

LISTENING

Aim
To give practice in listening and note-taking, and listening for detail.

Step 1 Tell students they are going to hear a short talk on playing cards (cards you use to play games). They should take notes on the key points as they listen. Play the recording.

76 OUTCOMES

11 PLAY

> **Suggested answers**
> 1 origins unclear, possibly from Chinese dominoes, possible mix of origins
> 2 52-card deck, four suits; *baraja* from Spain, 40 cards, different suits representing positions of power in the Middle Ages; East Asian flower cards, no numbers just pictures, 10 suits, from 17th century, designed to beat ban on gambling
> 3 huge variety of games, different rules – hence enduring popularity of playing cards

🔊 11.2
Playing cards are popular the world over, but their origins and development are far from clear. It's possible they originated from Chinese paper dominoes, China having invented paper some thousand years before its use in Europe. However, the multitude of designs that existed in the past suggests they are an amalgam of various traditions. There are three types of deck widely used today. The 52-card deck is the most widespread particularly with the popularity of poker. The four suits – hearts, clubs, spades and diamonds – each have thirteen cards: numbers two to ten followed by jack, queen, king and ace as the highest-ranking card. Then there's the Spanish baraja. These decks use different suits which supposedly represent different power groupings in the Middle Ages. There are coins which represented merchants, clubs representing peasants, gold cups for the church and swords symbolizing the military. There are only 40 cards. That's one to seven plus a jack, a knight and a king. Finally, there are the East Asian flower cards. They have 12 suits, one for each month of the year with four cards each. They don't have numbers, just pictures. These cards originally came into existence in the 17th century to avoid a ban on gambling with 'western' cards that had been introduced from Portugal.

Playing cards are still so popular because they offer an infinite variety of games. In some games, you have to collect sets of cards, while others require you to shed the cards in your hand so you have none left. Alternatively, you may sometimes have to accumulate points or the whole pack. They range from simple games of chance to ones with complex rules and strategy using trumps, which are a suit or cards that have an added value; or jokers, cards which can replace any other, as well as the opportunity to bluff or team up with other players. And all that varied entertainment for less than the price of a cinema ticket.

Step 2 Put students in pairs to compare their notes. They should discuss whose notes they think are better and why, and how they could make their notes better. Conduct feedback and point out that notes should be brief and on key points only. They should be written in note form (not full sentences) and include abbreviations. You might want to give some targeted practice on this as a follow-up.

Step 3 Put students in pairs to discuss what the items in exercise C are. Play the recording again for them to check.

> **Answers**
> *deck* = pack of cards (52); *suits* = groups of cards i.e. clubs, diamonds, hearts, spades; *clubs* = a suit, which looks like a trefoil; *jack* = a colour card, like a prince (worth 11 points); *trumps* = the strongest suit; *a joker* = a 'wild' card, which can be used at any time to replace another card

Step 4 Put students in pairs or threes to discuss the questions in D. Conduct brief feedback.

GRAMMAR Linking words

Aim
To focus on different kinds of linking words.

Step 1 Read out the explanation in the box. Elicit a few examples of linkers. Ask students to look at the linkers in A and put them in the correct category according to their meaning. Check in pairs and then with the whole group.

> **Answers**
> the purpose / result: *so, so as to*
> conditions: *if, unless, provided, whether*
> contrasts: *even though, although, even if, otherwise*
> order / time: *then, until*

Step 2 Ask students to complete the sentences in B using the correct linking word from A. Direct them to the grammar reference on page 146 if they need help. Check in pairs and then with the whole group.

> **Answers**
> 1 Then, whether   6 If, unless
> 2 so   7 although
> 3 so as to   8 even though
> 4 otherwise   9 until
> 5 provided   10 even if

Step 3 Put students in pairs. Ask them to tell each other about games they know and try to find one they know, but their partner doesn't. Then ask them to take turns telling each other the rules of their game. They should try to use linking words where appropriate. Monitor and take notes for a correction slot at the end.

> 👥 **11A** see Teacher's notes p. 125.

11 PLAY 77

11 PLAY

LISTENING 2

Aim
To listen for gist and intensively.

Step 1 Tell students they are going to hear five people talking about games. Ask them to look at the items in exercise A and number them according to which speaker talks about each one. Play the recording.

Answers
a speaker 3
b speaker 4
c speaker 3, speaker 5
d speaker 1
e speaker 1, speaker 5
f speaker 2

🔊 **11.3**
Speaker 1
We used to play this game me and my brother made up for long journeys, but it kind of spread through friends at school. The aim was to spot a particular kind of car and be first to shout out say 'yellow car no returns'. The one who's first then has the right to punch the other on the shoulder and the 'no returns' mean that they can't punch you back. It sounds a bit brutal, but in practice you didn't do it that hard because you knew they could get their own back at any moment and you didn't want to get hurt.

Speaker 2
We used to play Parchis at home. It's a board game where you move your counters all round the board and back home, to win. The people playing can capture each other and send each other back to the start. My parents actually banned it for a while because it kept ending in fights. My brothers used to gang up on me ... you know, they wouldn't capture each other so they could catch me! I remember once, I was on the point of winning – I was two places short of safety and Miguel landed on my square. My brothers all burst out laughing and teased me and I just tipped over the board and stormed out of the room.

Speaker 3
I can't play any card games now, because it just triggers that desire. It's a shame because there are some great games that don't involve gambling and it really brings families or friends together. There's always a bit of banter around it. It's educational even. The problem lies when there are stakes involved. I started off with blackjack for small change with my mates, but it escalated when I played poker online. I kept thinking I'm bound to win next time and I became ever more desperate – bluffing badly when I couldn't win.

Speaker 4
I woke up this morning and my shoulders were really stiff. I could hardly raise my arm or even clench my fist. It felt like I'd been beaten up, but then I remembered I'd been playing boxing with my son on this sports game. You have to punch madly at the screen with the controller to try and knock the other figure out and I guess I'm just not used to using those muscles. I had to take the day off!

Speaker 5
On one level, you look at it and you just wish the roles they take on weren't so awful – gunning down cops, mugging people for cash and the like. It's hardly a good example for life. And you do hear negative stories in the press. Then again, it's a very open game. You know, you can choose the tasks or quests you undertake and it involves different skills, and a bit of strategy and you can team up with other players. I mean, my son plays with people in Korea, Mexico, all over. It's amazing, really. And my son's pretty level-headed and has reached the age of 16 without becoming a mass murderer or gang leader, so I guess he distinguishes fact from fiction OK.

Step 2 Ask students to look at the sentences in C and complete them, as in the recording. Check in pairs, then play the recording again for them to check.

Answers
1 a was to spot   b their own back
2 a gang up on   b tipped over
3 a there are stakes   b bound to win
4 a been beaten up   b used to using
5 a tasks or quests   b fact or fiction

SPEAKING

Aim
To personalise the topic and give fluency practice.

Step 1 Ask students to look at the questions in A and think about how they would answer them. Then put them in small groups to discuss the questions. Conduct brief feedback.

pp. 80–81

Next class Make photocopies of **11B** p. 149.

READING

Aim
To practise reading for specific information and detail.

Step 1 Tell students they are going to read an article about different kinds of word play. Put them in pairs and ask them to discuss which of the items in A they are familiar with. They should try to think of an example of each. Do not conduct feedback as they are going to find out by reading.

78 OUTCOMES

11 PLAY

Step 2 Ask students to read the article and find examples of the items in A. They should then think of another example of each of the items. Check in pairs. Then check with the whole group.

> **Answers**
> advertising slogans = Men can't help acting on impulse; I'm loving it
> puns = impulse; Sunny daze
> word games = Taboo; scrabble
> comic insults = your mum's so fat people jog round her for exercise; you stink
> tongue twisters = we surely shall see the sun shine soon; she sells seashells on the seashore
> riddles = what gets wetter the more it dries? (a towel); when is a door not a door? (when it's ajar = a 'jar')
> metaphors = moving the goalposts; up in the air
> idioms = put your finger on something; once in a blue moon
> alliteration = don't just drive it – dream it; lovely Linda
> nursery rhymes = hey diddle diddle; Baa baa, black sheep

Step 3 Put students in pairs or threes to discuss the questions in exercise C. Conduct brief feedback.

> **Answers**
> 1 playing with sounds, songs, chants, noises to accompany motor activities, nonsense words, playful language in poetry and prose, banter, pop lyrics, movie dialogue, crosswords, word games
> 2 It is part of our development as humans; for entertainment; it can be memorable (e.g. advertising)
> 3 It was a fun way of gently pulling his leg, a way of making others laugh and bonding with each other
> 4 a towel

LANGUAGE PATTERNS

Aim
To focus on patterns used to talk about range.

Step 1 Ask students to read the examples in the box and check they understand. Ask them to translate the sentences into their own language and notice any similarities / differences. In a monolingual class, ask students to compare their translation. In a multilingual class, ask students to work in pairs and tell each other if the sentences were easy to translate.

Step 2 Then ask them to close their books and translate the sentences back into their own language. At the end, they should open their books again and compare their translations with the original sentences. Ask them to discuss in pairs who had the least mistakes. What mistakes did they make? Why?

Alternatively If you prefer not to use translation, ask students to look at the sentences and tell you what patterns they notice (different words / expressions to talk about range). Elicit a few more examples.

SPEAKING

Aim
To extend the topic and give fluency practice.

Step 1 Ask students to look at the questions and think about how they would answer them. They might like to make a few notes.

Step 2 Put students in small groups to discuss the questions. Conduct brief feedback.

VOCABULARY
Sports and games metaphors

Aim
To introduce, and give practice in, metaphors based on sports and games.

Step 1 Ask students to look at the sentences in exercise A and decide where the metaphors come from and what they mean in the context. Check in pairs, then check with the whole group.

> **Answers**
> 1 boxing; unnecessarily hurtful
> 2 poker or gambling game; risky
> 3 football or other field game; fairness, equal treatment
> 4 card game; reveal your true feelings or opinion
> 5 racing; level, equal
> 6 poker or similar card game; pretend, act confident
> 7 chess; something or someone used or exploited by someone more powerful
> 8 card games; not reveal your secrets
> 9 tennis; it's your turn to make a decision or take responsibility
> 10 boxing; when something happens to interrupt a difficult situation (the bell ends the round)
> 11 athletics; obstacles to be overcome
> 12 running; a long-term (rather than a quick) decision or situation

Step 2 Put students in pairs or threes to discuss the questions in B. Conduct brief feedback.

11B see Teacher's notes p. 125.

12 HISTORY

UNIT OVERVIEW
In this unit, students practise **describing key events in people's lives and talking about how they have built success, discussing historical events, presenting ideas and theories, asking for clarification and using similes to make descriptions more interesting**. They **read about the Roman Empire** and **listen to conversations about an amazing life**, and **important events in recent history**. The main grammar aim is the use of **dramatic inversion**.

Next class Make photocopies of **12A** p. 150.

VOCABULARY Personal histories

Aim
To introduce words / phrases commonly used to talk about people's biographies.

Step 1 Ask students what some key moments in people's lives are. In pairs ask them to explain what the key moments in their lives have been and why. Conduct brief feedback.

Step 2 In the same pairs ask students to look at the sentences in B and help each other with any new words. Tell them to check in the *Vocabulary builder* on page 46. They should then discuss the positive and / or negative effects each situation could have on someone's life. Conduct brief feedback.

Step 3 Ask students to work in the same pairs and tell each other about people they know who fit the descriptions in C. Conduct brief feedback.

LISTENING

Aim
To practise predicting and listening for specific information.

Step 1 Tell students they are going to hear a conversation in which someone describes his girlfriend's father's amazing life. Put students in pairs and ask them discuss how the words / phrases in A might be connected with the father's life. Play the recording for them to check.

Answers
He's from a *first-generation* immigrant family; they lived in total *poverty*; he *dropped out* of school when his father died and sold *ice cream* on the street; he moved on to selling *textiles*; he moved to *the capital* when he was 21; he started his own company *selling outboard*

motors for boats; he can now afford to have his children educated in *the States*; he eats like a *peasant*.

🔊 **12.1**
A: So how did it go with Sara's parents, George?
B: Oh, it was surprisingly good, actually. The whole visit passed off far better than I'd dared to hope it would.
A: Yeah? Even with her father?
B: Yeah. It turns out his bark is much worse than his bite. We had a long talk over dinner on Saturday and got on really, really well. He's a pretty amazing guy, actually.
A: Yeah? In what way?
B: Well, he's just had an incredible life. I mean, he's from a first-generation immigrant family, grew up in a very strict, very close-knit immigrant community, not really speaking the local language, and basically living in total poverty. Then when he was 13 his dad passed away and as the oldest son he found himself having to support the family.
A: Seriously? Is it a big family?
B: Yeah, colossal. Twelve brothers and sisters! So he had to drop out of school and start working.
A: That's VERY young to be working. What was he doing?
B: He started off selling ice creams on the street of the town he was living in, and then moved on to selling textiles door-to-door and by the time he was about 17, he was going off all round the island selling and making deals.
A: That's amazing. I was still living at home stressing about my end-of-school exams at that age.
B: Yeah, exactly. Then when he was about 21 he decided that if he really wanted to get ahead, he'd have to move to the capital, and set off to make his fortune. He got there, somehow managed to start up his own company selling outboard motors for boats and then just slowly built things up until he got to where he is today, where he can afford to have all his kids educated in the States and go off on holiday whenever he feels like it.
A: So he really is a proper self-made man, then.

80 OUTCOMES

> B: Yeah, completely, but what was great about him is that he's still quite rough around the edges. I mean, he eats like a peasant still and burps after dinner and everything, all of which I found strangely endearing.
> A: And what did he make of you and the idea of his daughter dating an artist, then?
> B: Well, he's still coming to terms with that, obviously, trying to get his head round it all, but his eyes lit up when I told him how much I got for that portrait I sold last year. Basically, I think he just wants to see that she'll be provided for.
> A: Despite the fact she's earning twice as much as you are already!
> B: Yeah, well. I didn't dwell on that fact too much.

Step 2 Ask students to complete the phrases in C with the correct form of the phrasal verbs, as used in the conversation. Play the recording again to check. Check meaning by asking for synonyms or examples.

> **Answers**
> 1 passed off
> 2 turns out
> 3 passed away
> 4 drop out
> 5 started off, moved on
> 6 get ahead, set off
> 7 start up, built (things) up
> 8 lit up
> 9 dwell on

Step 3 Put students in small groups to discuss the questions in exercise D. Conduct brief feedback.

Native speaker English

get your head round it

Ask students what they think the speaker meant by *he's still trying to get his head round it all*. Read out the explanation in the box. Try to elicit a few more examples.

Developing conversations

Similes

Aim
To draw students' attention to similes and give practice.

Step 1 Read out the explanation, checking students understand as you read. Try to elicit a few more examples. You could use prompts to help them e.g. *drink like a ...? (fish) sleep like a ...? (log).*

Step 2 Ask students to match the beginnings 1–5 with the correct ending a–e. Check in pairs, then with the whole group. Concept check by asking for examples of when you would use each expression. Then ask them to repeat the procedure with 6–10 and f–j.

> **Answers**
> **A** 1 c (a bad memory, full of holes)
>   2 e (he smokes a lot)
>   3 b (I felt very uncomfortable or awkward)
>   4 a (I try extremely hard to avoid him)
>   5 d (they're very different)
> **B** 6 h (very tough)
>   7 f (it's completely dead or over)
>   8 j (extremely pale)
>   9 g (very old)
>   10 i (not clear at all)

Step 3 Put students in pairs. Ask them to discuss what each simile means, and whether they have similar expressions in their own language

Step 4 Put students in AB pairs. A should say some of the beginnings 1–10 and B, with book closed, should say the correct ending. Then swap.

Step 5 Ask students to complete the sentences in E with their own similes. These can be as poetic, funny or serious as they like. Ask students to read out a few sentences at the end and comment on each other's sentences.

Conversation practice

Aim
To give practice in the target language.

Step 1 Ask students to think of someone they know who has had an incredible life. Ask them to make notes on what they know about their personal history, using similes if possible.

Step 2 When students are ready, put them into small groups to tell each other about the people they have chosen. Monitor for a correction slot at the end.

Tip You could ask students to do this exercise for homework and bring to the next lesson.

👥 12A see Teacher's notes p. 125

pp. 84–85

Speaking

Aim
To give fluency practice and lead in to *Reading*.

Step 1 Put students in groups and ask them to discuss the questions in A. Check they understand *World Heritage Site* = a place declared of special interest and protected by UNESCO (United Nations Educational, Scientific and Cultural Organisation) e.g. Greenwich in London, Luang Prabang in Laos). Conduct brief feedback.

Tip In a multilingual class, try to have different nationalities in each pair.

12 HISTORY

READING

Aim
To give practice in reading for gist and specific information, and guessing meaning from context.

Step 1 Tell students they are going to read an article about the fall of the Roman Empire. Ask them to answer the questions in A as they read. Tell them not to worry about the words in bold. Check in pairs, then as a class.

> **Answers**
> 1 decadence, economic problems, external pressures, division and infighting, Christianity and cultural change
> 2 because of lack of evidence
> 3 because new discoveries are made that shed more light

Step 2 Ask students to read the text again and answer the questions in B. Check in pairs and then with the whole group.

> **Answers**
> 1 some scholars suggest many advances were lost – quite strong evidence as examples are given – more examples would help
> 2 no evidence really, just the writer's opinion – more scientific evidence about why would help
> 3 the joke from *The Life of Brian* suggests this but this is only a film; also there were no popular uprisings but this could be for a number of reasons; you would need more eye witness accounts
> 4 a new book on the subject comes out nearly every year and over 200 different theories have been suggested; quite strong evidence; you could also ask how many university courses include the study of the Roman Empire
> 5 no evidence – only possibly referred to indirectly as part of *environmental causes* and then thought to be unlikely; you would want more scientific proof of the link
> 6 the mention of green movements and theories – not very strong evidence – *it is argued*; you would want more concrete examples

Step 3 Put students in pairs to discuss the meanings of the words in bold. Check with the whole group.

> **Answers**
> whip up = provoke; culminating = ending; uprisings = rebellions; crumble = gradually be destroyed; to date = up to now; scarcity = lack; sacked = raided; contended = argued; outlook = point of view

Step 4 Put students in pairs or threes to discuss the questions in D. Conduct brief feedback.

DEVELOPING CONVERSATIONS
Asking for clarification

Aim
To focus on ways of asking for clarification in an academic context.

Step 1 Tell students they are going to hear different ways of asking for clarification. Read out the explanation in the box. Ask students to complete the sentences in A as they listen. Play the recording.

> **🔊 12.2 and answers**
> 1 You cited someone called Edward Gibbon. Could you provide us with a reference for that?
> 2 When you were talking about changes in construction techniques, you mentioned thatching. Could you just explain exactly what that is?
> 3 You referred to a theory that lead poisoning contributed significantly to the demise of the empire. Could you elaborate on that a little?
> 4 You mentioned some findings that suggested that environmental degradation was a cause. Do you have any statistics available on that?

Step 2 Ask students to write three similar questions about the article. Check in pairs then check a few examples with the class.

Step 3 Tell students they are going to read different bits of information about the Roman Empire. Divide them into AB pairs. Ask As to look at File 4 on page 153 and Bs to look at File 9 on page 155 and read their information.

Step 4 When students are ready, they should take turns to ask each other questions about the other text, using the questions they wrote in exercise B. Their partner should give the relevant information, invent an answer or apologise for not knowing. Monitor and take notes for a correction slot at the end.

Alternatively Ask students to take turns giving a brief resume of their text and a few clues about details. They should then take turns asking for further information, using the clues and the questions practised in exercise A and B. Their partner should give the relevant information, invent an answer or apologise for not knowing. Monitor and take notes for a correction slot at the end.

VOCABULARY
Presenting arguments and theories

Aim
To focus on ways of presenting arguments and theories.

Step 1 Put students in pairs. Ask them to look at the words in italics in the sentences in A and discuss whether they have the same or different meanings. If they are different, they should discuss how. Check with the whole class.

12 HISTORY

Answers
1 *put forward* / *advanced* = same; *established* / *claimed* = different; *established* = proved, found to be true, *claimed* = said (but it may not be true)
2 *asserts* / *demonstrates* = different; *asserts* = claims, *demonstrates* = shows, proves; *stemmed from* / *gave rise to* = different; *stemmed from* = came about because of, *gave rise to* = prompted something to happen
3 *allegedly* / *supposedly* = same; *questioned* / *cast doubt on* = same
4 *challenged* / *accepted* = opposite; *highlighting* / *emphasising* = same
5 *argues* / *contends* = same; *significant* / *minor* = opposite

Step 2 Ask students to choose one of the people in B or a person or theory they already know about. They should research and prepare a short presentation (2–3 minutes). They should try to use verbs from this part of the unit. If you have access to computers / research books, you can do this in class time; otherwise, set the preparation for homework.

SPEAKING

Aim
To give presentation practice, tying together the verbs in *Vocabulary* and the questions in *Conversation practice*.

Step 1 Put students in groups of five or six and tell them to take turns presenting their information to each other. The other students should listen and ask questions at the end, using questions similar to those in *Conversation practice*. Conduct brief feedback at the end.

Alternatively You could conduct this as a whole group activity, with students taking turns to present to the whole class. The other students should take notes on each presentation and ask questions at the end of each one.

📖 **pp. 86–87**

Next class Make photocopies of **12B** p. 151.

SPEAKING

Aim
To move into a new topic (recent history).

Step 1 Ask students to think about what they know about each of the items in A. Then put them in small groups to discuss what they think happened in each case and what they think the causes and results were. Conduct brief feedback.

Suggested answers
Berlin Wall – divided East and West Berlin (Communist bloc and the West). After much civil unrest in 1989, people started climbing over it, finally came down on 9th Nov 1989 – Germany was reunified in 1990.
9/11 attacks Sept 11th, 2001. Four planes involved – two flew into Twin Towers of World Trade Centre, one into the Pentagon in Washington, one landed in a field in Pennsylvania. Al-Queda claimed responsibility. No survivors on planes. 2,995 people killed in total.
The euro – used in 16 countries and is official currency of the eurozone – not all EU countries use it e.g. UK. Introduced in 1999, coins and banknotes entered circulation 2002. Some problems because of the different strengths of the economies involved.
Iraq conflicts – first Gulf War was in 1990/91 in response to Iraqi invasion of Kuwait. Led by USA / UK but other allied countries involved. Second conflict March–May 2003, led by USA / UK despite very strong popular opposition. Official reason was to destroy the dictatorship of Saddam Hussein – he was toppled in May 2003.
Tsunami – 26/12/04 in the Indian Ocean, following a very strong earthquake. Waves up to 30 metres high. Main countries affected were India, Indonesia, Sri Lanka, Thailand, The Maldives. Estimated death toll 230,000, huge destruction.
Genocide – Rwanda – 1994 – mass killing of an estimated 800,000 in approximately 100 days. Mostly Hutu tribe killing Tutsi people as part of civil war. Estimated that 20% of the total population was wiped out; Darfur (Sudan) – ongoing guerrilla conflict. Different tribes and government and police involved. Conflict between black Africans and those of Arab origins. Estimated between 20,000 and several hundred thousand dead, either through direct combat or starvation / disease.

VOCABULARY Recent history

Aim
To introduce verbs associated with historical events.

Step 1 Ask students to complete the sentences in A using the correct form of the verbs from the box. Check in pairs, then with the whole group. Concept check by asking for other examples.

Answers
1 called
2 was assassinated
3 declared, gain
4 went, dented
5 was abolished
6 was overthrown
7 issued
8 were massacred
9 carried out
10 have been pushing

Step 2 Put students in pairs or threes to discuss the questions in B. Conduct brief feedback.

12 HISTORY

LISTENING

Aim
To practise listening for gist and specific information.

Step 1 Tell students they are going to hear four people talking about milestone events in the recent history of different countries. Check they understand *milestone events* = important, often changing the situation significantly. Ask them to answer the questions in A as they listen. Play the recording.

> **Answers**
> 1 Attack on Anna Lindh, a government minister in Sweden, who later died; significant because she might have become Prime Minister, and because it changed people's views of Sweden as a safe country.
> 2 Poland's entry into the EU; significant because it meant Poland was accepted as a mature member of Europe, it drew a line under the past and meant that a lot of people left the country.
> 3 The opening of the Baku–Tbilisi–Ceyhan pipeline in 2005; significant because it gave Azerbaijan economic independence and Turkey more recognition.
> 4 The apology by the Australian government to Aborigine communities; significant because of the suffering of Aborigines under successive governments; it removed the stain on the nation.

⏵ 12.3

1   Back in 2003, I came home from college one day and turned on the TV – and saw that Anna Lindh had been attacked. She was the Swedish minister for foreign affairs and a woman I'd always admired. She'd always taken a strong stand against injustice and had campaigned against apartheid and the arms trade and that kind of thing. She'd even started being talked about as a possible future prime minister. Then one day – it was September the eleventh, I remember, because it was the second anniversary of the World Trade Centre bombings – she went out shopping in Stockholm and was stabbed in the chest and the stomach by this random guy with a history of mental illness. She was rushed to hospital, but they were unable to save her. It was just such a senseless murder and it kind of sounded the death knell for this notion we'd had of Sweden being a safe country where even leading politicians could go out during their lunch break without fear of abuse or assault.

2   For many Poles of my generation, joining the European Union was a huge event. It represented the moment we moved closer to the west in all manner of ways – mentally, economically, politically. It symbolised a kind of rite of passage, a moment when we were finally recognised by the elder statesmen of Europe, by Germany and the UK and France and so on. It implied we were somehow mature enough now to be accepted into the unifying structure and after so much bad blood between so many European countries all through the twentieth century, it felt like we were drawing a line under the past and moving on into the future. In the referendum, over three-quarters of the population voted to join the EU and the changes since then have been enormous.

One of the most remarkable phenomena was the number of people who went to live overseas. No sooner had we been granted full membership than literally hundreds of thousands of young Poles headed off abroad. I spent three years living in the north of England, and while I loved it and learned a lot there, it was also good to come home. I had money in the bank, my language skills had improved and I'm now proud to help develop my nation's economy. The freedom of movement that our accession to the EU allowed me has really helped me kick-start my business back home.

3   Probably the most significant event of recent times in my country, Azerbaijan, was the opening of the Baku–Tbilisi–Ceyhan pipeline back in 2005. It's a pipeline transporting oil over one thousand miles from our capital, Baku, to Ceyhan, on the Mediterranean coast in Turkey. It was a very historic event for us because it signalled a kind of financial and economic independence. Because the Caspian is a landlocked sea, all the movement of oil in the past went through Russia, but this pipeline bypasses the old trade routes and goes through Georgia instead. It's placed us closer to the heart of the global oil market, and of course it gives Turkey greater geo-political clout as well. The income that's been generated is so substantial that it's forced us to allow greater transparency and to introduce tighter checks against corruption as well. All of that can only be for the good.

4   For me, the standout event of recent years was the apology issued to the Aborigine community a few years ago. A motion was passed in Parliament, followed by a speech from Prime Minister Rudd and it was the first time that we as a nation had really acknowledged the mistakes of the past with regard to the treatment of our indigenous population. I don't know how much you know about it, but over the years successive governments carried out a kind of cultural genocide. Just to give one example, throughout most of the twentieth century, any mixed-race kids were forcibly removed from Aborigine communities and basically forced to live in white-only communities, thus losing all knowledge of their cultural heritage. A lot of the kids who were removed didn't get properly educated and so face higher levels of unemployment today and plenty of them suffered chronic abuse in care as well. The apology for all of this was long overdue, but at least it was an attempt to start removing the stain this has been left on the whole nation.

Step 2 Ask students to decide if the statements in exercise B are true or false. Then play the recording again for them to check. Check with the whole group. Ask students to correct the false statements.

84 OUTCOMES

12 HISTORY

> **Answers**
> 1 a T
>   b F – it was a random attack
>   c F – she died in hospital
> 2 a T
>   b F – over three quarters of the population voted for it
>   c T
> 3 a F – it bypasses the old trade routes
>   b F – it has generated a substantial income
>   c T
> 4 a T
>   b F – they face higher levels of unemployment today
>   c T

Step 3 Ask students to look at C and match 1–10 with a–h, as they were used in the recording. Ask them to check with the audioscript on page 174. Then put them in pairs and ask them to discuss who or what did each of the things in C.

> **Answers**
> 1 e – Anna Lindh (against injustice)
> 2 f – Anna Lindh's death caused the end of the notion that Sweden was safe
> 3 a – Poland's EU entry
> 4 g – Poland's EU entry
> 5 b – the pipeline
> 6 h – the pipeline (to Turkey)
> 7 c – the Australian government
> 8 d – the Australian government

Step 4 Put students in groups to discuss the questions in exercise D. Conduct brief feedback.

LANGUAGE PATTERNS

Aim
To draw students' attention to some patterns using *for the* + adjective or comparative/superlative of *good / bad*.

Step 1 Ask students to read the examples in the box and check they understand. Ask them to translate the sentences into their own language and notice any similarities / differences. In a monolingual class, ask students to compare their translation. In a multilingual class, ask students to work in pairs and tell each other if the sentences were easy to translate.

Step 2 Then ask them to close their books and translate the sentences back into their own language. At the end, they should open their books again and compare their translations with the original sentences. Ask them to discuss in pairs who had the least mistakes. What mistakes did they make? Why?

Alternatively If you prefer not to use translation, ask students to tell you what pattern they notice = *for the* + *good*, *better*, *best* or *worse* (but not *worst*), meaning having that kind of result. Try to elicit a few more examples.

GRAMMAR Dramatic inversion

Aim
To revise dramatic inversion.

Step 1 Read out the explanation in the box and check that students understand. Elicit which tense is used after *no sooner* (usually past perfect) and which linker joins the two clauses (*than*). Ask students to look at the sentences in A and re-write them using *no sooner*, and making any necessary changes. Check in pairs then check as a class.

> **Answers**
> 1 No sooner had the President been overthrown than civil war broke out.
> 2 No sooner had we adopted the euro than prices went up.
> 3 No sooner had the earthquake struck than the looting began.
> 4 No sooner had Brazil equalised than we went up the other end of the pitch and scored the winner.

Step 2 Try to elicit a few examples of other phrases which are followed by inversion. You could prompt students with *hardly…? little …?* You could point out / elicit that these are all adverbs / adverbial phrases with a negative or restrictive meaning. Read out the explanation in the box. Then ask students to look at the sentences in B and complete them using the correct word / phrase from the box. Direct them to the grammar reference on page 147 if they need help. Check in pairs, then check with the whole group.

> **Answers**
> 1 Not only   4 Not until
> 2 at no time   5 Nowhere else, only
> 3 Never before

SPEAKING

Aim
To round off the unit and give fluency practice.

Step 1 Tell students they are going to discuss important historical events. Ask them individually to think of three major events from their country in recent years and make some notes, thinking about why they were significant. When ready, put students in small groups to discuss their events. Encourage students to develop conversations by asking questions. Conduct brief feedback.

Tip In a multilingual class, mix up the nationalities as much as possible. In a monolingual class, ask students to discuss how they would explain the events to a foreigner.

> 🗣🗣 **12B** see Teacher's notes p. 125.

03 REVIEW

Two minutes, game, conversation practice & act or draw

For aims and suggested procedure, see Review 01, pages 32–35.

Quiz

Answers
1. People **network** to build up business contacts.
2. The opposite of **upholding** a decision is *overturning* a decision.
3. Jobs which might be **emotionally draining** often involve troubled people e.g. social worker.
4. People **bluff** when they have bad cards and they want to convince their opponents their cards are good (e.g. at poker).
5. A person, a car, a computer could be **temperamental**, i.e. mood-changing or unreliable.
6. It's good if cancer **goes into remission**.
7. People **flee** an area because there is war, an earthquake or a flood.
8. You might need a **skin graft** when you have burns.
9. A drain / sink could **clog** / **clog-up** with mud, food or rubbish.
10. If a town or city is **sacked** it is attacked and valuable goods are destroyed / stolen.
11. You could **confess to** a crime, an accident (when you broke something), an affair, etc.
12. Hare Krishna is a **chant**. There are also football / sport chants.
13. If a team is **relegated**, it goes down to the next division. The opposite is *promoted*.
14. You might **glare** at someone who has been rude.
15. Shops might get **looted** during a war or after a natural disaster.

Collocations

For aims and suggested procedure, see Review 01, pages 32–35.

Idioms

Answers
1. We're all in the same situation.
2. He's teasing you.
3. I've been terribly busy.
4. Maybe you can show me around and explain how things work?
5. It was unnecessarily cruel and direct.
6. He is more aggressive verbally than physically.
7. I don't think he's contributing enough.
8. I had to stop myself from saying what I wanted to say.
9. It's a way of marking a change from one stage of life to another.
10. She is secretive.
11. They keep changing the rules or parameters.
12. Let me check what you mean.
13. We are being used by more powerful people.
14. Her parents are separated or divorced.
15. It's up to you / It's your decision.

pp. 90–91

Listening

For aims and suggested procedure for the rest of the review, see Review 01, pages 32–35. The audio is R3.1.

Exercise A answers
a Speaker 5
b Speaker 2
c Speaker 1
d –
e Speaker 3
f –
g Speaker 4

Exercise B answers
a –
b Speaker 3
c –
d Speaker 5
e Speaker 1
f Speaker 2
g Speaker 4

86 OUTCOMES

Grammar

Exercise A answers
1 Under no circumstances **are you** to leave your post unattended.
2 If it hadn't been for my old Chemistry teacher, I wouldn't be **working** here now!
3 Only after a full enquiry **did** we understand the full horror of the incident.
4 That **can't** have been much fun. I would've gone crazy if it'd happened to me.
5 I wouldn't work for that firm even **if** the money was amazing.
6 It was awful. My phone **went** off while I was being interviewed.
7 I can't believe he failed. He **must** be feeling dreadful now.
8 I don't mind you answering the call in class **as long as** it's quick.

Exercise B answers
1 shouldn't have been texting
2 can't have been feeling well
3 No sooner had I started there
4 At no time did he
5 a day goes by without
6 'm not very adept

Language patterns

Answers
1 be
2 longer
3 better
4 from
5 worse
6 more

Prepositions

Answers
1 on
2 of
3 for
4 of
5 on
6 on
7 to
8 on

Opposites

Answers
1 civilian
2 conservative
3 malignant
4 significant
5 good
6 quick
7 privileged
8 substantial

Missing words

Answers
1 impact
2 grasp
3 award
4 spiral
5 hand

Verbs

Answers
1 draw up
2 retain
3 put forward
4 exacerbate
5 bypass
6 administer
7 forge
8 cite

Forming words

Answers
1 findings
2 redundancy
3 occurrence
4 dealings
5 scarcity
6 recurrent
7 workers

Vocabulary

Answers
1 C hurdles
2 B transition
3 C formality
4 B rigorous
5 C painstaking
6 A leadership
7 C witty
8 A delegate

13 NEWS AND THE MEDIA

UNIT OVERVIEW
In this unit, students learn how to **understand news stories better** and practise **commenting on news stories and talking about the media**. They practise **recognising and using rhetorical questions**. They read a text about **popular newspapers** and listen to conversations about **TV programmes**, part of a programme about **the future of news publishing** and **the evening news**. The main grammar aim is revision of **reporting verbs**.

VOCABULARY News headlines

Aim
To introduce and practise words commonly used in headlines.

Step 1 Begin by showing students some real headlines and eliciting what they mean, or you could write some invented headlines on the board. Ask students what the main characteristics of headlines are. Then read out the explanation in the box.

Step 2 Ask students to look at the words in bold in the sentences in A and try to work out what they mean. Direct them to the *Vocabulary builder* on page 50 if they need help. Check in pairs, then check with the whole group.

Answers
1 *blast toll* = number of dead from explosion
2 *hails* = praises
3 *bars* = bans, prohibits from entering; *crackdown* = stricter policy
4 *cleared* = freed from
5 *seize* = take; *raid* = sudden entry and search
6 *brink* = edge, very close to
7 *leak* = revelation; *slash* = cut a large number of
8 *ups* = increases; *bid* = attempt
9 *clash* = fight, disagree violently
10 *rule out* = dismiss the possibility of; *halt* = stop
11 *pulls out of* = withdraws from
12 *blow* = setback
13 *vows* = promises

Step 3 Put students in pairs and ask them to look again at the headlines in A and discuss what they think happened in the story, if they think this is good or bad news, and whether they would like to read more. Conduct brief feedback.

Step 4 Put students in pairs or small groups and ask them to discuss the questions in C. Conduct brief feedback.

LISTENING

Aim
To extend the topic and practise listening for gist.

Step 1 Tell students they are going to hear five conversations about some of the headlines from *Vocabulary* exercise A. Ask them to decide which headline the speakers are talking about and whether they agree or disagree with each other as they listen. Play the recording.

Answers
Conversation 1
1 Sanders cleared of bribery charges 2 agree
Conversation 2
1 Email leak reveals secret plan to slash jobs
2 initially speaker one has a different opinion, but agrees with second speaker in the end
Conversation 3
1 Kohl pulls out of Open over sex scandal 2 agree
Conversation 4
1 Hector vows to continue despite outburst
2 disagree about the seriousness of the situation
Conversation 5
1 Club bars fans in crackdown on hooliganism
2 agree

♦ 13.1
Conversation 1
A: Have you seen the news today?
B: Yeah. Did you see that MP got off?
A: Well, what did you expect? It's one rule for us and another for them, isn't it?
B: It makes me sick. It was so obvious he's been lining his own pockets. I don't know how he's got away with it.
A: Apparently, the case was dismissed on some kind of technicality.
B: Typical. As you say, if it'd been someone lower down, they'd have been convicted.

Conversation 2
C: What do you think of this story about cutting back the public sector workforce?
D: I'll believe it when it happens.
C: You don't think it will?
D: No. I mean, look at it from the government's point of view. Why would they? What do they have to gain? There's an election coming up in just over a year. It'd be a disaster for them.
C: That's true. Maybe the opposition is just stirring up trouble.
D: More likely. I don't think they've said the source of the story.
E: I can't believe they're still going on about this guy and his affair. It's such a fuss about nothing.
F: I don't think she'd see it like that!
E: No, I know. It's obviously a big deal for her, but I don't see how having it all over the papers will help. What's it got to do with us? And what's it got to do with playing tennis?
F: Nothing. It's all to do with money and sponsorship, isn't it?
E: Exactly. As if anyone cares. It's such nonsense.

Conversation 3
G: Did you see that thing about the Secretary of State and what he said?
H: Yeah. I can't believe he's refusing to resign!
G: I don't know. Put yourself in his shoes. Can you imagine the pressure politicians are under when there's so much news coverage? It amazes me they don't make more slips.
H: I know, but it's not the first time and I think it undermines our standing in the world. What are other countries going to think?
G: Ah, it's just a storm in a teacup. It'll all blow over quickly enough.
H: You think so?

Conversation 4
I: Did you see that business with the Hampton supporters?
J: Yeah, it was a disgrace. They're just animals. They should do something about them.
I: Didn't you hear? They have! A whole load of them have had their season tickets confiscated.
J: Well, it's about time, though why on earth aren't they being prosecuted? The amount of damage they caused! Not to mention the intimidation.
I: I know. They're thugs. They should be locked up.

Step 2 Ask students to look at the sentences in B and try to complete them, as in the conversations. Check in pairs, then play the recording again for them to check.

Answers
1 a pockets   b technicality
2 a election   b trouble
3 a fuss   b sponsorship
4 a standing   b teacup
5 a season tickets b thugs

NATIVE SPEAKER ENGLISH *all over*

Ask students what they think the speaker meant by *having it all over the newspapers* = *the story is in lots of newspapers*. Read out the explanation in the box. Try to elicit a few examples from students.

DEVELOPING CONVERSATIONS
Rhetorical questions and common opinions

Aim
To draw students' attention to rhetorical questions.

Step 1 Read out the explanation, checking students understand as you read.

Step 2 Ask students to look at the audioscript on page 175 and decide which questions are real and which are rhetorical, and what opinions the rhetorical questions show.

Answers
The rhetorical questions are:
Conversation 1
Well, what did you expect? (= I'm not surprised)
Conversation 2
Why would they? What do they have to gain? (the speaker thinks the government will do what is good for them, especially before an election)
Conversation 3
What's it got to do with us? What's it got to do with playing tennis? (the speaker sees no connection between the guy's ability to play tennis and the fact that he has had an affair)
Conversation 4
Can you imagine ... news coverage? (politicians are under a lot of pressure from the media)
What are other countries going to think? (this is bad for our international reputation)
Conversation 5
Why on earth aren't they being prosecuted? (I think they should be prosecuted)

Step 3 Put students in groups. Ask them to look at the opinions in B and discuss which ones they could imagine saying themselves and in what situations. Conduct brief feedback.

13 NEWS AND THE MEDIA

CONVERSATION PRACTICE

Aim
To give practice in the target language and in talking about the news.

Step 1 Tell students they are going to have similar conversations to the ones they heard in *Listening*. Ask them to think of different news stories they have heard about recently. Ask them to think about what they can say, and to write a question to begin a conversation about each one.

Step 2 Put students in small groups and ask them to tell each other about their news stories. One of them should begin by asking a question, and they should take turns to tell their stories. Conduct brief feedback by asking which was the funniest / most interesting / most surprising story they heard.

Alternatively You could conduct this as a mingle. Ask students to stand up and move around, asking their questions and telling different students their stories. Conduct feedback as above.

pp. 94–95

Next class Make photocopies of **13A** p. 152.

SPEAKING

Aim
To extend the topic of talking about news, give fluency practice and lead in to *Listening*.

Step 1 Ask students to read the short text in A. Then put them in small groups and ask them to discuss the questions. Conduct brief feedback.

LISTENING

Aim
To give practice in listening for gist and specific information.

Step 1 Tell students they are going to hear part of a news programme about the future of newspaper publishing. Ask them to note what reason is given for the continued existence of newspapers, what other reason is given, and why this is described as ironic. Play the recording.

Answers
1 Because newspapers are still responsible for most news gathering.
2 Because of the income generated by advertising on newspaper companies' websites.
This is ironic because the websites are free to access but newspaper companies can still make a profit by advertising on them – despite possibly selling fewer newspapers as a result of them – because of the number of people who see these advertisements.

13.2
It would obviously be absolute folly for newspaper owners and publishers to ignore current technological developments, but it should also be acknowledged that newspaper companies are still alive and well and doing quite nicely, thank you. Whilst it is obviously true that technology has changed potential modes of delivery, the fact remains that there is no content without a news organisation to gather and edit news.

Indeed, Internet-only sites that have attempted to publish solely their own content have struggled, while the online news sites that HAVE thrived have done so almost entirely as a result of others' labours. Newspapers are still very much the main news-gatherers as well as being the primary suppliers of news to Internet-based companies and the bottom line is that this will continue to be the case until online journalism becomes as profitable as print-based media. Even bearing in mind reduced delivery and printing costs, such parity is probably still many, many years away.

Another important factor in the continued survival of newspapers has ironically been the new income generated from advertising placed on the companies' websites. The vast majority of newspaper websites are still free to access, as efforts to monetise them have had decidedly mixed results. As a result, they are attractive to advertisers keen to hit as wide a range of potential customers as possible. Most companies have strong brand identities, are in healthy financial positions and have access to a deep well of content, all of which suggests that rumours of the death of the newspaper have been somewhat exaggerated!

Step 2 Ask students to look at the statements in B and decide which ones the speaker claims are true. Check in pairs, then play the recording again for them to check.

Answers
2, 5

LANGUAGE PATTERNS

Aim
To draw students' attention to some patterns using (*not*) *as ... as*.

90 OUTCOMES

13 NEWS AND THE MEDIA

Step 1 Ask students to read the examples in the box and check they understand them. Ask them to translate the sentences into their own language and notice any similarities / differences. In a monolingual class, ask students to compare their translation. In a multilingual class, ask students to work in pairs and tell each other if the sentences were easy to translate.

Step 2 Then ask them to close their books and translate the sentences back into their own language. At the end, they should open their books again and compare their translations with the original sentences. Ask them to discuss in pairs who had the least mistakes. What mistakes did they make? Why?

Alternatively If you prefer not to use translation, ask students to look at the sentences and tell you what pattern they notice = (*not*) *as* + adjective + *as* to make comparisons. Try to elicit a few more examples.

VOCABULARY Newspapers

Aim
To introduce words / phrases commonly used to talk about newspapers, and lead into *Reading*.

Step 1 Ask students to look at the sentences in A and try to work out the meaning of the words / phrases in bold from the extra information given. Ask them to translate them into their own language.

Alternatively If you prefer not to use translation, put students in pairs and ask them to come up with a definition, near-synonym or example to show the meaning of each of the items. Check with the whole class.

> **Answers**
> 1 *tabloids* = smaller, more sensational newspapers also called *red tops* e.g. *The Sun*; *broadsheets* = serious newspapers e.g. *The Times*
> 2 *supplements* = extra sections e.g. Travel, magazine
> 3 *circulation* = number of readers
> 4 *sensationalist* = concerned with scandals, accidents, celebrity gossip etc; *the lowest common denominator* = the most basic, least sophisticated level of taste of the readers
> 5 *bias* = preference; *editorials* = opinion pieces written by the editor
> 6 *invasion of privacy* = interference in people's private lives; *acting in the public interest* = giving the public what they want, for the good of the public
> 7 *retract* = withdraw; *substantiate* = prove to be true
> 8 *free press* = total liberty for newspapers and the media; *harassment* = assaults on someone's privacy by following them, bothering them, asking them personal questions, etc.

Step 2 Put students in groups and ask them to discuss how far each of the sentences in exercise A are true for their country. Conduct brief feedback.

Tip In a multilingual class, mix up the nationalities as much as possible.

> 13A see Teacher's notes p. 126.

READING

Aim
To give practice in reading for detail and responding to text.

Step 1 Tell students they are going to read about three different newspapers. Ask them to answer the questions in exercise A as they read. Check they understand: *disseminate propaganda* = spread politically biased information; *diversify* = add more variety to a brand; *meddling* = interfering.

> **Answers**
> 1 The Sun, Marca
> 2 Marca, Helsingin Sanomat
> 3 The Sun
> 4 Helsingin Sanomat
> 5 The Sun
> 6 Helsingin Sanomat
> 7 Marca
> 8 The Sun
> 9 Helsingin Sanomat
> 10 Marca
> 11 Helsingin Sanomat
> 12 The Sun

Step 2 Put students in pairs or small groups to discuss the questions in C. With a multilingual group, mix up the nationalities as much as possible. Conduct brief feedback.

> pp. 96–97

> **Next class** Make photocopies of 13B p. 153.

SPEAKING

Aim
To give fluency practice and lead in to *Listening*.

Step 1 Ask students to look at the items in A and think about how they would answer the questions in relation to news stories they've heard in the last year. If they wish, they could make a few notes.

Step 2 Put students in pairs or threes. Ask them to tell each other about their choices and agree / disagree, or explain the story if their partner hasn't heard about them.

13 NEWS AND THE MEDIA

Listening

Aim
To give practice in listening for gist and specific information.

Step 1 Tell students they are going to hear headlines for five news items. They should note down the subject of each item as they listen.

> **Answers**
> 1 retirement of minister
> 2 award for sniffer dog
> 3 riots in Manova
> 4 rising interest rates
> 5 sports player out of match
> 6 two people have won a libel case against a newspaper

🔊 13.3
This is the six o'clock news with SBC, I'm Natalie Davies. The headlines this evening: Finance Minister Carol Dixon announces her retirement; medal awarded to sniffer dog; two dead as rioting continues in Manova; Interest rates to rise; Jermaine Johnson is out of the final world cup qualifier; and Simon Crouch and Jennifer Ponting have won their libel case against *News Enquirer*.

Step 2 Put students in pairs. Ask them to look at the noun / noun phrases in exercise B and decide which two they think go with each news item. Play the recording again for them to check. Then play the full bulletin to check their answers and to find out what happened in each story.

> **Answers**
> 1 health grounds, a private matter
> 2 bomb disposal, bravery
> 3 petrol bomb, tear gas
> 4 base rate, inflation
> 5 thigh strain, good form
> 6 sham marriage, an appeal

🔊 13.4
N = Newsreader, **CD** = Carol, **I** = Interviewer,
HC = Hassan, **NS** = Nico, **FH** = François, **AK** = Anita,
L = lawyer

N: In an interview with SBC, Finance minister Carol Dixon has confirmed rumours that she is to retire on health grounds. She categorically denied that her retirement was connected to recent criticism of the government's decision to build two new nuclear power stations, although she acknowledged there had been division on the issue.

CD: Of course there was a dispute over nuclear energy. I've been a long-term opponent and I've never hidden that, but I lost that argument. On broad policy – hand on heart – I remain totally behind this government.

N: However, she refused to comment further on the health reasons for her departure.

I: And will you be giving more details on your health? Otherwise, it's bound to fuel speculation.

CD: No. I really think that's a private matter between my family and me.

N: A sniffer dog has received a medal for bravery for its work in a bomb disposal unit. Bodge has worked in several war zones over the last six years and has helped find over 200 bombs and mines to be deactivated. His handler, Corporal Hassan Cleaver, said it was a proud day and praised the work of the whole unit.

HC: It's just fantastic. We're so proud of him. And he deserves it, as do lots of the dogs we work with. What they do is just unbelievably important. They're fantastic.

N: Rioting over government reforms has continued in Manova, with two men being killed. Crowds throwing missiles confronted police armed with batons in the main square and conducted running battles in the surrounding streets throughout the day. Nico Smith reports:

NS: There are conflicting reports about the deaths. A police spokesman assured reporters that the men died when a car exploded after being set alight by a petrol bomb that had been thrown by rioters. Meanwhile, demonstrators, claim they were crushed when police fired tear gas to disperse the crowd in the square, forcing people down narrow side streets. As the news of the deaths spread, protesters rampaged though the surrounding area, smashing things in anger. The rioting lasted most of the day until an uneasy calm fell upon the city this evening. Addressing the country on television, the president blamed the rioting on subversive groups trying to destabilise the country and rejected demands for the government to change tack. He urged what he termed a silent majority to make their voices heard. However, there are no signs that that call will be heeded. Nico Smith, Manova.

N: Interest rates are set to rise half a per cent, taking the base rate to a ten-year high of 4%. The central bank refused to rule out further increases this year as it bids to control inflation.

Sport, and the national football team has been dealt a further blow in the run up to its crucial World Cup qualifying match against Russia. The goalkeeper and team captain Jermaine Johnson has been ruled out with a thigh strain. The team has struggled and must win if they are to go through to the finals next year. The manager, François Houllier, expressed confidence in Johnson's replacement, Paul Harrison.

FH: Obviously it is not a great preparation, but Paul is a great keeper and has been in good form, so I am not so worried.

92 OUTCOMES

13 NEWS AND THE MEDIA

> N: The Hollywood couple Simon Crouch and Jennifer Ponting have won their libel action against the paper News Enquirer, following allegations that theirs was a sham marriage. Anita Karaji reports.
> AK: During the compelling three-day hearing, the court heard claim and counter-claim about the state of Crouch and Ponting's marriage, but in the end the judge found in their favour, awarding £560,000 damages. Outside the court, in a statement read by their lawyer, the couple thanked supporters and vowed to donate the money to charity.
> L: Simon and Jen would like to thank all those fans who sent well wishes and never doubted the outcome of this case. They would also like to make clear that all the proceeds from this decision will be given to good causes, because this case was never about personal gain, only about personal truth.
> AK: News Enquirer said it disagreed with the decision and was considering an appeal.
> N: And that's the news from SBC. It's five past six.

Step 3 Put students in small groups and ask them to look at the statements in D. They should discuss whether they are definitely true, definitely false or still unclear – and why. Play the recording again and ask students to read the audioscript on page 176 as they listen, to check their ideas. Check with the whole class at the end.

> **Answers**
> 1 T – there had been division on the issue
> 2 not clear – she would not give details
> 3 F – he works for the bomb disposal unit of the army
> 4 not clear – two men were killed, there are conflicting reports how
> 5 not clear – he thinks so, but this is not a fact
> 6 not clear – the bank refused to rule it out
> 7 not clear – not stated
> 8 F – they must win to go through
> 9 T – they will give it to good causes
> 10 not clear – not stated

GRAMMAR Reporting and verb patterns

Aim
To revise reporting verbs and give practice.

Step 1 Begin by eliciting some reporting verbs and the patterns that follow them. Prompt students if necessary e.g. *suggest?* = (verb + *ing* or (*that*) clause) *promise?* = (+ *to* infinitive). Then read out the explanation in the box.

Step 2 Put students in pairs and ask them to discuss which pattern followed the reporting verbs in the news bulletin. Ask them to look at the audioscript on page 176 to check. Check with the whole group.

> **Answers**
> verb + (*that*) clause = *acknowledge, claim, deny*
> verb + object + (*that*) clause = *assure*
> verb + *to-* infinitive = *vow, refuse*
> verb+ object + *to-*infinitive = *urge*
> verb + noun / noun phrase = *express, reject, praise, confirm, blame,* (+ *on something / someone*)

Step 3 Ask students to write five sentences about things they have heard in the news recently, using reporting verbs from exercise A. Direct them to the grammar reference on page 148 if they need help. Put them in pairs to compare their sentences. Check a few examples with the whole group at the end.

> **13B** see Teacher's notes p. 126.

SPEAKING

Aim
To round off the unit and give fluency practice.

Step 1 Ask students to look at the news stories in exercise A and choose five that they would publish. Then put them in small groups to discuss their ideas and reach an agreement.

Step 2 Ask groups to put their five stories in order of importance and write a headline for each. Ask students to share their ideas with the rest of the class.

Alternatively Groups could read out their headlines to each other and the rest of the class could guess which stories they chose.

Optional activity Ask the groups to tell each other their reasons to publish what they've chosen, then try and get the whole class to come to an agreement on the five stories they would choose to publish, and the order of importance of the stories.

14 BUSINESS AND ECONOMICS

UNIT OVERVIEW
In this unit, students practise **talking about running a business and about how a business is doing**. They learn how **to hold a meeting and take minutes** and how to **network, make small talk** and describe **problems with banks**. They read an article about **banking practices** and listen to **phone calls between colleagues** and to a **business meeting**. The main grammar aim is revision of **relative clauses**.

Next class Make photocopies of **14A** p. 154.

Speaking

Aim
To lead in to the topic and get students thinking and talking about running a business.

Step 1 Begin by asking students what different kinds of business they can think of. Then ask them to look at the questions in exercise A and think about how they would answer them. Check they understand: *start-up funds* = money needed to start a business; *implementing a business plan* = putting a business plan into action; *hiring and firing* = recruiting and sacking staff; *team morale* = motivation and enthusiasm of the staff; *networking* = making contacts; *bookkeeping* = accounting; *cash flow* = money coming in and out.

Step 2 Put students in small groups and ask them to discuss the questions in A. Conduct brief feedback.

Vocabulary *How's business?*

Aim
To introduce words / phrases commonly associated with business.

Step 1 Put students in pairs and ask them to look at the pairs of words / phrases in italics in A and decide whether they mean basically the same thing or something different. Ask them to explain differences in meaning to each other. Check with the whole group.

Answers
1. *inundated* / *flooded* = same
2. *relocating* / *moving* = same
3. *rents* / *overheads* = different; *rents* = payments for properties; *overheads* = total costs
4. *upturn* / *decline* = different; *upturn* = increase; *decline* = decrease
5. *a solid client base* / *loyal customers* = same
6. *lay off* / *employ* = almost opposite; *employ* = take on; *lay off* = make redundant
7. *floating* / *launching* = same
8. *pick up* / *get better* = same; *end up going under* / *have to make serious cutbacks* – similar, *end up going under* = go out of business; *have to make serious cutbacks* = have to save money, almost go out of business
9. *hanging in* / *surviving* = same, but *surviving* is more formal
10. *diversify* / *consolidate* = different; *diversify* = broaden, add more variety to; *consolidate* = make stronger
11. *take on staff* / *make staff redundant* = opposite (see 5)
12. *downturn* / *drop* = same
13. *terminating* / *pitching for* = different; *terminating* = ending; *pitching for* = bidding for

Step 2 Put students in pairs or threes. Ask them to discuss what might cause each of the possible options in A, as in the example. Conduct brief feedback.

14A see Teacher's notes p. 126.

Listening

Aim
To extend the topic and to give practice in listening for gist and intensively.

Step 1 Tell students they are going to hear two telephone calls between colleagues. Ask them to look at the questions in A and answer them as they listen. Play the recording.

Answers
Conversation 1
1. to check whether a delivery has arrived
2. not bad – picking up a bit
3. family and a holiday

94 OUTCOMES

> **Conversation 2**
> 1 to arrange a meeting
> 2 not bad – they may relocate
> 3 football – the European championships

> ♺ **14.1**
> **Conversation 1**
> A: Hello. InTech Corporation. Maria speaking. How can I help you?
> B: Oh hello there, Maria. It's me, Delphine.
> A: Oh, hi. How're you?
> B: Not too bad, thanks. Listen, I'm just calling to check whether the delivery we sent out on Monday has reached you yet.
> A: It has, yeah. It came in this morning, I believe.
> B: Oh, that's good. I was panicking over nothing, then.
> A: Well, better safe that sorry, isn't it?
> B: Exactly. Anyway, how're you? How're things your end?
> A: Oh, you know. We're hanging in. Sales have actually picked up a bit this quarter, so that's good, and we've actually taken on a couple of new people, so can't complain, you know. How's life with you? How's the little one?
> B: Oh, she's good. She's just coming up to one now, so she's crawling around everywhere and babbling away to herself all the time.
> A: Oh!
> B: Yeah. I'll send you pictures if you want.
> A: That'd be lovely, yeah. And how's Majid?
> B: He's OK. He's been away a lot with work recently, actually, which has been a bit of a pain, but hopefully that'll ease off a bit soon.
> A: And how was your holiday? Didn't you go away somewhere recently?
> B: Yeah, that's right, we did. Two weeks in Crete. It was lovely. Over far too quickly, of course, but much needed.
> A: Oh, that's good, though.
> B: Yeah.
>
> **Conversation 2**
> C: Hello. CNC.
> D: Hi, is that Matt?
> C: Yeah. Dietmar. Hi. I was just thinking of you, actually. I saw the draw for the European Championships.
> D: Oh yeah. I'm sorry, but England have to lose to someone.
> C: Don't count your chickens yet! Let's wait and see.
> D: I admire your optimism.
> C: Well, you have to look on the bright side, don't you – especially in our line of work.
> D: Tell me about it! How're things, anyway?
> C: Oh, not too bad, all things considered.
> D: And what's happening with the relocation?
> C: Well, it's still on the cards, apparently. We've told them it's a bad idea, but they just won't listen!
> D: Well, just think of all the savings you'll make on your overheads.
> C: And on wages if half the staff who're threatening to walk actually do!
> D: A lot of that's just talk, I'd imagine. They'll soon come round.
> C: I hope you're right. Anyway, what can I do for you today?
> D: Well, I was just wondering if we could maybe sort out a time for a meeting during the trade fair next week. It'd be good to talk though Mexico with you.
> C: Yeah, of course. ... Is Thursday any use to you?
> D: I could squeeze you in in the morning, if you want. Say 10? 10.15?
> C: Yeah, 10.15 should be fine. I'll pencil it in.

Step 2 Put students in pairs and ask them to discuss what the speakers said about each of the items in B. Then play the recording again for them to check.

> **Answers**
> **Conversation 1**
> 1 She was panicking over nothing because the delivery has arrived.
> 2 Sales have improved this quarter.
> 3 They have taken on two new staff.
> 4 Her daughter is crawling everywhere.
> 5 Her husband is away a lot, which has been a bit of a pain.
>
> **Conversation 2**
> 6 He's just seen the draw for the European championships.
> 7 He tells him not to count his chickens – i.e. England won't necessarily lose to Germany.
> 8 They'll save on their overheads if they relocate.
> 9 Half the staff are threatening to leave if they relocate.
> 10 They arrange the meeting for Thursday.

NATIVE SPEAKER ENGLISH *on the cards*

Ask students what they think the speaker meant by *it's still on the cards, apparently*. Read out the explanation in the box. Try to elicit a few examples from students.

Note In American English the expressions is *in the cards*.

DEVELOPING CONVERSATIONS Small talk

Aim
To draw students' attention to small talk.

Step 1 Begin by asking students what is meant by *small talk* and when we use it (talk about unimportant things to break the ice or make the atmosphere more relaxed). Then read out the explanation, checking students understand as you read.

14 BUSINESS AND ECONOMICS

Step 2 Put students in pairs or threes and ask them to discuss the questions in A. Conduct brief feedback.

Step 3 Put students in pairs and ask them to discuss what questions produced the answers in exercise B. Check with the whole group.

> **Answers**
> (variations are possible)
> 1 How's the company doing?
> 2 How's the economy doing?
> 3 How are your children?
> 4 Isn't the weather lovely?
> 5 How's work?
> 6 How's the team doing?
> 7 Are you doing anything this evening?
> 8 How was your holiday?

Step 4 Put students in pairs and ask them to practise. They should take turns asking the questions from exercise B and inventing different answers.

CONVERSATION PRACTICE

Aim
To give practice in the target language and round off this part of the unit.

Step 1 Put students in pairs. Ask them to imagine they both work for the same company and to decide what kind of company it is and what their roles are. Tell them they are going to role-play telephone conversations about four of the situations in exercise B. Ask them to choose the situations, then individually to think about what they can say about them. Tell them to try to engage in plenty of small talk before and after the serious business.

Step 2 When they are ready, students should take turns to begin the conversations. Monitor and take notes for a correction slot at the end.

Optional activity If time permits, ask a selection of pairs to role-play one of their conversations for the class.

pp. 100–101

SPEAKING

Aim
To give fluency practice and lead in to *Reading*.

Step 1 Ask students to look at the problems connected to banks and think about them. Check they understand *defaulted* = missed a payment. Then put them in small groups to discuss the questions. Conduct brief feedback.

READING

Aim
To give practice in reading for gist and specific information.

Step 1 Tell students they are going to read a blog entry about banks and banking. Begin by asking them what they think about banks and bankers and why. Then ask students to read the main blog entry – not the comments – and answer the questions in exercise A. Check in pairs, then check with the whole group.

> **Answers**
> 1 It is a play on the expression *laughing all the way to the bank* – used when someone makes a lot of money, often effortlessly. This is used ironically and suggests someone has lost a lot of money – possibly to the bank itself.
> 2 The news that the National bank is on the brink of bankruptcy and may need bailing out (rescuing financially).
> 3 Angry because banks have changed and now behave dishonestly.
> 4 a because it was so different then
>   b that is when things began to change because of deregulation
>   c those services began to be provided by banks
>   d despite this huge profit they are still going bankrupt
>   e taxpayers' money will be used to bail them out.

Step 2 Ask students to look at the sentences in B and complete them with nouns from the blog entry. Check in pairs. Then check with the whole group.

> **Answers**
> 1 asset
> 2 period
> 3 profit
> 4 beast
> 5 bankruptcy
> 6 bailout

Step 3 Put students in pairs or threes. Ask them to discuss what the main message of the blog entry is and whether they agree or disagree with it. Conduct brief feedback as a class.

> **Suggested answer**
> Banks have changed a lot since being deregulated in the 1980s. They are no longer community minded, but profit focused and greedy. They no longer serve the public, but the taxpayer has to bail them out.

96 OUTCOMES

14 BUSINESS AND ECONOMICS

GRAMMAR Relative clauses

Aim
To revise and practise relative clauses.

Step 1 Begin by eliciting some modal relative pronouns and ask what they are used for (*which*, *who*, *where*; used to join two clauses). Ask students to look at the sentences in exercise A from the blog entry and correct the mistakes. Check in pairs. Then ask them to check by reading the blog entry again. Direct them to the grammar reference on page 149 if they need help. Check with the whole group.

Answers
1 a period in which
2 places you went to not only
3 services that had
4 a beast that fed off
5 the ways in which
6 which means us

Step 2 Read out the explanation box. Then ask students to complete the sentences in C with one word in each gap. Check in pairs, then check with the whole group.

Answers
1 why   2 where   3 where   4 which   5 where   6 in

SPEAKING

Aim
To give fluency practice and practice in responding to text.

Step 1 Ask students to read the comments on the blogs, ignoring the words in bold, and think about their response. Then put them in pairs or threes to discuss their opinions, giving reasons. Conduct brief feedback.

Step 2 Ask students in the same pairs to discuss what they think the words in bold in the blog entries mean in the context. Check with the whole group.

Answers
1 obscene = very high and unfair
2 jeopardise = put at risk
3 lax = not very controlled
4 seductive = leading to temptation
5 bear a share = carry part of the blame
6 legitimised = made to seem legal
7 daylight robbery = stealing in an open and excessive way
8 exceeded = gone over
9 hole = bad situation
10 threw = offered on very easy terms
11 a killing = a huge profit
12 servicing = paying the interest on

Optional activity Ask students to write their own comment to add to the blog. They could then pass the comments around or stick them on the walls and walk round and read them. Ask students at the end which comments they liked most / least and why.

pp. 102–103

Next class Make photocopies of **14B** p. 155.

VOCABULARY Business situations

Aim
To introduce words / phrases commonly used in the context of business.

Step 1 Ask students to look at the sets of words / phrases in exercise A and match them with one of the situations in the box. Put them in pairs to check their answers and discuss possible connections. Check with the whole group.

Answers
1 a new product
2 an industrial dispute
3 a takeover
4 cutting costs
5 sales
6 business taxes

Step 2 Put students in pairs or threes to discuss the questions in exercise B. Conduct brief feedback.

LISTENING

Aim
To give practice in listening for gist and detail, and taking minutes at a meeting.

Step 1 Tell students they are going to hear a business meeting in a footwear company. Put them in pairs and ask them to look at the words in bold in A and discuss what they mean, and discuss the answers to the questions in A.

Answers
agenda – list of items to be discussed, *the chair* – conducts the meeting, *the minute taker* notes the main points made and who made them

Step 2 Ask students to listen to five speakers and complete the table with the correct role from the box for each of them. Play the recording.

Answers
Peter – chair
Henry – finance
Rachel – sales
Alex – product development

14 BUSINESS AND ECONOMICS

♫ 14.2

Katrin: I've also been approached by the unions, but perhaps that can wait till the end of the meeting.
Peter: Right. Let's move on to the next item on the agenda.
Henry: OK. Well, I've handed out the spreadsheet of current figures and, as you can see, we're set to make a substantial loss this year.
Rachel: We exceeded our sales targets in Eastern Europe.
Alex: Yeah, this is a prototype of what we're calling the shoe saver.

Step 3 Read out the explanation in the box. Check students understand they need to get the main points and who made them, and that they should use note form and abbreviations where appropriate. Then ask students to take the minutes of the meeting as they listen. Play the recording.

♫ 14.3

K = Katrin, P = Paul, H = Henry, R = Rachel, A = Alex

K: I've also been approached by the unions, but perhaps that can wait till Any Other Business, at the end of the meeting.
P: Right. Let's move on to the next item on the agenda, then. We've already touched on the background to this, but perhaps Henry, if you could just restate the situation.
H: OK. Well, I've handed out the spreadsheet of current figures and, as you can see, we're set to make a substantial loss this year. Obviously, it's been a volatile year for everyone in the industry, but we can't simply blame economic problems. We've also underperformed.
R: Not entirely! We exceeded our targets in Eastern Europe.
H: Yes, that offers some hope, but that was starting from quite a low base. I know Alex sees great possibilities with his new product, but I really feel the way forward is to cut back on costs.
K: Cutting costs? I would've thought we were at the limit, to be honest. People are already overstretched.
H: It doesn't have to mean more work. We could renegotiate deals with suppliers and then scale back operations.
K: You mean layoffs?
H: Some redundancies, maybe, but hopefully they'd be voluntary.
K: Really? I ...
P: ... OK. Katrin, I think we're getting ahead of ourselves here. Let's see what Alex has to say first and we'll take it from there. Alex.
A: Yeah, this is a prototype of what we're calling the shoe saver. As you see, it's basically a compact box. This is a basic design, but we're planning others. Essentially, you pop your shoes inside and give it a blast to remove all the smells. I've bought along a pair of my son's trainers to demonstrate.
R: Oh, they smell dreadful!
A: Yeah. They've been left damp in a bag to show you just how effective the box is. So I put them in. ... And switch it on. It takes a minute. Yes, Rachel?
R: How does it work?
A: It uses tiny particles of silver, which have anti‑bacterial properties once ionised. They essentially kill the microbes that cause the odours.
R: Right. OK. I'm not sure what ionised means, but isn't the silver expensive?
A: Yeah, but we're talking tiny amounts. ... OK. ... There. Done. Have a sniff.
R: Wow! That's amazing.
K: Very impressive.
H: Very. So what margins are we looking at with this?
A: Well, unit costs are between 35 and 45 euros and we're looking for it to retail at between 100 and 120 euros.
R: That'd certainly improve our bottom line.
H: Why such uncertainty about production costs? That's quite a big range you've given.
A: Well, we're looking at a deal to outsource production, which could bring significant savings. The higher figure would be if we used our own factories and that's also very much erring on the side of caution.
H: Sure. And what kind of sales projections do you have?
A: We've estimated something in the region of 10,000 units in the first year, followed by 30,000 in year two, 100,000 in year three and quarter of a million by year four.
R: Gosh.
P: I know it's ambitious, but we really are excited about this product. Henry, you don't look convinced.
H: Yeah, I don't want to be the bad guy, but have you really thought this through? You know, there's already a range of products that can solve this problem. Will people really want to pay a hundred and twenty euros for this?
A: Fair question. I think the first point is that this is far more effective than the sprays and insoles currently on the market. We estimate it could extend a shoe's life by up to 50%, so it'd pay for itself. Secondly, our initial market is not actually homes, but health clubs and gyms. Longer term, growth would come from high‑end consumers and we've already had some positive feedback from focus groups.
P: I think Katrin wants to come in.
A: Sure.
K: Yes. What about patents? Is this original technology?
A: Well, no. In fact, the technology's been around for a while, so that's not something we control, but we have patented a couple of the manufacturing processes that we think will give us an edge over any competitors. Plus, of course, we'll have a head start in establishing the brand.

Step 4 Put students in small groups to compare their minutes. Ask them to decide whose were the clearest and most accurate, and how they could improve their own minutes. Conduct brief feedback.

Step 5 Put students in pairs or threes and ask them to discuss the questions in exercise E. Conduct brief feedback.

Step 6 Ask students to look at the statements in F and decide whether they are accurate, using their minutes. They should correct the inaccurate ones. Ask them to look at the audioscript on page 177 to check. Then ask them to underline any expressions they think are useful for managing a meeting, ask them to compare answers / ideas briefly in pairs before checking as a class.

> **Answers**
> (A – accurate, I – inaccurate, PA – partly accurate)
> 1 I – he says they can't entirely blame the economy
> 2 I – she says they have exceeded their targets
> 3 A
> 4 I – he says there may be redundancies but he hopes they will be voluntary
> 5 A
> 6 PA – retail at 100–130 euros
> 7 A
> 8 A
> 9 A
> 10 PA – main market gyms / health clubs. Initial reaction good.
> 11 A
> 12 A

Language patterns

Aim
To draw students' attention to some patterns using *side*.

Step 1 Ask students to read the examples in the box and check they understand. Ask them to translate the sentences into their own language and notice any similarities / differences. In a monolingual class, ask students to compare their translation. In a multilingual class, ask students to work in pairs and tell each other if the sentences were easy to translate. Why / Why not?

Step 2 Then ask them to close their books and translate the sentences back into their own language. At the end, they should open their books again and compare their translations with the original sentences. Ask them to discuss in pairs who had the least mistakes. What mistakes did they make? Why?

Alternatively If you prefer not to use translation, ask students to look at the sentences and tell you what pattern they notice = *side* used in different ways and with different meanings. Check the meaning of each one by asking students to paraphrase. Try to elicit a few more examples.

Speaking

Aim
To round off the unit and give fluency practice.

Step 1 Tell students they are going to role-play a meeting similar to the one they heard in *Listening*. They should imagine they are managers in an electronics company. Divide the class into small groups and allocate one of the items in the box to each group. Each group should prepare a short proposal, or update, on their point.

Step 2 When they are ready, ask students to choose a chair and a minute taker. They should then conduct the meeting as a whole group. Each point should start with the proposal / update from the relevant group and anyone may interrupt or ask questions at any time. Monitor and take notes on their use of language for a correction slot at the end.

> **14B** see Teacher's notes p. 126.

15 FASHION

UNIT OVERVIEW
In this unit, students learn how to **describe hairstyles and clothes**, discuss **media and fashion images** and talk about **trends**. They also practise **correcting misunderstandings** and **giving opinions on style**. They read an extract from a **book on fashion** and a text about a **costume museum**, and listen to **conversations about style** and a **lecture on fashion and society**. The main grammar aim is revision of **prepositions**.

Next class Make photocopies of 15A p. 156.

Speaking

Aim
To lead in to the topic and give fluency practice.

Step 1 Lead in by asking students what they think of current fashions. Put students in pairs or threes and ask them to discuss the questions in A. Conduct brief feedback.

Alternatively You could begin by showing some pictures of controversial styles from magazines and asking students what they think.

Vocabulary Style and design

Aim
To introduce and practise words commonly used about clothes and hairstyles.

Step 1 Put students in pairs and ask them to look at the words in exercise A and match them with a definition a–h and then say which is the odd one out. Check with the whole class and check the meaning and pronunciation of a few of the other words, e.g. *lapel* = front, lower part of collar on jacket or coat; *bangle* = bracelet; *shades* = sunglasses; a *bob* = short, straight haircut; *sturdy* = strong; *slinky* = flowing, clinging to the body and sexy; *pinstripe* = narrow stripe pattern, often used in suits; *frizzy* = very curly e.g. after rain; *wedges* = high shoes with solid thick sole; *frilly* = with narrow layers of material added to form pattern e.g. flamenco dresses.

Answers
1 g – laces
2 c – blouse
3 a – shawl
4 b – sturdy
5 f – linen
6 e – baggy
7 h – flared
8 d – frilly

Step 2 Ask students to look at the photos and say which of the words in exercise A can be seen. You could make this a race to find the most words (total number = 28). Check with the whole group.

Answers
collar, pocket, lining, lapel, sleeve, laces, ribbon, bangle, purse, a bob, highlighted, summery, sturdy, low-cut, strapless, knee-length, slinky, lining, spotted, thick, baggy, red, wavy, ripped, frilly, faded, skinny, designer

Step 3 Put students in pairs or threes and ask them to discuss the questions in C. Conduct brief feedback.

15A see Teacher's notes p. 127.

Listening

Aim
To give practice in listening for specific information and guessing meaning from context.

Step 1 Tell students they are going to hear four conversations about style. Ask them to look at the statements in exercise A and decide if they are true or false as they listen. Play the recording. Check in pairs, then check with the whole group.

Tip For extra practice, ask students to correct the false statements.

Answers
1 a F – Tatiana has long hair
　b T
2 a F – she's trying on a dress or a blouse
　b T
3 a T
　b F – one thinks they show off her legs, one thinks they make them look thin
4 a F – he looks smart
　b T – though she doesn't say so directly

100 OUTCOMES

15.1
Conversation 1
G = Gail, T = Tatiana

G: Hey, Tatiana
T: Gail! Gosh! I hardly recognised you. It's a bit radical, isn't it?
G: You don't like it?
T: No, no you look fantastic. It's just that it's so different. What brought that on?
G: Oh, I just fancied a change. I was getting sick of it, especially with the summer and I've taken up running again. I mean, you can have it in a ponytail or tie it up but ... I don't know...
T: No, I know what you mean. ¹I wish I could get away with it short like that – it'd be so much easier.
G: You don't think you could?
T: No – ²my face is too round. I'd look like a lollipop!
G: That's a bit of an exaggeration! You could have it a bit shorter – a wavy bob like just above shoulders. That'd work.
T: You think?
G: Yeah, definitely. Not that you need to change.

Conversation 2
C = Colette, D = Diana

C: How do I look?
D: Hmm.
C: You don't like it. I have to say I'm not sure about the sleeves. They're a bit frilly.
D: No, I think they're OK, I just think you need something else. ... I don't know – some beads or something to set it off. Here, try these. ... And maybe these bangles.
C: OK.
D: Lets see. Yeah, that's better. What do you think?
C: Yeah, ³they work well together.
D: It's great. ⁴It really shows off your curves.

Conversation 3
E = Ella, F = Fiona

E: Oh, my gosh! Look at her outfit.
F: You don't like it?
E: A flowery dress with checked shirt? And the ribbon in her hair – and then those army boots!
F: Hey, ⁵it wouldn't work for me, but I think ⁶she pulls it off. It's quite a funky look. I might lose the ribbon, but those kind of ⁷clashing patterns are really in at the moment.
E: Well, it's not a trend I like. And the boots?
F: Well, they kind of ⁸show off her legs in a funny way.
E: I think they make them look like sticks. ⁹She'd be better off in some strappy heels or some wedges.

Conversation 4
G = Gunilla, H = Harry

G: Are you going like that?
H: Why? What's wrong with it?
G: Nothing. You look very smart. It's just that I don't think it's going to be that kind of do.
H: Oh, right. ¹⁰Shall I lose the tie, then?
G: Yeah, I mean, I'm just going to wear these jeans and that green top.
H: Right, so you want me to change then?
G: Well ... I just don't want you to feel awkward, because ¹¹you're sticking out.

Step 2 Put students in pairs and ask them to look at the audioscript on page 178 and discuss what they think the underlined expressions mean. Ask them to translate them into their own language. Conduct feedback on what the expressions mean.

Alternatively If you prefer not to use translation, ask students to come up with a definition or an example to illustrate the meaning of each expression.

Answers
1 I wish I could get away with it = I wish I had the shape or looks to carry off that style
2 My face is too round. I'd look like a lollipop = it wouldn't suit the shape of my face
3 They work well together = they look good together
4 It really shows off your curves = it shows the shape of your body in a positive way
5 It wouldn't work for me = it wouldn't suit me
6 She pulls it off = it suits her, it is a successful look even though it may be a bit strange
7 clashing patterns are really in = different bright colours together are in fashion
8 show off her legs = make her legs look good
9 she'd be better off = she'd look better
10 lose the tie = take off my tie
11 sticking out = looking noticeable or different

Step 3 Put students in small groups to discuss the questions in exercise C. Conduct brief feedback.

NATIVE SPEAKER ENGLISH *funky*

Ask students what they think the speaker meant by *funky*. Read out the explanation in the box. Ask students whether they think this is positive or negative (positive). Try to elicit a few examples from students (e.g. music, furniture, a nightclub, a room could all be described as *funky*).

15 FASHION

DEVELOPING CONVERSATIONS
Backtracking and correcting

Aim
To draw students' attention to ways of correcting misunderstandings, and give practice.

Step 1 Read out the explanation, checking students understand as you read.

Step 2 Ask students to look at the sentences in A and complete them in such a way as to correct the misunderstanding. Check in pairs, then check with the whole class.

> **Suggested answers**
> 1 ... that it's very colourful.
> 2 ... you really suit having dark hair.
> 3 ... I think we need to wear something more formal to the dinner.
> 4 ... sometimes he comes across as being quite abrupt.
> 5 ... that your skills would be best suited elsewhere.
> 6 ... you already have three skirts that are quite similar at home.

Step 3 Put students in pairs. Ask them to take turns saying sentences 1–6 and responding with their completed sentences. Conduct brief feedback.

Step 4 Ask students to write three 'misunderstandings', as in the example. Then put them in pairs to practise. They should take turns reading out their misunderstandings and repairing them. Monitor and make notes on their use of language for a correction slot at the end.

CONVERSATION PRACTICE

Aim
To give practice in the target language and in talking about fashion.

Step 1 Ask students to look at the photos on page 158, or ask them to come prepared with magazine photos. Put them in new pairs or threes and ask them to discuss if they like the looks or not, and why. Conduct brief feedback.

Tip If you have access to computers, ask students to look at fashion websites for this exercise.

pp. 106–107

Next class Make photocopies of **15B** p. 157.

READING

Aim
To give practice in reading for gist and detail.

Step 1 Tell students they are going to read the opening to a book on fashion by Elizabeth Wilson. Ask them to look at the questions in A and answer them as they read. Check in pairs, then check with the whole class.

> **Answers**
> 1 She feels moved and a bit frightened or spooked.
> 2 Because it is full of dead things or things once used by people who are now dead.
> 3 Because they are between life and death and they are waiting for the music to begin – presumably for the next show.

Step 2 Put students in pairs or threes to discuss the questions in exercise B. Conduct brief feedback.

Step 3 Ask students to look at the descriptions of exhibits in exercise C and match them with the correct picture 1–8 (three pictures are not described). Check in pairs, then check with the whole class.

> **Answers**
> Picture 1   Picture 5
> Picture 2   Picture 6
> Picture 3   Picture 7
> Picture 4   Picture 8

Step 4 Put students in pairs and ask them to discuss which of the items goes with each description in exercise D. Check with the whole group.

> **Answers**
> 1 Napoleonic dress, mini-dress
> 2 Mini-dress
> 3 Ottoman dress
> 4 sagging jeans
> 5 the mini-dress
> 6 the turban, the fez (Ottoman), the hoodie
> 7 the mini-dress, the hoodie
> 8 the ruff (starch), the mini-dress (tights)

SPEAKING

Aim
To extend the topic and give fluency practice.

Step 1 Put students in pairs or threes and ask them to discuss the questions in A. Conduct brief feedback.

Tip In a multilingual class, mix up the nationalities as much as possible.

GRAMMAR Prepositions

Aim
To revise and practise various uses of prepositions.

Step 1 Read out the explanation in the box, checking students understand as you read.

Step 2 Ask students to complete the sentences in A with the correct preposition. Direct them to the grammar reference on page 150 if they need help. Check in pairs, then check with the whole group.

> **Answers**
> 1 at
> 2 as
> 3 throughout
> 4 With
> 5 to
> 6 from
> 7 to, of
> 8 for, in
> 9 with, on
> 10 On

15B see Teacher's notes p. 127.

pp. 108–109

LISTENING

Aim
To give practice in listening and note-taking.

Step 1 Tell students they are going to hear a lecture about fashion and society. Ask them to look at the questions in A and think about how they would answer them. Then put them in small groups to discuss the questions.

Step 2 Ask students to note the order in which the five different kinds of image are mentioned and to make notes on the main points made about each one. Play the recording. Put students in pairs to compare their notes and come up with a summary of the main point of the talk. Check with the whole class.

> **Answers**
> 1 stick-thin models – hangers to hang clothes on – rise in eating disorders
> 2 very thin men – called 'manorexia' – more male models these days
> 3 Asian and black models undergoing treatments e.g. skin bleaching – 'deracialising' and obscene
> 4 range of different shapes and sizes of model – used by Dove
> 5 Beth Ditto – overweight but popular – only because it is unusual and different
>
> **Main point** – we see a number of unhealthy images in fashion, and it depicts the world mainly as white, young and thin

15.2
L: We live in an age of unprecedented visual saturation. We are bombarded with more images than ever before, images transmitted by an ever-growing range of technologies, and because of the explosion of such technologies, the phenomenon is no longer unique to developed countries, but is penetrating every corner of the world. I shall be arguing that this is not a neutral occurrence and shall be attempting to give you an overview of some of its results.

There are two slightly different ways we can conceptualise the growth in visual representation. On the one hand are those who argue that what is going on is simply an attempt to represent reality, to depict or show the world – or at least portions of it – as it really is. However, it can also be argued that these images shape our reality. They stand in for us in the way that our political representatives do, and so become symbolic of some kind of idealised or perfected parallel world.

Obviously, a large number of the images that confront us on an hourly basis are produced and disseminated by the fashion industry and over recent years what this has meant is that a particular kind of image of beauty has dominated our consciousness: that beauty is predominantly young, white, and almost impossibly thin! Driven by the big fashion houses' need to sell clothes in a cut-throat market, models become little more than human hangers – something stick-thin and lovely that products are 'hung' from. I'm sure we're all familiar with the kind of thing I mean here.

15 FASHION

Now obviously cause and effect are nigh-on impossible to prove conclusively, but it seems to me to be no coincidence that this has coincided with a huge rise in the incidence of eating disorders – and what we've seen in particular is anorexia and bulimia among teenage girls, the main consumers of fashion magazines. However, as images of men have also multiplied, and in particular since the move towards thinner and thinner models, as opposed to the more muscle-bound images of a previous generation, we've also started seeing a rise in what's being termed 'manorexia'.

On top of all that, both sexes are increasingly turning to cosmetic surgery and we're seeing younger and younger people opting for procedures such as Botox that were once the preserve of much older patients. As if this wasn't disturbing enough, there's growing evidence that young black and Asian girls are so deprived of role models in the world of high fashion that they are undergoing extreme procedures such as skin bleaching and eyelid reshaping operations in an attempt to simulate what they see as Western standards of beauty. It's a kind of deracialisation process and verges on the obscene.

The degree to which images of the body beautiful has become the norm can perhaps best be demonstrated by the fact that token alternative representations can now be used as a selling point. Brands such as *Dove* had huge success with their 'real beauty' campaign, which uses a far broader range of woman in its advertising, and which seems to have struck a chord with women fed up with the pressure on them to be young and slim. Similarly, singer Beth Ditto, who weighs in at around a hundred kilos, has attracted massive amounts of publicity as she has launched her fashion range for sizes 14 to 32. Nevertheless, as refreshing as it may be to see such images reach the mainstream, it should not be forgotten that they only have impact due to the fact they swim so strongly against the dominant tide.

Step 3 Put students in pairs and ask them to discuss why the lecturer mentioned the items in C. Play the recording again for them to check. Check with the whole group.

Answers
1 the spread of fashion and images associated – no longer simply in developed countries
2 fashion is as important/ influential as political representatives
3 the big fashion houses are driving the trends – they need to sell in a cut-throat market
4 teenage girls are the biggest consumers – and most vulnerable
5 younger and younger people using Botox shows seriousness of the problem
6 extreme cosmetic procedures that non-western women submit themselves too also highlights the seriousness of the problem
7 *Dove* campaign and Beth Ditto both are example of representations of normal, healthy women
8 but they only have impact because they are not the norm (swimming against the tide)

Step 4 Ask students to look at the verbs 1–10 in exercise E and match them with a noun phrase a–j, as used in *Listening*.

Step 5 Put students in pairs to check their ideas and discuss who / what the phrases describe. Ask them to check in the audioscript on page 178.

Answers
1 g penetrate every corner of the world (fashion images)
2 a depict the world as it really is (images in fashion)
3 b disseminate images (fashion industry)
4 c cut-throat market (the fashion market)
5 h nigh-on impossible
6 e opt for procedures (to make oneself more 'attractive' e.g. Botox)
7 f undergo extreme procedures (young black and Asian girls)
8 j become the norm (unrealistic images of body beautiful)
9 d strike a chord (*Dove* campaign)
10 i attract publicity (Beth Ditto with her fashion range for larger women)

Step 6 Put students in pairs. Ask them to read the statements in exercise G and decide which of the statements the lecturer would agree with. Ask them to explain why, and to discuss how far they agree with each statement. Conduct brief feedback.

Suggested answers
The lecturer would strongly agree with statement 3, and to a degree with statement 2.

15 FASHION

LANGUAGE PATTERNS

Aim
To draw students' attention to some patterns using *no* + noun phrase.

Step 1 Ask students to read the examples in the box and check they understand. Ask them to translate the sentences into their own language and notice any similarities / differences. In a monolingual class, ask students to compare their translation. In a multilingual class, ask students to work in pairs and tell each other if the sentences were easy to translate.

Step 2 Then ask them to close their books and translate the sentences back into their own language. At the end, they should open their books again and compare their translations with the original sentences. Ask them to discuss in pairs who had the least mistakes. What mistakes did they make? Why?

Alternatively If you prefer not to use translation, ask students to look at the sentences and tell you what pattern they notice = *no* + noun phrase to give emphasis. Try to elicit a few more examples (*it's no wonder, there's no doubt, no laughing matter*).

VOCABULARY Fashion and the media

Aim
To introduce words / phrases commonly used to talk about fashion and the media.

Step 1 Ask students to look at the sentences in A and complete them using the correct form of the word in bold. Check in pairs, then check with the whole class.

> **Answers**
> 1 repre<u>sen</u>tative
> 2 <u>dom</u>inant
> 3 <u>im</u>agery
> 4 <u>broad</u>ened
> 5 in<u>flu</u>ential
> 6 ex<u>ploi</u>tative
> 7 perpetu<u>a</u>tion
> 8 de<u>pic</u>tion
> 9 <u>age</u>ist, <u>sex</u>ist
> 10 represent<u>a</u>tion, por<u>trayed</u>

Step 2 Ask students to choose two sentences from A they strongly agree with, and one they strongly disagree with. Then put them in pairs or threes to compare their choices and explain their ideas. Conduct brief feedback.

Step 3 Put students in pairs. Ask them to think of other forms of the words in bold in exercise A, and write a sentence to illustrate each one. Ask them to compare their sentences in pairs. Check some of their ideas at the end.

> **Suggested answers**
> 1 unrepresentative, representing
> 2 domination, dominated
> 3 imagine, imaginary, imagination
> 4 breadth, broader
> 5 influencing, influenced
> 6 exploitation, exploiting
> 7 perpetuate, perpetuity
> 8 depicting, depicted
> 9 ageing, aged; sexual, sexuality
> 10 see answer 1; portray, portrait

SPEAKING

Aim
To give fluency practice and round off the unit.

Step 1 Ask students to look at the quotes in exercise A and think about how far they agree / disagree with each, and why. If they wish, they could make a few notes. Remind them to use the *Vocabulary builder* on page 59 if they need help with some of the language used.

Step 2 Put students in pairs or threes to discuss their ideas. Take notes on their use of language for a correction slot at the end. Conduct brief feedback.

16 DANGER AND RISK

UNIT OVERVIEW
In this unit, students learn how to describe **accidents and injuries** in more detail, talk about **risk**, **safety and laws** and the **pros and cons of Internet use**. They also practise **interjections**. They read a text about **health and safety measures** and listen to conversations about **scars**, to a health and safety officer and to a **radio phone-in programme**. The main grammar aim is **more unusual future forms**.

Next class Make photocopies of 16A p. 158.

Speaking

Aim
To lead in to the topic and give fluency practice.

Step 1 Ask students to look at the activities and places in A and think about what accidents might be associated with each one. Put them in pairs to discuss their ideas and which of the activities they think are the most risky and why.

Listening

Aim
To practise listening for gist and specific information.

Step 1 Tell students they're going to hear two conversations about accidents which left scars. Ask them to answer the questions in A as they listen. Play the recording.

Answers
Conversation 1 leg – cut it with a scalpel while making an architectural model
Conversation 2 forehead – walked into a shelf while on summer camp; chin, blown by wind between two parked cars – whacked chin on road

16.1
Conversation 1
A = Annabel, B = Belinda
A: Well played. I thought I might stand a chance after you blew that second set, but you thrashed me!
B: Ah, you played OK … . You just need to work on your serve!
A: And my backhand and my footwork and everything else!
B: Yeah, well … maybe a bit! By the way, I hope you don't mind me asking, but what happened to your leg? That's one hell of a scar!
A: What? This?
B: Yeah?
A: Oh, it's a long story.
B: Go on, then. I've got time!
A: Oh, it's stupid, really. It happened when I was in my final year at university. You know I did architecture, yeah?
B: Yeah.
A: Well, we had to make a lot of models and present them and one time I was up half the night trying to finish off this one particular model and it was about four in the morning and I was more dead than alive and my hand slipped and I somehow managed to cut a huge great big slice out of my thigh with the scalpel I'd been using.
B: Oh! Nasty.
A: Yeah, but I was so out of it that I was just staring at this gaping great hole, half in shock, half in complete exhaustion, and in the end I just wiped the blood off with a tissue, tried to super-glue it all together and crashed out. Next morning, I woke up early, went along to A and E to get it cleaned up and stitched – and still managed to present my model in the afternoon.
B: And who said students are lazy, eh!

Conversation 2
C = Chloe, D = Doug
C: How did you get that scar, if you don't mind me asking?
D: Which one? The one on my chin?
C: No, I meant the one on your forehead. It's pretty nasty.
D: Oh, that. Yeah, well, I was smart enough to somehow walk straight into a head-height shelf when I was 18. I was working at this summer camp in the States and I'd been out to a party with some friends one night, stumbled home and whacked myself when I got back to my cabin. I decided that while it hurt a bit, it'd probably be OK and that what I really needed was my bed. I woke up in the morning to find there was blood everywhere – all over the bed, the floor – and most shockingly, when I looked in the mirror, I realised my face was covered in dried blood, which I really hadn't been expecting! The doctor said he could've stitched it if I'd seen him right away, but that it was unstitchable the following day! Just my luck.
C: Oh, that's awful.
D: Yeah, well, it's my own stupid fault, really.
C: And … um … I'm scared to ask now, really, but what about that other one?
D: You won't believe me when I tell you. Honestly.

106 OUTCOMES

> C: Um ... OK. Is it gruesome?
> D: Not really. Just odd. I don't know if you remember, but a couple of years ago, there were all these reports of people getting blown off their feet by high winds, and even someone getting killed from being blown head first into a door.
> C: No! That must just have completely passed me by somehow.
> D: Yeah? Well, it was pretty crazy. What happened with me was that one night I just got totally blown down the drive at the side of my house, completely out of control! I somehow managed to go head first between two parked cars, whacking my head on both of them and landing on my chin in the middle of the road.
> C: Ouch!
> D: Yeah – and when I came to, I found my chin completely split open ... and my wisdom teeth weren't too happy either!
> C: Woah! You're fairly accident-prone, really, aren't you?
> D: I've got another one, actually, if you want to hear about it ...

Step 2 Put students in pairs to discuss whether the statements in B are true or false. Ask them to correct the false statement. Play the recording again for them to check.

> **Answers**
> 1 T
> 2 F – she studied to be an architect and made models
> 3 F – she was tired
> 4 T
> 5 F – she went to A and E (Accident and Emergency), got stitches and presented the model on time
> 6 F – he was working at summer camp
> 7 T
> 8 F – it was too late to stitch
> 9 F – the woman doesn't remember it
> 10 F – he hit it on the road

Step 3 Read out the explanation in the box. Then put students in pairs to look at the sentences in C and discuss what they think is meant by the words / phrases in italics in the context of the conversations. Check as a class.

> **Answers**
> 1 a a very big or serious scar
>   b very tired
>   c almost unconscious, extremely tired
>   d fell asleep
> 2 a sufficiently clever (sarcastic)
>   b staggered, walked with difficulty; hit myself
>   c I was unlucky and I usually am
>   d hurt, were suffering

Step 4 Put students in small groups to discuss the questions in D. Conduct brief feedback.

LANGUAGE PATTERNS

Aim
To draw students' attention to some patterns using double adjectives to give emphasis.

Step 1 Ask students to read the examples and check they understand. Ask them to translate the sentences into their own language and notice any similarities / differences. In a monolingual class, ask students to compare their translation. In a multilingual class, ask students to work in pairs and tell each other if the sentences were easy to translate.

Step 2 Then ask them to close their books and translate the sentences back into their own language. At the end, they should open their books again and compare their translations with the original sentences. Ask them to discuss in pairs who had the least mistakes. What mistakes did they make? Why?

Alternatively If you prefer not to use translation, ask students to look at the sentences and tell you what pattern they notice = two adjectives of similar meaning used together to give emphasis (the more extreme adjective always comes first). Try to elicit a few more examples (*soaking wet, starving hungry, filthy rich!*)

DEVELOPING CONVERSATIONS

Interjections

Aim
To draw students' attention to interjections.

Step 1 Ask students if they know what interjections are and whether they remember any from *Listening*. Read out the explanation, checking understanding as you read.

Step 2 Put students in pairs. Ask them to listen to the interjections and, after each one, discuss what they think it means. Play the recording. Don't check the answers yet.

Step 3 Tell students they are going to hear the whole exchange for each of the interjections so they can check their ideas. Play the recording. Check as a class (answers in square brackets).

> **🔊 16.3 and answers**
> 1 A: She speaks six different languages.
>   B: Wow! That's impressive. [I'm impressed]
> 2 A: I was running and I heard something in my knee just snap!
>   B: Fff! Ouch! Painful! [that must've hurt]
> 3 A: His false teeth fell out onto the floor and he just picked them up and put them straight back into his mouth again.
>   B: Yuk! That's disgusting! [that's disgusting]
> 4 A: I've still got a scar. Look.
>   B: Gosh! That's awfully big! [I'm surprised]

16 DANGER AND RISK

> 5 A: The doctor I went to for a second opinion said I'd been given the wrong diagnosis and it wasn't as serious as they'd thought.
>   B: Phew! That's a relief, then.
> 6 A: Mmm! This is delicious! What's yours like?
>   B: Yeah, not bad.
> 7 (sound of door opening)
>   A: Ahem! [you are disturbing me]
>   B: What? ... Oh, sorry. (sound of door closing)
> 8 A: And then she said, like, you know, that she thought it was a bit too revealing, but I wasn't sure so ... are you listening to me?
>   B: Mmm. Yeah. Course. [I'm not really listening]
> 9 A: So how come you decided to do that, then?
>   B: Umm. That's a good question, actually. I'd have to think about that. [I'm not sure]
> 10 A: Oi! What do you think you're doing? [getting someone's attention]
>   B: Quick! Run!
> 11 A: (sound of a mobile phone going off).
>   B: Sshhh! The baby's sleeping. [be quiet]
> 12 A: And then I realised I'd copied my boss in on the email by mistake!
>   B: Oops! That wasn't very clever. [what a mistake]

Step 4 Put students in pairs or threes to discuss the questions in C. Conduct brief feedback.

VOCABULARY Accidents and injuries

Aim
To focus on words associated with accidents and injuries.

Step 1 Ask students to look at the sentences in A and replace the words in italics with one of the synonyms from the box. Check in pairs, then with the whole group.

> **Answers**
> 1 ripped   4 panicked   7 sliced   10 fainted
> 2 came to   5 banged   8 cut   11 break
> 3 pouring   6 heavily   9 burnt   12 terrible pain

Step 2 Put students in AB pairs and ask them to test each other. Student A should say six of the words in the box and Student B, with book closed, should try to remember the correct synonym. Then swap.

Step 3 Ask students to decide which of the pairs of synonyms in A they like best and why. Put them in pairs / threes to compare their ideas.

👥👥 **16A** see Teacher's notes p. 127.

CONVERSATION PRACTICE

Aim
To extend the topic and give fluency practice.

Step 1 Ask students to think of scars they have and how they got them. If they don't have any, they can invent them. Ask them to think about what they can say about each one. Then put them in small groups to tell each other about their scars. Conduct brief feedback.

📖 pp. 112–113

SPEAKING

Aim
To extend the topic and give fluency practice.

Step 1 Put students in small groups to discuss the questions in A. Conduct brief feedback.

READING

Aim
To practise reading for detail and responding to text.

Step 1 Tell students they are going to read about different examples of health and safety. Ask them to read the first two paragraphs. Put them in pairs to discuss the questions in A.

> **Answers**
> 1 Bureaucrats or civil servants from the EU have abandoned the idea of trying to stop people exposing part of their flesh to sunlight on health grounds.
> 2 It is biased because it says they have seen sense and they should use common sense more often.
> 3 They wanted to include sunlight because it is a form of bright light and it can be dangerous.

Step 2 Ask students to read the other eight examples of health and safety 'madness' and mark each one with a tick if they agree with the writer of the article, a cross if the disagree and a question mark if they are not sure. Put them in pairs to compare their ideas and discuss the questions in C.

Step 3 Ask students to read the short reports in D, ignoring the words in bold, and then in pairs / threes discuss what they think the newspaper would say about each one.

VOCABULARY Laws and regulations

Aim
To introduce words / phrases commonly used to talk about laws and regulations.

Step 1 Ask students to look at the words in bold from *Reading* exercise D and try to work out the meaning. Ask them to translate them into their own language.

Alternatively If you prefer not to use translation, put students in pairs and ask them to come up with a definition or example to show the meaning of each item.

108 OUTCOMES

16 DANGER AND RISK

Answers
1 <u>loop</u>holes = anomalies in the law that often allow someone to avoid doing the right thing
2 non-compliance = not keeping the law
3 legis<u>la</u>tion = set of rules or laws about something
4 <u>li</u>able = responsible
5 <u>law</u>suits = when someone sues someone else or takes them to court
6 <u>dam</u>ages = compensation
7 <u>neg</u>ligence = carelessness or not doing their job properly
8 an ap<u>peal</u> = an attempt to get a ruling overturned by retrying the case

Step 2 Ask students to complete the sentences in B using the correct form of the verb from the box. Check in pairs, then check with the whole class.

Answers
1 held   3 sued   5 filed   7 exp<u>loit</u>
2 a<u>ward</u>ed 4 over<u>turned</u> 6 ad<u>mit</u>ted 8 opposed

Step 3 Put students in pairs / threes to think of real examples of 1–8 in exercise B, and explain to each other what happened. Conduct brief feedback.

LISTENING

Aim
To practise listening for specific information.

Step 1 Tell students they are going to hear a health and safety officer talking about her job. Put them in pairs to discuss the questions in A.

Step 2 Ask students to listen and tick the arguments in B that Eva, the health and safety officer, gives. Play the recording. Then put students in pairs to compare and explain their ideas. Check with the whole group.

Answers
2, 4, 5, 8, 9

🔊 16.4
I = interviewer, EC = Eva Chakrabati

I: So I'm here in a school in Chipping Sodbury where I'm talking to Eva Chakrabati, who's a Health and Safety officer. Now I have to say, Eva, I was a bit surprised to see what you were doing there. You were holding bubbles of methane and setting them alight. Exploding gases in front of children isn't what we expect from people like you.

EC: No? Well, that's very much the kind of misconception we're trying to combat here. Health and Safety is not about removing all risk from life. Personally, I'm into rock climbing and I'm all for people having fun and excitement. Society relies on people doing hazardous jobs, whether it be working in quarries, on oil rigs or in farming, but there's a difference between risks and recklessness. We analyse risk and set legal guidelines to reduce it.

I: OK, but that's the issue – those guidelines. We constantly hear stories of the reams of paperwork involved in setting up, say, a school trip. Doesn't it turn basic pleasures and education into a bureaucratic nightmare?

EC: I wouldn't deny some forms are excessive, but I would query whether that's really down to us. We've produced templates for risk assessment for school trips that are just three pages long. However, some bodies in charge of implementation produce one form covering every type of assessment, with the result that they're overlong and contain much that's irrelevant to individual events.

I: Why don't you force the use of your forms, then?

J: Well, they are widely available and we're running a campaign on health and safety myths, but really we're caught between a rock and a hard place. On the one hand, we have these hysterical stories in the media that we're imposing a nanny state, but then here you're saying we should override local people on the ground. Actually, I think we should stick to our policy, which is providing standards that generally have the caveat that common sense should apply and changes only made where the cost is appropriate to the benefits.

I: So you're saying that many of the stories we hear – banning snowballs; stopping clowns blowing bubbles; punishing staff for moving chairs round a room – all those are essentially nonsense.

E: Well, yes! They may have a grain of truth, but they're usually over-generalised or wrongly blamed on us. It's possible some schools have banned snowballs, but I think that's likely to have been a response to a particular incident and maybe fears of litigation. It's certainly not the result of anything we've said. The clown story is something similar. He was using a bubble-making machine and he couldn't get insurance – we didn't stop him. Actually, there IS a risk there because the machines create lots of soapy liquid and on smooth surfaces they're a hazard, but we'd say used on grass, gravel or some other non-slip surface they're great fun – go ahead! As for the furniture in our office, we have chairs and desks fitted with lockable wheels that can be moved by anyone, but yes we do have porters to shift other, heavier furniture.

I: And you don't think that's excessive?

E: No, as I say, we're raising awareness and giving workers options. Literally thousands of people are injured at work because of disregard for safety standards. Helping avoid that saves heartache and millions in lost revenue.

I: Eva Chakrabati. Thank you very much. Back to the studio.

Step 3 Put students in pairs to discuss the questions in D. Conduct brief feedback.

16 DANGER AND RISK 109

16 DANGER AND RISK

> **pp. 114–115**
>
> **Next class** Make photocopies of **16B** p. 159.

SPEAKING

Aim
To give fluency practice and lead in to *Listening*.

Step 1 Ask students to think about how they would answer the questions in A. Ask them to make a few notes and a list for the last question. Put students in pairs / threes to discuss their ideas. Ask them to decide which is the most serious risk and why. Conduct brief feedback.

VOCABULARY Dangers and risks

Aim
To introduce and practise phrases about risk.

Step 1 Ask students to choose the correct alternative for the phrases in italics in A. Check in pairs, then as a class.

Answers							
1	threat	4	the menace	7	risk	10	danger
2	peril	5	threat	8	danger		
3	hazard	6	menace	9	risk		

Step 2 Ask students to underline the adjective–noun, verb–noun and preposition–noun collocations in the sentences in A. Put them in pairs to discuss which ones are new for them. Check with the whole class.

Step 3 Put students in pairs / threes to discuss how far they agree with the statements in A. Conduct feedback.

LISTENING

Aim
To listen for gist and specific information.

Step 1 Tell students they are going to hear a radio phone-in programme about the dangers of the Internet. Ask them to list the dangers mentioned. Play the recording. Put students in pairs to compare and discuss which risks were not included in *Vocabulary* exercise A. Check as a class.

Answers
1 people are losing ability to think for themselves
2 pornography
3 people are sucked in to dangerous political or religious groups
4 online gambling
5 online fraudsters

16.5
M = Michael, J = Joyce, N = Nigel

M: With the news that the Internet penetration rate is set to reach 80% sometime in the next month coming hot on the heels of revelations that children as young as eight are now receiving treatment for Internet addiction, today we're turning our attention to this most modern of phenomena and asking whether the Internet has become more of a curse than a blessing. As ever, if the show is to work, we need YOU to call up and tell us what's on your mind. And I think we have our first caller, on line one. It's Joyce in Crawley. Joyce. Hello.

J: Oh hello, Michael. Thank you. Yes. Well, I've been a secondary school teacher for some forty years now and I'm on the verge of retiring. I'm due to stop work in the summer, and I must say I'm awfully glad about it.

M: Why's that, then, Joyce?

J: Well, to be frank, I think the Internet has ruined childhood and created a generation of idiots and I honestly don't think things are likely to get any better in the foreseeable future.

M: Well, that's a fairly bleak appraisal. What is it about the web that particularly concerns you?

J: Well, the first thing is simply the ease of access it provides. I'm obviously not opposed to people being able to access useful information, but most students nowadays have lost the ability to construct their own essays or think their own way through a question. They simply cut and paste and hand things in, which appals me.

M: So plagiarism, in short?

J: Exactly. And in addition to that, the Internet basically dangles all manner of temptation in front of young people, often very vulnerable young people, and that's bound to cause problems.

M: I'm guessing you're talking about pornography and the like here, Joyce?

J: Well, of course that's a worry, but there's so much more to it than that. I've heard tales of students getting sucked into white supremacist sites and religious extremist sites. Then there are sites offering assistance with weapon making and I've had students of my own get involved in online gambling. They run up huge debts and end up having to be bailed out by their parents. And to put it mildly, none of this exactly helps them perform academically.

M: The chances of it helping are pretty slim, I'd imagine. (laughter) Anyway, Joyce, thanks for that. Next up is Nigel, in Manchester. Hello.

N: Hello there, Michael. Nice to be with you. Long-time listener here. What I wanted to say was it's time we got tough and cracked down more on the web.

M: And how do you propose we do that, then?

N: Well, if it were up to me, I'd arrest anyone caught looking at banned websites. I mean, they must know who these people are, mustn't they, the government.

M: That's a huge online policing presence you're suggesting there, Nigel, and in all probability, most

110 OUTCOMES

> offenders are actually pretty harmless when it comes down to it.
> N: Yeah, OK, but maybe we should make an example of one or two people, then, you know. Hit them with the toughest sentences we can. Like spammers and online fraudsters and what have you. Do that and the odds are you'll put others off.
> M: Or, do that and there's a distinct possibility you'll end up embroiled in a lengthy legal dispute about proportionate punishments, I would've thought, to be honest.

Step 2 Ask students to answer the questions in B. Play the recording for them to check. Check in pairs, then as a class.

> **Answers**
> 1 Internet penetration (i.e. the number of people connected) will soon reach 80%; children as young as eight are addicted to Internet use.
> 2 She is going to retire from her job as a teacher and she is glad.
> 3 They can't write essays or think through a question.
> 4 pornography, white supremacists (those who believe white people are superior to black people), religious extremists, weapon making, online gambling
> 5 We should control the use of the web more.
> 6 It would require a huge online police force.
> 7 Make an example of a few people by punishing them severely.
> 8 There may be legal battles about the severity of punishments.

Step 3 Put students in pairs or threes to discuss the questions in C. Conduct brief feedback.

NATIVE SPEAKER ENGLISH

and the like / and what have you

Read out the explanation in the box and check understanding. Try to elicit a few more examples.

GRAMMAR Other future forms

Aim
To look at more unusual ways of expressing the future.

Step 1 Ask students to look at the sentences from *Listening* and try to complete them by putting the verbs in brackets in the correct form. Check in pairs, but not as a class.

Step 2 Ask students to complete the phrases in B with nouns from *Listening*. Check in pairs, but not with the whole group. Then play the recording again for them to check both A and B.

> 🔊 **16.6 and answers**
> 1 The Internet penetration rate is set to reach 80% sometime in the next month.
> 2 If the show is to work, we need YOU to call up and tell us what's on your mind.
> 3 I'm due to stop work in the summer.
> 4 I honestly don't think things are likely to get any better in the foreseeable future.
> 5 The Internet dangles all manner of temptation in front of young people, and that's bound to cause problems.
> 6 I'm on the verge of retiring.
> 7 The chances of it helping are pretty slim, I'd imagine.
> 8 In all likelihood, most offenders are actually pretty harmless.
> 9 Hit them with the toughest sentences we can. Do that and the odds are you'll put others off.
> 10 Do that and there's a distinct possibility you'll end up embroiled in a lengthy legal dispute.

Step 3 Put students in pairs to discuss the questions in E. Direct them to the grammar reference on page 151 if they need help. Check with the whole group.

> **Answers**
> 1 is / are due to   3 is / are set to   5 is / are likely to
> 2 is / are bound to   4 is / are to

Step 4 Ask students to rewrite the sentences in F using the words in bold. Check in pairs, then as a group.

> **Answers**
> 1 The situation is bound to deteriorate.
> 2 Our jobs are highly likely to be at risk.
> 3 They are on the verge of finalising the deal.
> 4 If you gamble online, there's a strong likelihood of losing / that you will lose.
> 5 The work is due to be finished by May.
> 6 Inflation is set to rise over 10% next month.

👥 **16B** see Teacher's notes p. 127.

SPEAKING

Aim
To give fluency practice and round off the unit.

Step 1 Put students in pairs to discuss the questions about the headlines in A. Conduct brief feedback – note there are no set answers, just ask students to explain their decisions.

Step 2 Tell students they are going to role-play a radio phone-in programme about current issues. In small groups ask them to choose one of the issues in A to discuss. Ask them to choose a presenter. The presenter should think about how to manage the programme / calls and what kind of questions to ask. The other students should think about what they are going to say. They should try to comment on what they think will happen in future and on other callers' opinions. When groups are ready, ask them to role-play the programme. Monitor for a correction slot at the end.

04 REVIEW

Two minutes, game, conversation practice & act or draw

For aims and suggested procedure, see Review 01, pages 32–35.

Quiz

Answers
1. Someone might **pull out of** a race or competition because they are ill or injured.
2. Three things that are now **obsolete** (no longer in use) are record players, Routemaster buses, pesetas.
3. The opposite of **denying** an allegation is *admitting* (to) an allegation.
4. Someone might make a **prototype** when they are inventing something.
5. The weather, a cancellation of some kind, your friend not showing up etc. can all **ruin** your day.
6. To **libel** someone you would write something untrue about them.
7. Companies can **outsource** factory workers, IT or call centre workers because it is cheaper.
8. You might find **loopholes** in the law which could save you from being prosecuted. *Lawyers* might look for them.
9. When people **rampage** through the streets they make a lot of noise and may damage things.
10. People might **freak out** if they are scared or panicking.
11. A government may need to **bail out** a company or bank because they are at risk of going bankrupt.
12. A type of behaviour or dress might be **frowned on** because someone disapproves of it.
13. You find **inmates** in prison.
14. Most companies have to pay **overheads** for rent, utilities, supplies, etc.
15. You might give someone a **head start** in a race because you have an unfair advantage over them e.g. a child.

Collocations

For aims and suggested procedure, see Review 01, pages 32–35.

Idioms

Answers
1. He's in a predicament / a difficult situation.
2. They're stealing the profits.
3. I fell asleep.
4. It's very expensive.
5. It's been likely to happen for a while.
6. He's always been a non-conformist.
7. They make a huge profit.
8. I really identified or sympathised with it.
9. It's a big fuss about nothing.
10. It's a good example of the government controlling people's lives.
11. I wouldn't be so sure it will happen.
12. It's an attack on people's personal lives.
13. It is of interest to the baser side of humanity.
14. I could find a space for you (e.g. for an appointment).
15. We are in a very difficult situation in which neither course of action is desirable.

pp. 118–119

Listening

For aims and suggested procedure for the rest of the review, see Review 01, pages 32–35. The audio is R4.1.

Answers
1. F – film industry's big annual award night
2. T
3. T
4. F – outfit showed off her curves
5. F – the crowd was stunned by her haircut
6. T
7. F – she categorically denies the accusations
8. F – many observers felt she looked worn down
9. F – she looked in absolute agony
10. T

112 OUTCOMES

GRAMMAR

Exercise A answers
1 where
2 Besides
3 whom
4 due
5 with
6 likely / liable
7 to
8 during

Exercise B answers
1 the vast majority are able to
2 urged them not to
3 the way in which
4 with regard to
5 blame government
6 on the verge of

LANGUAGE PATTERNS

Answers
1 correct
2 This isn't as **hard** an exercise as might be imagined. / This exercise **isn't as hard** as might be imagined.
3 There's **no** demand for that kind of fabric anymore.
4 At least he saw the funny side **of** the situation.
5 correct
6 He's got this **great big scar/ huge scar** down one side of his face.

PREPOSITIONS

Answers
1 from
2 with
3 throughout
4 of
5 for
6 on
7 in
8 at

OPPOSITES

Answers
1 positive
2 final
3 off-putting
4 simple
5 volatile
6 lax
7 specific
8 mainstream

MISSING WORDS

Answers
1 bid
2 clash(es)
3 appeal
4 base
5 leak

VERBS

Answers
1 confirm
2 retract
3 implement
4 slash
5 switch
6 regain
7 enhance
8 jeopardise

FORMING WORDS

Answers
1 technicality
2 coverage
3 policing
4 circulation
5 symbolic
6 authority
7 directive

VOCABULARY

Answers
1 C bid
2 A hailed
3 C seize
4 B Witnesses
5 A terminate
6 B floated
7 A consolidate
8 C defaulted

AN INTRODUCTION TO WRITING IN *OUTCOMES*

In this section we will look at two broad reasons for writing in a foreign language: to practise and play, and for the real world. We explain what we mean by them and how they may differ in teaching, tasks and feedback.

PRACTICE AND PLAY

The first reason for writing in a foreign language is simply to practise new language, experiment and learn more English. Writing may have significant benefits for students learning English. In contrast to speaking, students have time to plan what they want to say; they can look words up in a dictionary, they can check and rewrite grammar and they may be more able to notice how English works. That might then give benefits in terms of their overall competence in English.

Writing for the purpose of practice and play does not depend on any particular genre or standard organisation in writing; it could be short sentences, paragraphs, dialogues, etc; it could be about anything the student wants or it could be on a theme the teacher chooses; it could be random connections of sentences – true or imagined. Some grammar and vocabulary tasks in the Student's book are of this nature, with students having to complete sentences using their own ideas. Below are some more tasks. The ideas focus on revising language, but it doesn't have to be so. Here are some ideas your students could try:

- Write a diary about your day, trying to include new words or structures that you've learnt.
- Write five to ten lines of English every day about anything you like.
- Write every day / week about a story in the news you saw or read about.
- Write a poem or story using a new word you've learnt.
- Write a conversation based on one you had with someone during the class.
- Write an imagined conversation with someone you know based on a topic you've studied.
- Write an imagined conversation that takes place in a particular place.

As these kinds of writing tasks are unconnected to any particular genre, they require no 'teaching' or preparation, and can be set at any time. In terms of feedback, you may want to simply write a personal response to what the student wrote such as, *This really made me laugh* or *That's interesting.* Alternatively, you could engage in a dialogue with the student by asking them genuine questions, which they answer in writing. You may want to correct aspects of the key structure or words that they practised, or use common errors from different students as a way to re-teach language in class. However, we feel correction should be kept to a minimum with these kinds of texts. The aim isn't assessment: it is to encourage students, to engage with them and get them to play with language.

FOR THE REAL WORLD

The second broad reason for writing is that students need to write a specific kind of text for an assessment or for a 'real life' task such as sending an email. These texts are generic in some way. They often have specific vocabulary (including large chunks or expressions) or grammar connected with them. They also have rules about the way they are presented, how they are paragraphed and ordered and other aspects of discourse. The problem for foreign learners of English is that these rules of discourse might be different in their languages. Unlike speaking, where listeners might accept errors because they can see other things to help interpret the message, with writing a reader may misunderstand a message or even be offended when the rules or conventions of a genre are broken. For this reason, students need careful preparation for writing such texts, and feedback should be more thorough.

The writing units in the Student's book aim to provide this careful preparation. They are based on genres commonly tested in international exams such as FCE, CAE and IELTS, or on functional writing tasks we may perform at work or when studying in an English-speaking context.

WHAT'S IN *OUTCOMES* WRITING UNITS?

Each double-page spread teaches a different style of writing. You can follow them in any order or do them after every two units in the main Student's book. The units contain:

Speaking The units aim to be interactive. Speaking activities provide a warmer, relate to the topic, discuss the text types or may be part of planning for writing.

Writing The writing sections present model texts. While there may be some basic comprehension questions around these, the main focus is noticing useful language for the genre and how the texts are organised.

Key words This section focuses on words / expressions which link sentences and clauses and give texts coherence. They follow a similar pattern to grammar exercises, with a short explanation or guided questions and a controlled practice.

Vocabulary and grammar There are often short grammar or vocabulary sections if there is a close relation to the text type. Note there's *no* link to the grammar reference or *Vocabulary builder*.

Practice This is a task for students to write a similar kind of text to the one they looked at in **Writing** and try to incorporate some of the other language they have learnt in the unit. This section can be set as homework or be done in class. Doing the practice in class can be interactive, particularly if using a 'process writing' approach.

PROCESS WRITING

Process writing approaches focus on the fact that good writers often go through several stages to produce a good piece of writing. They may:

- brainstorm ideas
- write a plan
- write a draft
- discuss their draft with someone
- write a second draft
- put it through a spell-checker
- have corrections made by someone
- write the final draft

Obviously, we don't always go through these stages when we write, but in the case of our students, having different stages and allowing for more than one draft gives more opportunity for teaching and learning. In fact, brainstorming and planning stages are often included in **Practice** or at some other stage of the lesson. However, there is no reason why any of the stages above shouldn't be done in pairs in class. Another way you might want to incorporate a process approach is to give the Practice task for homework *before* they do the actual writing lesson. They then rewrite their work in light of what they learn.

MARKING AND FEEDBACK

There are a number of options available to teachers to mark and give feedback on students' writing.

Using symbols You can mark essays using symbols above the inappropriate word or grammar. Here are some examples:

- t = wrong tense
- wf = wrong word form (e.g. noun not adjective)
- col = wrong collocation (e.g. the noun is the right meaning but doesn't go with the verb)
- voc = you have the wrong word (it makes no sense here)
- prep = you need a different preposition
- pl = plural is wrong or should be plural
- sp = wrong spelling
- wo = the word order is wrong
- art = the article is wrong or absent

The idea of doing this is to make students notice their errors and try to find answers. You could do this as a pair activity in class. It may help them to become more aware of their common errors and edit their own work more carefully. The difficulty is that mistakes don't fit neatly into categories and students may still get the language wrong. You should mark the text again.

Reformulation You may simply want to cross out and rewrite things that are 'wrong' in the text. This may have the advantage of teaching students the correct language (though note they may still be unclear *why* it was wrong). It may also be time-consuming for you and demoralising for students if they see lots of crossing out. In this case – and indeed with all cases of teacher feedback – you need to strike a balance. At Advanced level, you will expect a good degree of accuracy. Students should also be able to deal with a variety of text types, employing informal and formal registers. Students should also be able to structure their writing and use language appropriate to their readers.

Content and structure When you mark the texts you could ignore 'grammar' and individual vocabulary mistakes and focus only on whether the writing answers the question and is organised well. You simply write comments on the writing or at the end. This is often quicker for you, the teacher.

Marking this way trains students to appreciate the importance of these aspects of writing over basic 'accuracy'. Readers in fact will often ignore mistakes if the overall structure of the text is clear and the content is relevant, logical and / or interesting. However, students will want to know if their writing is correct unless you clearly warn them beforehand that you'll only deal with content and structure.

Peer correction Students can also give feedback. Get them to read each other's writing and evaluate the texts and / or suggest changes. To do this they really need a 'mark scheme'; this could be a list of statements they tick or adapt such as:

- *I enjoyed this.*
- *I wanted to know more about …*
- *I didn't understand the bit about …*
- *You used some words / grammar I didn't know how to use.*

Another way is to give them marking criteria from an established source such as the FCE exam. Check they're not too difficult for your students.

The advantage of peer correction is that it's interactive and based on genuine readers' responses. It's also easy on the teacher! However, it is not so good for dealing with language, apart from general statements, as students may not trust each other's judgement – often with good reason! However, it is a useful stage and may save you time by reducing mistakes or inconsistencies before you come to mark the texts.

WRITING AND PORTFOLIOS

Whichever way you choose to correct the students' texts, we suggest you get students to rewrite them. This would guarantee that the students focus on their errors and produce an improved text which they could then keep in a portfolio. Portfolios of work are recommended by the CEF and can provide evidence of students' progress and level.

WRITING LESSONS 1–8

01 DESCRIBING VISUAL DATA

WRITING

Answers A
1 by population (not by area)
2 not all cities expected to grow
3 rural to urban living (not the other way round)
4 not true that urban populations in the whole world are projected to rise by 25%
5 Mumbai will rise more than slightly
6 Dhaka will rise by 8.6% (not triple)

VOCABULARY Describing percentages

Answers A
1 the vast majority
2 almost a fifth
3 more than halved, fourfold
4 four out of five, slightly higher
5 a tiny percentage
6 a significant minority

GRAMMAR Describing changes

Answers A
1 By 2025, the population of Dhaka is projected to have risen to 22 million.
2 In the next 20 years the rural population is set to fall.
3 African cities are expected to grow rapidly over the next few years.
4 China is predicted to become the world's largest economy in the next ten years.

KEYWORDS FOR WRITING
of whom / of which

Answers
1 The government donates 0.6% of GDP as aid, the bulk of which goes to countries in Africa.
2 There were 2650 fatalities from car accidents last year, the vast majority of which were caused by driver error.
3 University entrees, of whom 12% will come from deprived backgrounds, are set to increase.
4 There was a significant fall in crime in the last decade, a large part of which was put down to rising living standards.
5 The survey interviewed 950 people altogether, most of whom were 18–25 years old.

02 EXPRESSING YOUR OPINION

WRITING

Answers F
1 so
2 Indeed
3 As such
4 However
5 Secondly
6 Whilst
7 In short
8 such

KEYWORDS FOR WRITING *indeed*

Answers A
1 + 3; 4 + 6; 2 + 5

Suggested answers D
1 they may have to make cuts.
2 they can usually use taxpayers' money to help if necessary.
3 the present government made many such promises in the run-up to the election.
4 it can be open to corruption.

WRITING LESSONS 1–8

03 A REVIEW

VOCABULARY Reviews

Answers A and B
1. based + set (film)
2. rhyme + collection (poetry)
3. album + encores (gig)
4. sets + choreography (ballet)
5. abstract + sculptures (exhibition)
6. production + plot (play)
7. technique + partner (musical)
8. prose + multi-layered (novel)
9. orchestration + role (opera)
10. symphony + finale (concert)

KEYWORDS FOR WRITING

nevertheless / given

Answers A
1. f
2. b
3. a
4. c
5. e
6. d

04 DESCRIBING PROCESSES

WRITING

Answers C
1. whereby
2. thus
3. meanwhile
4. as
5. which

VOCABULARY Processes

Answers A
1. Plastic is removed from the rubbish manually.
2. The pipes are insulated with foam to minimise heat loss.
3. The final product is screened for impurities.
4. The tea leaves are categorised into different grades according to size and quality.
5. Nothing is discarded through the process, to maximise efficiency.
6. The raw materials are delivered in a container ship.
7. The parts are assembled in a central plant.
8. The oranges are boxed and loaded on to lorries.
9. The turbines are powered by forcing water through them.
10. The microbes are used to break down the oil into droplets.

KEYWORDS FOR WRITING

whereby, thereby and *thus*

Answers B
1. whereby
2. thus / thereby
3. whereby, thus / thereby
4. whereby

WRITING LESSONS 1–8

05 A COVERING LETTER

WRITING

Answers A
1 am writing
2 as
3 would
4 having spent
5 worked
6 which
7 put
8 all
9 should
10 hearing

VOCABULARY Achievements at work

Answers A
1 arranged
2 promoted
3 advised
4 achieved
5 conducted
6 dealt with
7 implemented
8 diagnosed
9 devised
10 budgeted
11 negotiated
12 represented

KEYWORDS FOR WRITING should

Answers A
1 Please do not hesitate to contact me should you require further information.
2 References are available on request, should you require them.
3 Should any vacancies become available, please contact me at your earliest convenience.
4 After sixty days you can retake the test should you wish to do so.
5 Please phone to make an appointment should you wish to discuss the matter further.

Answers B
1 Feel free to get in touch if you want more information.
2 I've got references if you need them.
3 Please let me know as soon as possible if any jobs come up.
4 You can do the test again after a couple of months if you want to.
5 Phone and make an appointment if you want to talk any more about this.

06 A MAGAZINE ARTICLE

WRITING

Answers B
1 Paragraphs end at *Museum* and *maintenance*.
   paragraph 1 – introduces inventor and invention
   paragraph 2 – describes how he came to invent the Cat's Eye
   paragraph 3 – talks about applications of Cat's Eye and compares it with other inventions
2 1 I believe Percy Shaw is a great inventor and his Cat's Eye should be displayed in the Design Museum.
   2 How many of these were really invented by one man?
   3 It made its inventor millions of pounds, yet few people know his name.
   4 Their inventors 'stood on the shoulders of giants'.
   5 telephones, cars, computers, etc.
   6 *yet* – line 1, *surely* – last sentence, *besides* – last sentence but one
3 Possible title = *An invaluable invention*

KEYWORDS FOR WRITING

surely, yet, besides

Answers A
1 There was enormous interest in the new device, yet sales were sluggish.
2 It was cheap to produce. Besides, it was beautiful to look at. / Besides being cheap to produce, it was beautiful to look at.
3 Surely this is the greatest achievement in the 21st century so far.
4 Some may argue that many others were working on the problem, but surely his was the biggest and most decisive contribution.
5 The train was fast and comfortable, and besides, it was the cheapest option.
6 He made millions from his invention, yet he died in poverty.

GRAMMAR *few / a few, little / a little*

Answers A
1 little
2 few
3 little
4 a few
5 a little
6 few
7 a few

118 OUTCOMES

WRITING LESSONS 1–8

07 A WIKI GUIDE

VOCABULARY Evaluating

Answers A
1 c
2 a
3 h
4 g
5 e
6 d
7 f
8 b

WRITING

Answers B
1 largely
2 effectively
3 partially
4 predominantly
5 essentially
6 above
7 below
8 subsequently
9 deliberate
10 previously

KEYWORDS FOR WRITING *albeit*

Answers A
1 albeit conservative
2 albeit funny sometimes
3 albeit very slowly
4 albeit one I didn't wholly agree with
5 albeit he is an academic expert

08 GIVING INFORMATION

WRITING

Answers B
1 Housing
2 Founded
3 Situated
4 Following
5 entering
6 Walking
7 featuring

GRAMMAR

Participle clauses with adverbial meaning

Answers A
1 Entering the museum, we…
2 Walking round the museum, I…
3 Removed from Greece at the start of the 19th century, the Elgin Marbles…
4 Being redecorated, the galleries…
5 Not having long before closing time, we…
6 Being a regular visitor to the city, I'm…
7 Being about ten miles outside of town, the museum…
8 A new law was introduced about ten years ago, resulting in all entrance fees being scrapped.
9 Visiting the museum during the morning, you will find it much less crowded.
10 The guide, pretending not to hear her questions, carried on with the tour.

KEYWORDS FOR WRITING

among and *within*

Answers A
1 d
2 c
3 g
4 b
5 f
6 a
7 e

TEACHER'S NOTES

1A MATCHING ANAGRAMS

Aim
To revise adjectives associated with city life.

Before class
Make enough copies of Set A for half the class and enough copies of Set B for the other half.

In class
A Divide the class into AB pairs. Give out the correct set of words to each student. Tell students to look at their words (adjectives to describe cities) and write anagrams (write the letters in the wrong order) for each adjective on a piece of paper.
B Tell students to give their anagrams to their partners and race to unscramble them. When they have finished they should check together and find the matching pairs of opposites. The first pair to finish is the winner.

Answers (opposites)	
spotless – filthy	clean – polluted
compact – sprawling	safe – dangerous
affluent – deprived	vibrant – dull
well-kept – run-down	clear – congested
well-run – chaotic	cheap – expensive

1B SECRET QUESTIONS

Aim
To revise perfect forms and personalise the topic.

Before class
Make one copy for each student.

In class
A Tell students to write their name and short answers to the questions (not complete sentences) in random order on another piece of paper.
B Put them in small groups and ask them to swap papers. Each student should read out the name and the answers they have, one by one, and the others should guess which answer refers to which question, and ask follow-up questions e.g. *five – is this the number of careers you think you will have had? Yes. Why do you think that?* etc.
C Conduct feedback by asking what was the funniest / strangest / most surprising etc. thing they heard.

2A ONE THING THAT REALLY ANNOYS ME IS …

Aim
To give further practice in emphatic structures.

Before class
Make enough copies of the role cards for each student to have one, and one copy of the useful language box for each group.

In class
A Put students in threes, A, B and C. Give two identical role-cards to A and B in each group and a role-card 4 (scorer) to student C. Give a useful language box to each group. (Alternatively, you could dispense with the useful language box and elicit this language and put it on the board as an introduction.)
B Ask students to conduct the role-play according to the instructions on their cards. A and B have the conversation while C is the scorer. A and B should have a natural conversation but try to use as many examples of the target language as they can. C should award a point for each appropriate and correct use of the target language.
C When they have finished, ask the scorer to pass on the scorer role card to another student in the group. Give out two different same-number role cards to the other pair in each group and ask them to role-play again. Finally, repeat the role-play with the third set of role cards.

2B FIND YOUR PARTNER

Aim
To revise the names of common household objects.

Before class
Make enough copies of the sheet of pictures so that each student will receive one picture. For a class of twelve or less, make two copies of the page. For a class of more than twelve, make four copies. Cut the sheets into individual pictures, but make sure you keep them in matching pairs of pictures e.g. in envelopes or using paper clips.

In class
A Give out one picture to each student but make sure each student will be able to locate another student with exactly the same picture. Tell students not to show each other their pictures but to look at them and note what is in them. With an odd number, take one of the pictures yourself. With a larger class, there is no problem with using a picture more than once, but always make sure each picture has a match.

TEACHER'S NOTES

B Ask students to stand up and move around. They should try to find their partner by asking questions about each other's pictures e.g. *Is there a mop in your picture? Is it next to the bucket?* Point out that the pictures are all very similar and they must find the exact match.

C When they find their partner, they should sit down together. Ask them to turn the pictures over and write down all the objects they can remember.

3A *WOULD* PELMANISM

Aim
To revise uses of *would*.

Before class
Make a set of sentences for each pair.

In class
A Put students in pairs. Tell them they are going to play a game of pelmanism (finding matching pairs by turning over two sentences at a time and seeing if they match).

B Give out a set of sentences to each pair. Ask them to shuffle the sentences and lay them face down on the table.

C Students take turns turning over two sentences. If they match – according to the uses of *would* – they pick them up and keep them, and have another turn. If they don't match, their partner should have a turn.

D At the end, they count their sentences. The winner is the one with the most sentences. As a follow-up, ask students to imagine a scenario for each of the sentences.

> **Answers**
> 1–8, 2–12, 3–18, 4–7, 5–11, 6–17,
> 9–19, 10–15, 13–16, 14–20

3B COMPOUND ADJECTIVES

Aim
To revise compound adjectives from the unit.

Before class
Make one copy for each pair.

In class
A Tell students they are going to form as many compound adjectives as they can by putting the words from the box in the correct bubble. Point out that some of the words can go in more than one bubble.

B Put students in pairs and tell them to write the words in the correct box and discuss their meanings.

C Check with the whole class and concept check some of the newer compound adjectives. Alternatively, you could make this a race – the first pair to get all the words in the correct place win.

> **Answers**
> -minded = absent, broad, single, narrow, open
> -hearted = cold, warm, half, big
> -skinned = thick, thin, olive, clear
> -handed = left, right, even
> -headed = big, pig, clear

4A SPLIT SENTENCES

Aim
To revise conditional structures.

Before class
Make enough copies of the sentence halves for each student to have one, but make sure you have matching halves for each sentence.

In class
A Tell students they are going to have half a conditional sentence and they have to find their other half. Give out the sentence halves, making sure each one has a match. With an odd number, take one of the sentence halves yourself.

B Ask students to get up and walk around, and find their partner by saying their sentence half aloud, until they find a match.

C When they find their partner, they should sit down together and analyse the form and meaning of their sentence.

D When all students have sat down, they should take turns reading out their sentences and asking the rest of the class questions about the form and meaning.

> **Answers**
> 1 b   2 g   3 e   4 h   5 f   6 d   7 a   8 c

4B VOCABULARY RACE – POLITICS

Aim
To revise words / phrases about politics and politicians.

Before class
Make one set for each pair.

In class
A Put students in pairs and ask them to complete the word list with words / phrases from the unit. The first pair with all the answers correct is the winner.

B Ask students to mark the stress on the words / phrases.

C Check pronunciation and meaning with the whole class.

> **Answers**
> 1 cha<u>ris</u>ma; 2 e<u>lec</u>tion; 3 good communi<u>ca</u>tion skills;
> 4 inability to <u>com</u>promise; 5 <u>judg</u>ment; 6 <u>know</u>ledgeable;
> 7 M<u>P</u>; 8 o<u>pin</u>ion poll; 9 <u>par</u>ty; 10 question<u>naire</u>;
> 11 refer<u>en</u>dum; 12 <u>strike</u> ballot; 13 <u>turn</u>out; 14 <u>vic</u>tory;
> 15 <u>warn</u>ing; 16 <u>youth</u> vote

TEACHER'S NOTES

5A COLLOCATIONS DICTATION

Aim
To revise collocations formed of *a* + noun *of* + noun / noun phrase.

Before class
Make enough copies so that one half of the class has a Student A set and the other half has a Student B set.

In class
A Put students in pairs. Ask them to take turns dictating the noun / noun phrases they have in their box. Their partner should write them in the correct bubble.

B When they have finished, ask the pairs to check together and try to add one more noun / noun phrase to each bubble.

> **Answers**
> (suggested additional answer in brackets)
> **Student A**
> a bundle of: laughs, clothes (fun)
> a fraction of: the cost, an inch (a second)
> a risk of: flooding, accidents (failure)
> a flood of: replies, questions (people)
> **Student B**
> a sign of: the times, life (things to come)
> the supply of: blood to the brain, drugs (water)
> the abolition of: slavery, the death penalty (VAT)
> the tip of: the iceberg, my tongue (the island)

5B CROSSWORD – DESCRIBING BOOKS

Aim
To revise and consolidate vocabulary used to talk about books.

Before class
Make one copy of the crossword for each pair of students.

In class
A Tell students they're going to do a crossword with words related to talking about books. Hand out the photocopies and tell them to do the crossword in pairs.

B Get fast finishers to help other students.

C Extend the activity by getting students to write four definitions of other words from the unit and giving them to their partners to guess the answer.

> **Answers**
> **Across**   **Down**
> 2 minimal   1 tale
> 6 traces   3 insight
> 7 person   4 ranked
> 9 memoir   5 revolves
> 10 narrator   8 portrayal
> 12 protagonist   11 style
> 13 plot
> 14 tackles

6A WHOSE WISHES ARE THEY?

Aim
To revise *I wish* followed by a variety of structures.

Before class
Make one copy for each student.

In class
A Give out a set of instructions to each student. Ask them to write a complete sentence for each one, giving reasons or other details.

B Put students in groups of six to eight. Ask them to put all the sets of sentences in a hat or envelope and mix them up.

C Ask students to take turns pulling a set of sentences out and reading them aloud to the rest of the group. They should try to identify who wrote each of sentences and explain their choices to each other.

6B ADVERBS NOUGHTS AND CROSSES

Aim
To revise adverbs.

Before class
Make one copy of the grid for each group of three. To make it more challenging, you could cut out the sentence starters and lay them face down on a grid, so that players don't know what to expect.

In class
A Tell students they are going to play a game of noughts and crosses. Draw the grid on the board and explain / elicit the rules i.e. each player needs to get three answers in a line, which can be vertical, horizontal or diagonal. One student is noughts (0) and the other is crosses (X).

B Write in one of the boxes *I stupidly forgot ...* and elicit possible sentences. Explain that students will gain a square by forming a correct sentence.

C Divide the class into threes. They should choose a game master and the other two will play. Give out the grid. Ask the game master to conduct the game i.e. decide who starts and whether the sentences are correct. If they are not sure, they should ask you. Players should take turns choosing a square and forming a correct sentence. The first one with a line of three is the winner.

122 OUTCOMES

TEACHER'S NOTES

7A PASSIVES DICTATION

Aim
To revise passive forms.

Before class
Make enough copies of Student A for half the class and Student B for the other half.

In class
A Tell students they are going to do a paired dictation. They should dictate their text in chunks and give their partner time to write it down. When they get to the underlined parts they should say *blah blah blah* and their partner should leave a gap.
B When they have both finished, they should tell each other the verbs missing from their texts. They should try individually to fill in the gaps in the text they have written with the correct passive form of the correct verb.
C Ask them to look at the texts together and check the writing and the passive forms.

7B COMBINATIONS

Aim
To revise word formation.

Before class
Make one copy of each card for each pair.

In class
A Divide the class into pairs. Distribute one set of cards to each pair. Tell students they are going to form as many words as they can, using a root box + suffix box. Tell them the total number possible (32).
B Tell pairs to race to form as many words as they can. Alternatively, you could set a time limit of five minutes and stop them when the time is up. Check the answers and check parts of speech, meaning and pronunciation, especially stress. The pair with the most correct combinations is the winner.

> **Possible answers**
> explor: exploration, explored, exploratory
> prevent: prevented, preventive, prevention, preventable
> vari: varied, variety, variance, variable, variation
> aggress: aggressive, aggression
> manipulat: manipulated, manipulation, manipulative
> abund: abundant, abundance
> implic: implication, implicit, implicative
> cynic: cynicism, cynical
> fatal: fatalism, fatality
> prob: probable, probability
> divers: diversion, diversity
> cap: capability, capable

8A PICTURE DICTATION

Aim
To revise vocabulary about landscapes.

Before class
Make enough copies of picture A for half the class and picture B for the other half.

In class
A Put students in AB pairs and distribute the pictures according to letter. Tell students not to look at each other's pictures and tell them they are going to do a picture dictation. They should sit back to back and take turns describing their picture to each other. Their partner should draw the picture. Then swap.
B When they have finished, they should compare their drawings with the original and discuss any differences.

8B AUXILIARIES SNAP

Aim
To revise different uses of auxiliary verbs.

Before class
Make enough sets of cards for each group of four students.

In class
A Tell students they are going to play a game of snap. Explain the rules. Students in fours distribute all the cards face down equally among the group. They keep their cards in a pile face down in front of them and take turns turning the top card over and laying it face up in front of them. If any player sees a matching pair of cards at any point, they shout *snap*. They should identify which use the auxiliary verb has in the two sentences. If they are right, they collect the two cards and add them to the bottom of their pile. If they are wrong, the game continues. When players finish their pile of cards, they should turn them over and start again. If they run out of cards, they are out, but they can help to adjudicate the rest of the game. The winner is the player with all the cards at the end.
B Put students in groups and give out a set of cards to each group. Ask them to deal the cards and start when they are ready. Monitor and check they are playing correctly.
C If there is time at the end, you could ask students to form another sentence to illustrate the use of the auxiliary represented by each pair of cards.

> **Answers**
> 1 **question tags** = She lives here, doesn't she? They wouldn't know, would they? You haven't told him, have you? I'm not stupid, am I?
> 2 **substitution** – to avoid repeating whole phrase =
> A: He doesn't live here any more. B: Doesn't He?
> A: They aren't English. B: Aren't they? A: I met him in a pub. B: Did you? A: She can speak Japanese. B: Can she?

TEACHER'S NOTES

> 3 **emphasis** = I agree. I really do. I don't know. I honestly don't. She isn't my friend. She really isn't. He got up really early. He really did.
> 4 **as a response** = Yes I do. No it isn't. Yes we are. No they haven't.
> 5 **with *so* or *neither / nor*** – another type of substitution = So do I. Neither can he. So would she. Neither should you.

9A FIND SOMEONE LIKE YOU

Aim
To revise continuous forms.

Before class
Make one copy for each student.

In class
A Tell students they are going to find someone similar to themselves by asking questions. Give out the questions and ask them to write their own answers in the '*You*' column.

B Ask them to stand up and walk around and ask different students the questions. When they find someone with a similar answer to themselves (it doesn't have to be exactly the same but close), they should write their name in the right-hand column ('*Another student*').

C When they have finished, ask them to sit down and report to the rest of the class on some of the things they found out.

9B JOB INTERVIEWS

Aim
To revise vocabulary related to jobs.

Before class
Make enough copies of each card so that one student has either an Interviewee or an Employer card.

In class
A Tell students they are going to role-play a job interview. Divide them into AB pairs and ask them to decide who is the employer and who the interviewee. Give out the role cards. Tell them not to show their partner their card. Give them three / four minutes to prepare what they are going to say. They could make a few notes.

B Ask students to role-play the interview in closed pairs. Ask the employers to tell the interviewees at the end whether they have got the job or not and why. Monitor closely.

C If time, ask one or two pairs to act out their role-play in front of the class.

10A BODY CARDS

Aim
To revise body movements.

Before class
Make enough copies of Set A for half the class and enough copies of Set B for the other half.

In class
A Tell students they are going to play a card game to match parts of the body with the correct movement. Divide them into AB pairs and distribute the sets of cards accordingly. Ask students to shuffle their cards and deal themselves eight each. They should hold these in a fan facing them, and put the others in a pile in front of them.

B Student A should play a card and Student B should follow with the matching other half. If B makes a pair, they should collect the pair and have another go. If they can't make a pair, they should pick up a card from their pile. The player with the most pairs at the end wins.

10B BAD PATIENTS ROLE-PLAY

Aim
To revise modals in the past.

Before class
Make enough copies of each card for each group.

In class
A Tell students they are going to do a role-play between a doctor and a 'bad' patient. The patient has returned to the doctor for a second time because their symptoms are now much worse. The doctor should ask them if they followed each of the pieces of advice and they should confess that they didn't, in fact they did the opposite. The doctor should tell them off using past modals.

B Divide the class into threes – doctor, patient and scorer – and give out the Symptoms / Advice cards and a copy of the useful language to each group.

C The doctor and patient should choose one of the cards and think briefly about what they are going to say. The doctor should try to use the useful language in a natural way. The scorer should award points to the doctor for each appropriate use of the useful language. Then swap roles and repeat the role-play. Then swap again, so that each student has a turn taking each of the three parts.

124 OUTCOMES

TEACHER'S NOTES

11A FINISH MY SENTENCE

Aim
To revise linking words.

Before class
Make enough copies of the Student A card for half the class and enough copies of the Student B card for the other half.

In class
A Tell students they are going to dictate half-sentences to each other. Student A says one of their sentence beginnings and Student B finds the correct ending and dictates it back. If A thinks it is the correct ending they write it down to form a complete sentence. If not, they ask B to look again. After Student A has said all their sentence beginnings, they swap.

B When they have finished, ask them to check the sentences together.

Answers
Student A 1D
           2B
           3A
           4C
Student B 1B
           2A
           3C
           4D

11B ODD ONE OUT

Aim
To revise vocabulary related to games and sports.

Before class
Make one copy for each pair in the class.

In class
A Tell students they are going to play a game of odd one out. They should look at the sets of words and decide which is the odd one out and why. They should replace the odd word with one that fits with the set.

B Put students in pairs and give out a set of words to each pair. Ask them to play the game.

C Check answers, and check the replacement word is correct, with the whole class at the end.

Answers
1 tackle
2 goal
3 trumps
4 crossbar
5 bridge
6 dice
7 king
8 scrabble
9 suit
10 cheated

12A SIMILE STORIES

Aim
To revise and extend similes.

Before class
Make enough copies of Set A for half the class and Set B for the other half.

In class
A Tell students they are going to rewrite stories, using similes to make them more dramatic.

B Divide the class into AB pairs. Give out the stories according to letter. Tell students to rewrite their stories by replacing the underlined phrases with similes. They should choose from the similes in the box.

C When they have finished they should try to memorise their stories, including the similes. They should then take turns telling each other their stories. Their partner should write down all the similes they hear.

Answers
Set A
1 as old as the hills
2 as black as night
3 smoked like a chimney
4 as white as a sheet
5 as quick as a flash
6 a memory like a sieve
Set B
1 like a fish out of water
2 like chalk and cheese
3 avoid like the plague
4 as clear as mud
5 as cold as ice
6 as clear as muck

12B JUMBLED SENTENCES

Aim
To revise dramatic inversion.

Before class
Make enough copies of each set for half the students.

In class
A Tell students they are going to unscramble sentences with dramatic inversion. Elicit some phrases which introduce dramatic inversion in a sentence and what happens to the word order.

B Divide students into AB pairs, and give out the sets according to letter. Tell students not to look at each other's sentences and to unscramble their jumbled sentences as fast as they can. When they have finished, they check with their partner, who has their answers.

C Ask the pairs to invent a mini-scenario for each of the sentences by inventing a sentence before and after each one. Elicit some of their ideas at the end.

TEACHER'S NOTES

13A Just a minute!

Aim
To revise vocabulary about newspapers and give fluency practice.

Before class
Make one copy for each group of four or five students. You also need enough dice to give one to each group. And one counter for each student – these can be simple: a paperclip, a rubber, a coin etc.

In class
A Tell students they are going to play a game of 'Just a minute'. This is originally a radio game show in which contestants have to talk for one minute without stopping about a topic. Divide the class into groups of four or five and give out the boards and dice. Explain that they are to take turns rolling the die and when they land on a square, they have to talk about that topic for a minute. If they run out of steam, they go back to the beginning. If a student lands on a square already used, they should throw the die again. Ask students to provide counters.

B When they are ready, they should start. Monitor closely and check they are playing properly. The first student to reach **Finish** in each group is the winner.

13B Reporting verbs

Aim
To revise reporting verbs.

Before class
Make one copy of Student A for half the class and a copy of student B for the other half.

In class
A Tell students they are going to read a report of a conversation aloud to each other. Their partner has the lines of the actual conversation but in the wrong order. They should put the lines of the conversation in the correct order as they listen. Then swap.

B Divide the class into AB pairs and give out the strips of conversation / reports according to letter. Tell students not to look at each other's and to start when they are ready.

C Ask them to check together when they have finished. Check answers with the class.

Answers
Student A
6, 3, 4, 1, 5, 8, 7, 2
Student B
6, 5, 2, 7, 4, 1, 8, 3

14A Crossword – economy and business

Aim
To revise vocabulary related to the economy and business.

Before class
Make enough copies of the crossword for each pair to have one.

In class
A Tell students they are going to do a crossword about the economy and business. Put them in pairs and ask them to do the crossword together.

B The first pair to finish is the winner. They could help other pairs or you could go through the answers with them.

Answers

Across	Down
4 cut backs	1 make someone redundant
5 float	2 pitch
6 loyal	3 custom
8 minutes	4 clients
10 go under	5 flood
13 agenda	7 relocating
14 contract	9 take over
17 economic downturn	11 lay off
18 drop	12 balance
19 hit	15 pick up
	16 moving

14B Definitions game

Aim
To revise defining relative clauses and vocabulary from various units.

Before class
Make enough copies of each set for half the class.

In class
A Divide students into AB pairs and give out the sets according to letter. Tell students they are going to define words for each other using defining relative clauses, and guess each other's words. Ask them to look at their words and useful phrases and think about how to define them, without looking at their partner's.

B When they are ready, ask them to take turns defining and guessing. If their partner can't guess the word, they may give other clues but not say the word.

C Check a few of their ideas at the end.

TEACHER'S NOTES

15A SPOT THE DIFFERENCE

Aim
To revise vocabulary for clothes and accessories.

Before class
Make enough copies of Picture A for half the class and enough copies of Picture B for the other half.

In class
A Tell students they are going to play a game of spot the difference. They should look at their picture, but not their partner's, and try to find 10 differences by asking and describing. The first pair to finish is the winner.
B Give out the pictures according to letter. Monitor and check they are doing the activity properly.
C Elicit some of the differences at the end.

15B PREPOSITIONS SNAKES AND LADDERS

Aim
To revise various uses of prepositions.

Before class
Make one copy of the game for every three or four students. You also need dice – if you don't have dice, use slips of paper with numbers 1–6 for students to pick from an envelope.

In class
A Tell students they are going to play a game of snakes and ladders. They need a different counter each – a coin, ring etc.
B They should take turns to throw the dice and move that number of squares from the **START** square. If they land on a ladder they go up, on a snake they go down. If they land on a blank square, they stay there until their next turn. If they land on a square with a sentence, they should decide whether it is correct or incorrect. If they are right, they go forward two squares, if they are wrong they go back two squares.
C Give out the boards and dice to each group. All can play or one in each group can be the adjudicator, whose responsibility is to decide whether students are right or wrong. Monitor closely and help where necessary. When they are ready, they should take turns throwing the dice and moving round the board. The first player to reach **FINISH** is the winner.

Answers
(Incorrect sentences)
3 You did that **on** purpose.
7 This style has been popular **for** many years.
11 I've been living **on** my own.
13 I'm working **until** 8 p.m. this evening.
15 It's grown to **be** a very big company.
21 He is **like** a brother to me.
23 They are terribly **in** debt.
25 **In** the long term, things are sure to change.
31 She's working there **on** a temporary basis.

16A ACCIDENT AND EMERGENCY DICTATION

Aim
To revise vocabulary about accidents and injuries.

In class
A Tell students they are going to do a paired dictation. They should take turns to dictate their text. When they get to one of the underlined words / phrases, they should tell their partner, who should look for a synonym in the box and write the correct form of it in the text instead.
B Ask them to look together at the completed texts and check the spelling and the synonyms they have chosen.

Answers
Student A
1 cut 2 terrible pain 3 streaming 4 panic
5 passed out 6 regained consciousness
Student B
1 whacked 2 break 3 cut 4 broken 5 scalded

16B AGREE / DISAGREE

Aim
To revise ways of talking about the future.

Before class
Make one copy for each student.

In class
A Tell students they are going to do a questionnaire. They should read the questions and mark them 1 – *agree strongly*, 2 – *agree with reservations*, 3 – *disagree with reservations* 4 – *disagree strongly*. They should add two more questions of their own to ask other students.
B Put students in small groups to explain and discuss their answers and ask their additional questions. Conduct brief feedback at the end. Alternatively, ask students to get up and walk around and find someone with similar answers to themselves. They should sit down together and ask each other their additional questions.

1A Matching anagrams

Set A

| spotless | compact | deprived | clear | chaotic |
| well-kept | polluted | safe | expensive | vibrant |

Set B

| cheap | sprawling | dull | filthy | clean |
| congested | affluent | run-down | well-run | dangerous |

Set A

| spotless | compact | deprived | clear | chaotic |
| well-kept | polluted | safe | expensive | vibrant |

Set B

| cheap | sprawling | dull | filthy | clean |
| congested | affluent | run-down | well-run | dangerous |

Set A

| spotless | compact | deprived | clear | chaotic |
| well-kept | polluted | safe | expensive | vibrant |

Set B

| cheap | sprawling | dull | filthy | clean |
| congested | affluent | run-down | well-run | dangerous |

Set A

| spotless | compact | deprived | clear | chaotic |
| well-kept | polluted | safe | expensive | vibrant |

Set B

| cheap | sprawling | dull | filthy | clean |
| congested | affluent | run-down | well-run | dangerous |

© Heinle, Cengage Learning 2012

1B Secret questions

1. How many times do you think you may have been married by the time you are sixty?
2. How many careers do you think you will have had by the time you retire?
3. Name three things you would like to have done before your next birthday.
4. Name three important things you had achieved by the time you reached your last birthday.
5. Name something you are embarrassed about having done in the past.
6. Name something you are proud of having done.

---

1. How many times do you think you may have been married by the time you are sixty?
2. How many careers do you think you will have had by the time you retire?
3. Name three things you would like to have done before your next birthday.
4. Name three important things you had achieved by the time you reached your last birthday.
5. Name something you are embarrassed about having done in the past.
6. Name something you are proud of having done.

---

1. How many times do you think you may have been married by the time you are sixty?
2. How many careers do you think you will have had by the time you retire?
3. Name three things you would like to have done before your next birthday.
4. Name three important things you had achieved by the time you reached your last birthday.
5. Name something you are embarrassed about having done in the past.
6. Name something you are proud of having done.

---

1. How many times do you think you may have been married by the time you are sixty?
2. How many careers do you think you will have had by the time you retire?
3. Name three things you would like to have done before your next birthday.
4. Name three important things you had achieved by the time you reached your last birthday.
5. Name something you are embarrassed about having done in the past.
6. Name something you are proud of having done.

© Heinle, Cengage Learning 2012

2A One thing that really annoys me is ...

> **Useful language**
> One thing that annoys / worries / bothers / concerns / frightens me is...that / the fact that / the amount / number of...
> What annoys me is....
> The thing that really gets me is ...

Role card 1

You are talking to your neighbour about another neighbour. Tell your neighbour what you like and dislike about the third neighbour. Try to use as many examples of the useful language as possible, but in a natural way.

Role card 2

You are talking to your colleague about another colleague. Tell your colleague what you like and dislike about the third colleague. Try to use as many examples of the useful language as possible, but in a natural way.

Role card 3

You are talking to your colleague about your boss. Tell your colleague what you like and dislike about the boss. Try to use as many examples of the useful language as possible, but in a natural way.

Role card 4 – Scorer

You are the scorer. Listen to the conversation and note down each appropriate and correct use of the useful language. Award a point for each one. Tell your partners at the end how they did and who won.

© Heinle, Cengage Learning 2012

2B Find your partner

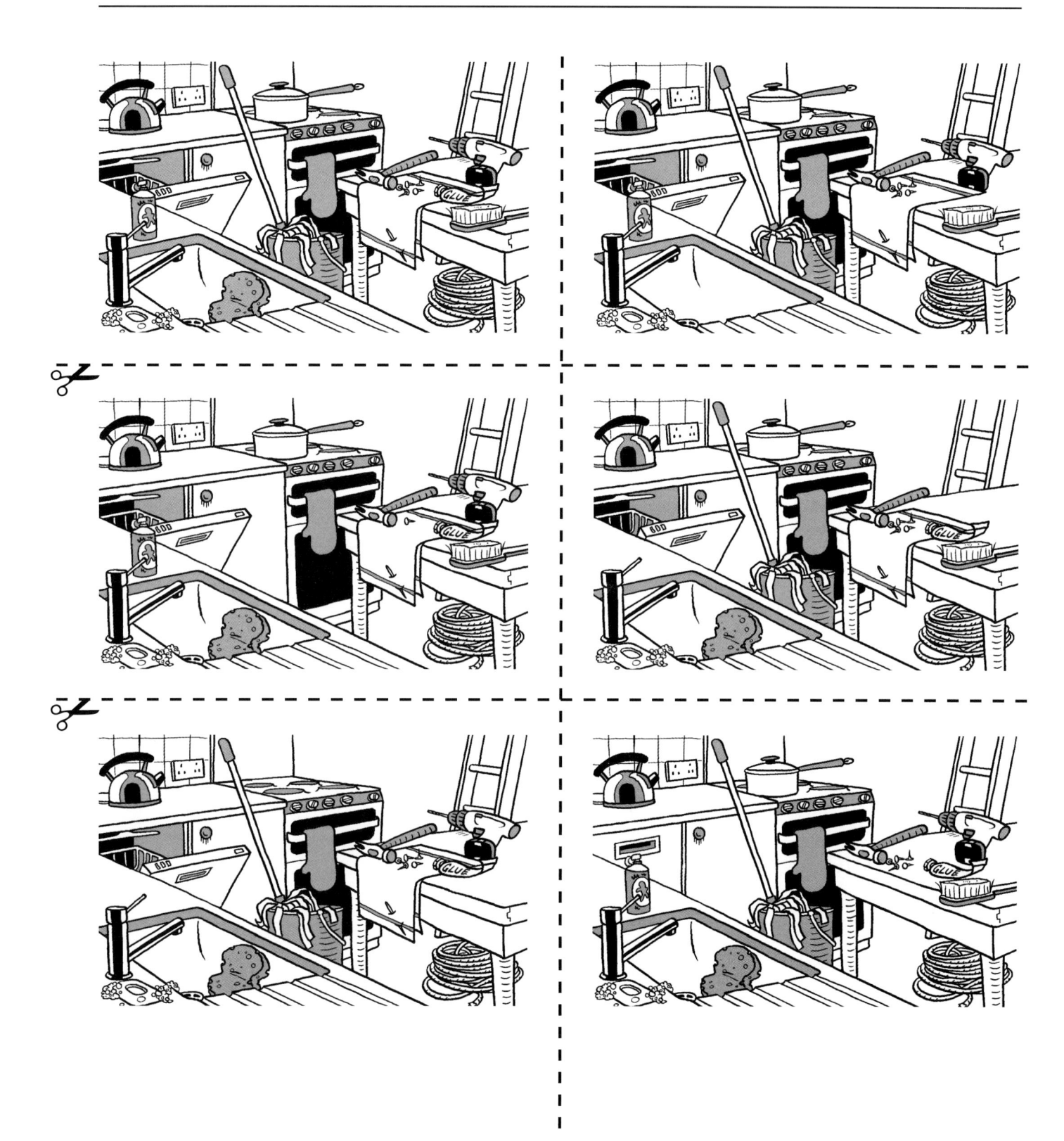

3A *Would* pelmanism

1 I would've thought that she's a really good boss.
2 Would you imagine that she could be so incompetent?
3 I'd expect her to stand up for what she believes in.
4 They knew she wouldn't come.
5 Would you care to explain?
6 Would you mind turning the music down?
7 I knew that would happen
8 I would have thought he might know how to deal with it.
9 I'm afraid I'd have to disagree with that.
10 Sorry I didn't call, my mobile wouldn't work yesterday.
11 Would you care to join us this evening?
12 I'd imagine that he's quite hard work.
13 If I were you, I wouldn't tell him.
14 I'd never have gone if I'd known.
15 The car wouldn't start this morning.
16 If he didn't have to leave, he could help.
17 Would you mind not talking?
18 Would you expect him to worry about that?
19 I'd have to agree with you.
20 If she hadn't worked so hard, she wouldn't have passed.

3B Compound adjectives

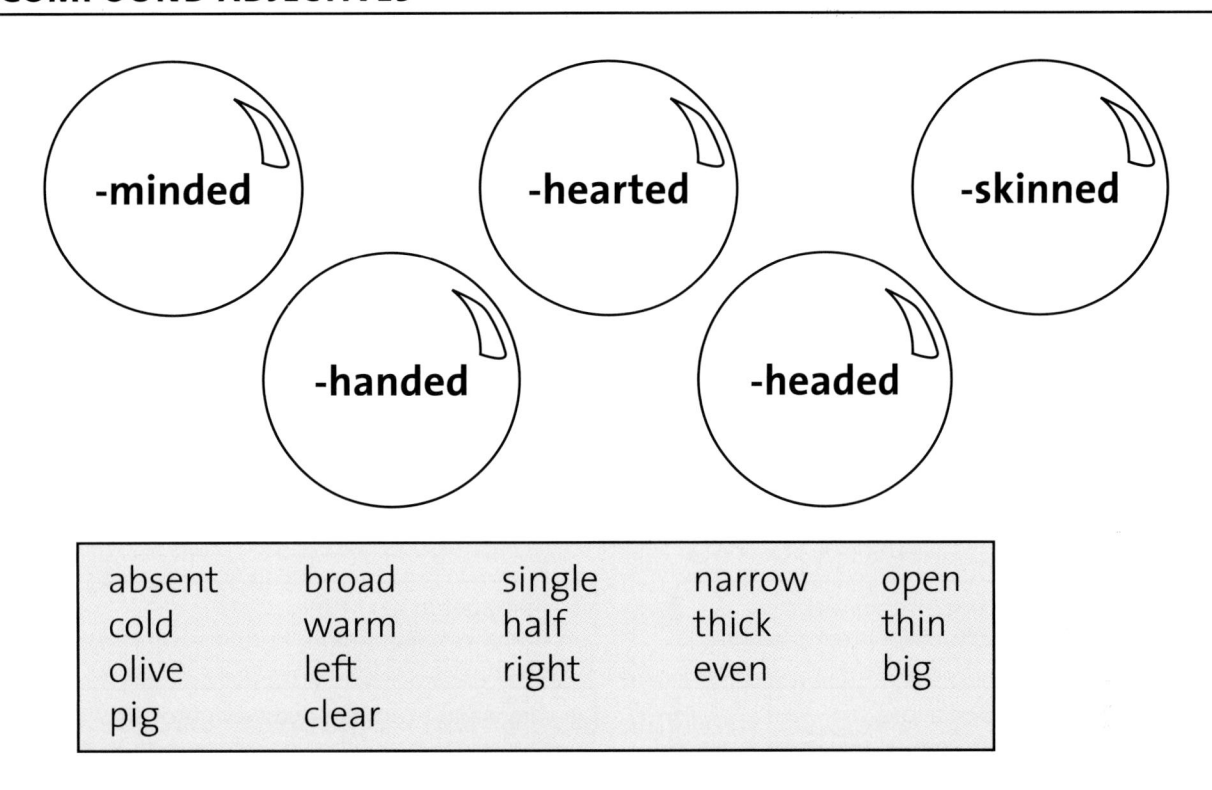

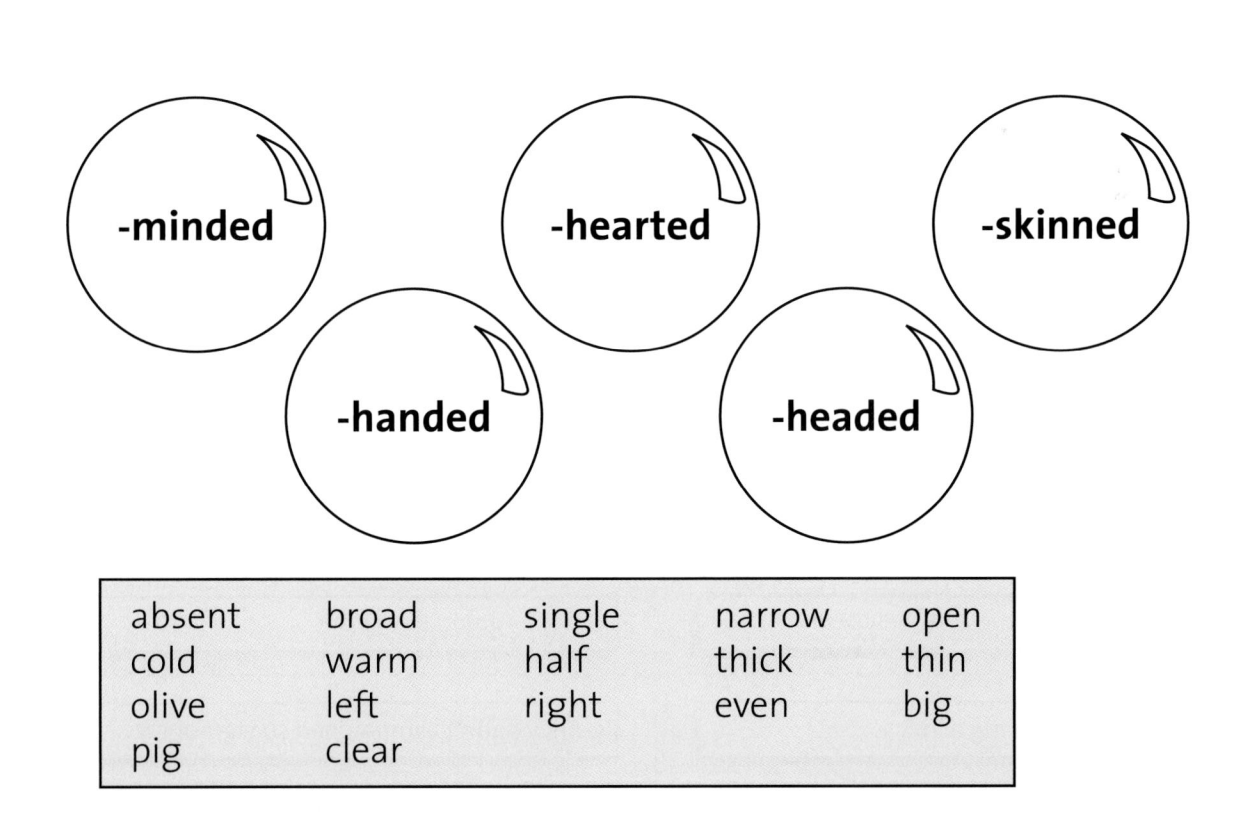

- -minded
- -hearted
- -skinned
- -handed
- -headed

absent	broad	single	narrow	open
cold	warm	half	thick	thin
olive	left	right	even	big
pig	clear			

- -minded
- -hearted
- -skinned
- -handed
- -headed

absent	broad	single	narrow	open
cold	warm	half	thick	thin
olive	left	right	even	big
pig	clear			

4A SPLIT SENTENCES

1 If it hadn't been for your stupidity, we	a the company may go bankrupt.
2 They mightn't have won the election, if	b wouldn't be in this mess today.
3 If they were more interested in green issues,	c you can't really complain about the result.
4 If they raised the minimum wage	d many of them will be more able to help themselves.
5 They say they're going to reduce taxation	e more people would have voted for them.
6 If we let poor countries off their debt	f if they get in next time.
7 If they carry on making a loss,	g they hadn't campaigned so vigorously.
8 Unless you vote	h fewer people would be living in poverty.

1 If it hadn't been for your stupidity, we	a the company may go bankrupt.
2 They mightn't have won the election, if	b wouldn't be in this mess today.
3 If they were more interested in green issues,	c you can't really complain about the result.
4 If they raised the minimum wage	d many of them will be more able to help themselves.
5 They say they're going to reduce taxation	e more people would have voted for them.
6 If we let poor countries off their debt	f if they get in next time.
7 If they carry on making a loss,	g they hadn't campaigned so vigorously.
8 Unless you vote	h fewer people would be living in poverty.

© Heinle, Cengage Learning 2012

4B Vocabulary race – politics

1 special quality of charm and ability to hold people's attention   c_____
2 when people vote   e_____
3 ability to talk and listen effectively   g___ c_____ s_____
4 being incapable of negotiating   i_____ t_ c_____
5 decision or choice   j_____
6 having learnt a lot   k_____
7 member of parliament   M_
8 survey about how people think, or the way they will vote   o_____ p___
9 political group standing for parliament   p____
10 method of collecting data   q_____
11 when the country has an opportunity to vote on a particular issue   r_____
12 vote on whether or not to stop work   s_____ b_____
13 number of people who vote   t_____
14 successful outcome   v_____
15 notification of something bad possibly happening   w_____
16 young members of the electorate   y____ v___

--- ✂ ---

1 having lost all your money   b_____
2 when people vote   e_____
3 ability to talk and listen effectively   g___ c_____ s_____
4 being incapable of negotiating   i_____ t_ c_____
5 decision or choice   j_____
6 having learnt a lot   k_____
7 member of parliament   M_
8 survey about how people think, or the way they will vote   o_____ p___
9 political group standing for parliament   p____
10 method of collecting data   q_____
11 when the country has an opportunity to vote on a particular issue   r_____
12 vote on whether or not to stop work   s_____ b_____
13 number of people who vote   t_____
14 successful outcome   v_____
15 notification of something bad possibly happening   w_____
16 young members of the electorate   y____ v___

5A Collocations dictation

Student A

a bundle of	a fraction of	a risk of	a flood of
the death penalty	my tongue	life	drugs
blood to the brain	the times	slavery	the iceberg

Student B

a sign of	the supply of	the abolition of	the tip of
laughs	replies	accidents	questions
the cost money	an inch	flooding	clothes

Student A

a bundle of	a fraction of	a risk of	a flood of
the death penalty	my tongue	life	drugs
blood to the brain	the times	slavery	the iceberg

Student B

a sign of	the supply of	the abolition of	the tip of
laughs	replies	accidents	questions
the cost money	an inch	flooding	clothes

© Heinle, Cengage Learning 2012

5B Crossword – describing books

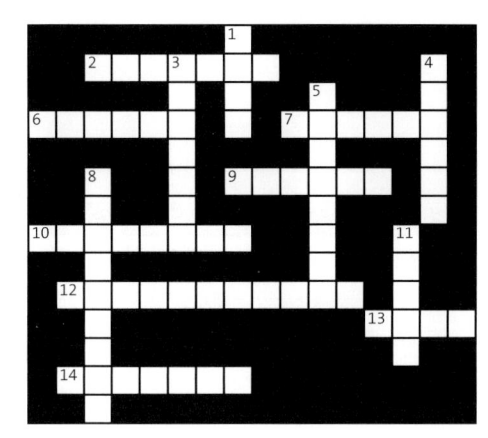

Across
2. There is space, ... dialogue in the novel.
6. It .... the family history right back to the 13th century
7. The story is told in the first ....
9. It's a moving .... about her life.
10. The .... is a thirteen-year-old girl.
12. The .... is a young man in need of love.
13. It's hard to put down it's got such a gripping...............
14. It .... really tough issues, but still manages to be funny.

Down
1. It's wonderful .... for children
3. It offers an .... into a different way to live.
4. It was .... number 1 on the best-seller list for three months.
5. The story .... around two lovers.
8. It's a vivid .... of love
11. He writes in a unique .... I've never read anything like it.

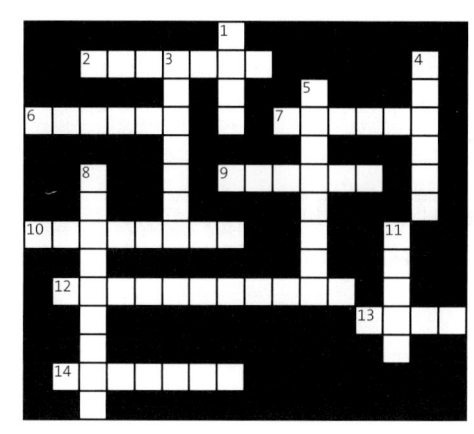

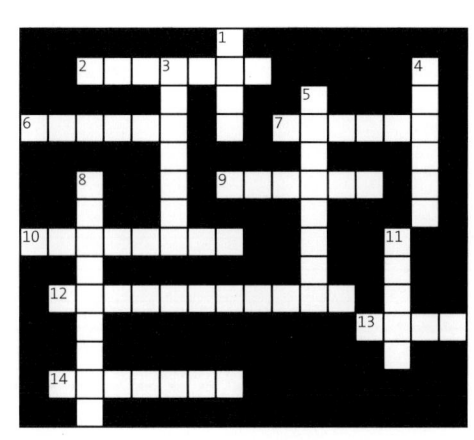

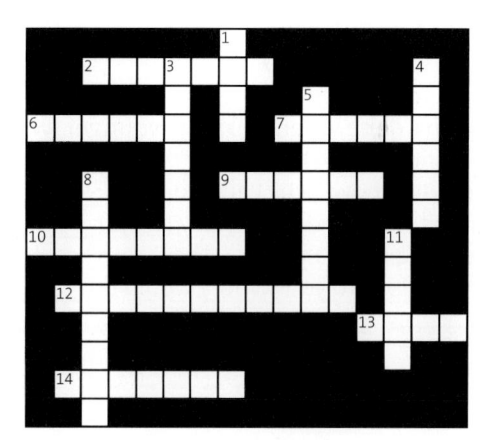

© Heinle, Cengage Learning 2012

COMMUNICATION ACTIVITIES **137**

6A Whose wishes are they?

Something you wish:

you had done when you were younger (why?) _____
you hadn't done when you were younger (why?) _____
you had now (why?) _____
you could do now (why can't you?) _____
you didn't have to do every day (why?) _____
you weren't (why?) _____
someone close to you (who?) would do _____

- -

Something you wish:

you had done when you were younger (why?) _____
you hadn't done when you were younger (why?) _____
you had now (why?) _____
you could do now (why can't you?) _____
you didn't have to do every day (why?) _____
you weren't (why?) _____
someone close to you (who?) would do _____

- -

Something you wish:

you had done when you were younger (why?) _____
you hadn't done when you were younger (why?) _____
you had now (why?) _____
you could do now (why can't you?) _____
you didn't have to do every day (why?) _____
you weren't (why?) _____
someone close to you (who?) would do _____

- -

Something you wish:

you had done when you were younger (why?) _____
you hadn't done when you were younger (why?) _____
you had now (why?) _____
you could do now (why can't you?) _____
you didn't have to do every day (why?) _____
you weren't (why?) _____
someone close to you (who?) would do _____

© Heinle, Cengage Learning 2012

6A Adverbs noughts and crosses

X

I bitterly regret ...	I desperately need ...	Presumably you ...
I expressly told you ...	I freely admit ...	Apparently they ...
I vaguely remember ...	I strongly recommend ...	Hopefully I ...

O

X

I bitterly regret ...	I desperately need ...	Presumably you ...
I expressly told you ...	I freely admit ...	Apparently they ...
I vaguely remember ...	I strongly recommend ...	Hopefully I ...

O

X

I bitterly regret ...	I desperately need ...	Presumably you ...
I expressly told you ...	I freely admit ...	Apparently they ...
I vaguely remember ...	I strongly recommend ...	Hopefully I ...

O

X

I bitterly regret ...	I desperately need ...	Presumably you ...
I expressly told you ...	I freely admit ...	Apparently they ...
I vaguely remember ...	I strongly recommend ...	Hopefully I ...

O

© Heinle, Cengage Learning 2012

7A Passive dictation

Student A

Many people believe the world will run out of fossil fuels before too long. It <u>is thought that</u> oil and gas supplies <u>will have been used up</u> by the end of the 21st century. Already people <u>are being encouraged</u> to use public transport more and new designs for electric cars <u>are being produced</u> every day. It is quite possible that all houses <u>built</u> in the near future <u>will be heated</u> by solar panels, and that central heating as we know it will become a thing of the past.

| encourage | build | use up |
| think | heat | produce |

Student B

A large number of species are in danger of becoming extinct and already many <u>have been destroyed</u> by man's cruelty and greed. According to research <u>carried out</u> recently, over 15,000 species are currently in danger of <u>being wiped out</u>, including the honey bee and the dormouse. If the honey bee <u>is lost</u> this will represent a natural catastrophe, as <u>described</u> in the book *A World without Bees*. Flowers will no longer <u>be pollinated</u>, which will have a disastrous effect on the food chain.

| pollinate | destroy | lose |
| wipe out | carry out | describe |

Student A

Many people believe the world will run out of fossil fuels before too long. It <u>is thought that</u> oil and gas supplies <u>will have been used up</u> by the end of the 21st century. Already people <u>are being encouraged</u> to use public transport more and new designs for electric cars <u>are being produced</u> every day. It is quite possible that all houses <u>built</u> in the near future <u>will be heated</u> by solar panels, and that central heating as we know it will become a thing of the past.

| encourage | build | use up |
| think | heat | produce |

Student B

A large number of species are in danger of becoming extinct and already many <u>have been destroyed</u> by man's cruelty and greed. According to research <u>carried out</u> recently, over 15,000 species are currently in danger of <u>being wiped out</u>, including the honey bee and the dormouse. If the honey bee <u>is lost</u> this will represent a natural catastrophe, as <u>described</u> in the book *A World without Bees*. Flowers will no longer <u>be pollinated</u>, which will have a disastrous effect on the food chain.

| pollinate | destroy | lose |
| wipe out | carry out | describe |

Student A

Many people believe the world will run out of fossil fuels before too long. It <u>is thought that</u> oil and gas supplies <u>will have been used up</u> by the end of the 21st century. Already people <u>are being encouraged</u> to use public transport more and new designs for electric cars <u>are being produced</u> every day. It is quite possible that all houses <u>built</u> in the near future <u>will be heated</u> by solar panels, and that central heating as we know it will become a thing of the past.

| encourage | build | use up |
| think | heat | produce |

Student B

A large number of species are in danger of becoming extinct and already many <u>have been destroyed</u> by man's cruelty and greed. According to research <u>carried out</u> recently, over 15,000 species are currently in danger of <u>being wiped out</u>, including the honey bee and the dormouse. If the honey bee <u>is lost</u> this will represent a natural catastrophe, as <u>described</u> in the book *A World without Bees*. Flowers will no longer <u>be pollinated</u>, which will have a disastrous effect on the food chain.

| pollinate | destroy | lose |
| wipe out | carry out | describe |

Student A

Many people believe the world will run out of fossil fuels before too long. It <u>is thought that</u> oil and gas supplies <u>will have been used up</u> by the end of the 21st century. Already people <u>are being encouraged</u> to use public transport more and new designs for electric cars <u>are being produced</u> every day. It is quite possible that all houses <u>built</u> in the near future <u>will be heated</u> by solar panels, and that central heating as we know it will become a thing of the past.

| encourage | build | use up |
| think | heat | produce |

Student B

A large number of species are in danger of becoming extinct and already many <u>have been destroyed</u> by man's cruelty and greed. According to research <u>carried out</u> recently, over 15,000 species are currently in danger of <u>being wiped out</u>, including the honey bee and the dormouse. If the honey bee <u>is lost</u> this will represent a natural catastrophe, as <u>described</u> in the book *A World without Bees*. Flowers will no longer <u>be pollinated</u>, which will have a disastrous effect on the food chain.

| pollinate | destroy | lose |
| wipe out | carry out | describe |

© Heinle, Cengage Learning 2012

7B Combinations

Roots

explor	prevent	vari
aggress	manipulat	abund
implic	cynic	fatal
prob	divers	cap

Suffixes

ed	ation	ety	ive
ion	ism	al	it
ative	ant	ance	ity
able	ability	atory	

- -

Roots

explor	prevent	vari
aggress	manipulat	abund
implic	cynic	fatal
prob	divers	cap

Suffixes

ed	ation	ety	ive
ion	ism	al	it
ative	ant	ance	ity
able	ability	atory	

- -

Roots

explor	prevent	vari
aggress	manipulat	abund
implic	cynic	fatal
prob	divers	cap

Suffixes

ed	ation	ety	ive
ion	ism	al	it
ative	ant	ance	ity
able	ability	atory	

- -

Roots

explor	prevent	vari
aggress	manipulat	abund
implic	cynic	fatal
prob	divers	cap

Suffixes

ed	ation	ety	ive
ion	ism	al	it
ative	ant	ance	ity
able	ability	atory	

© Heinle, Cengage Learning 2012

8A Picture dictation

Picture A

Picture B

Picture A

Picture B

Picture A

Picture B

Picture A

Picture B

8B Auxiliaries snap

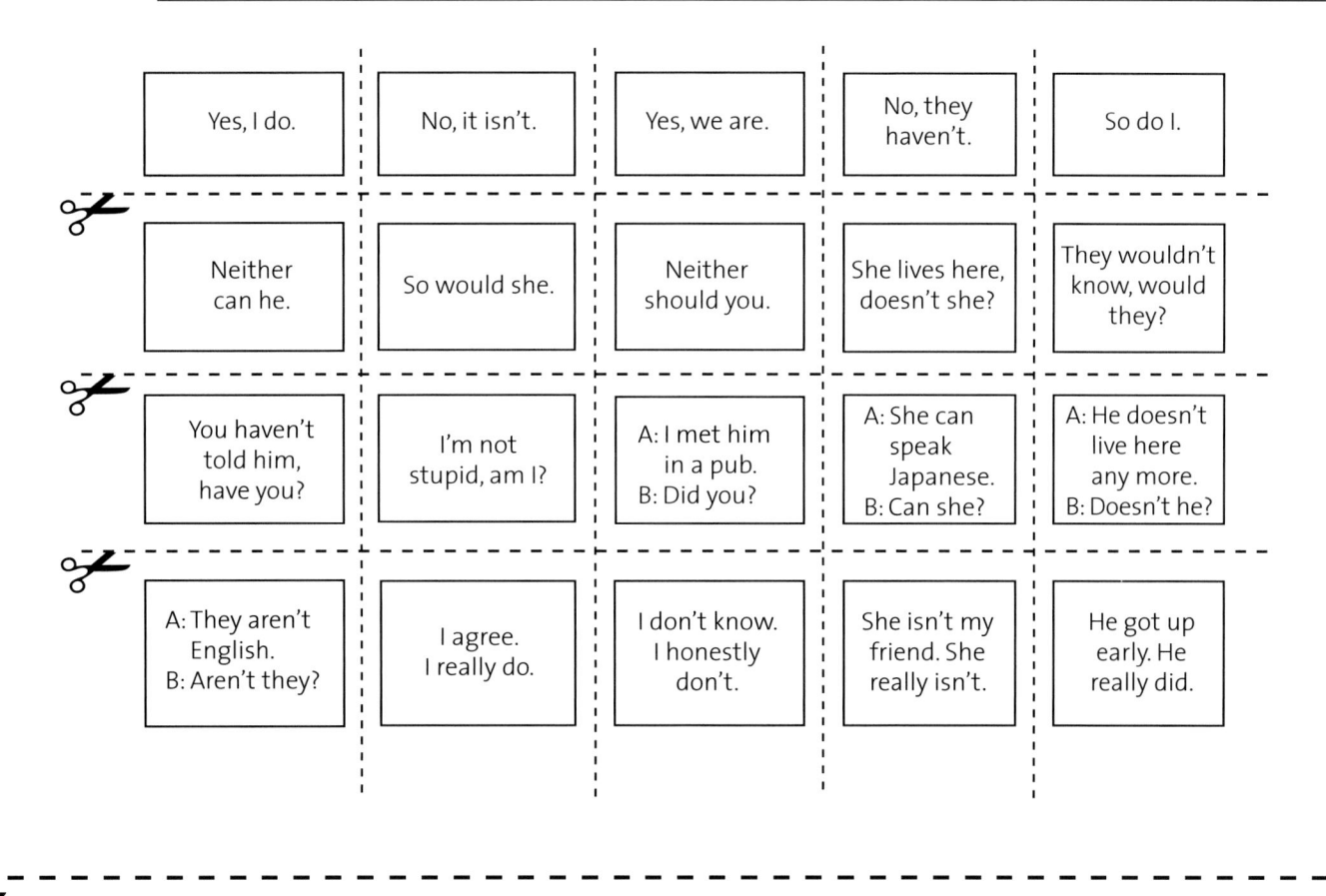

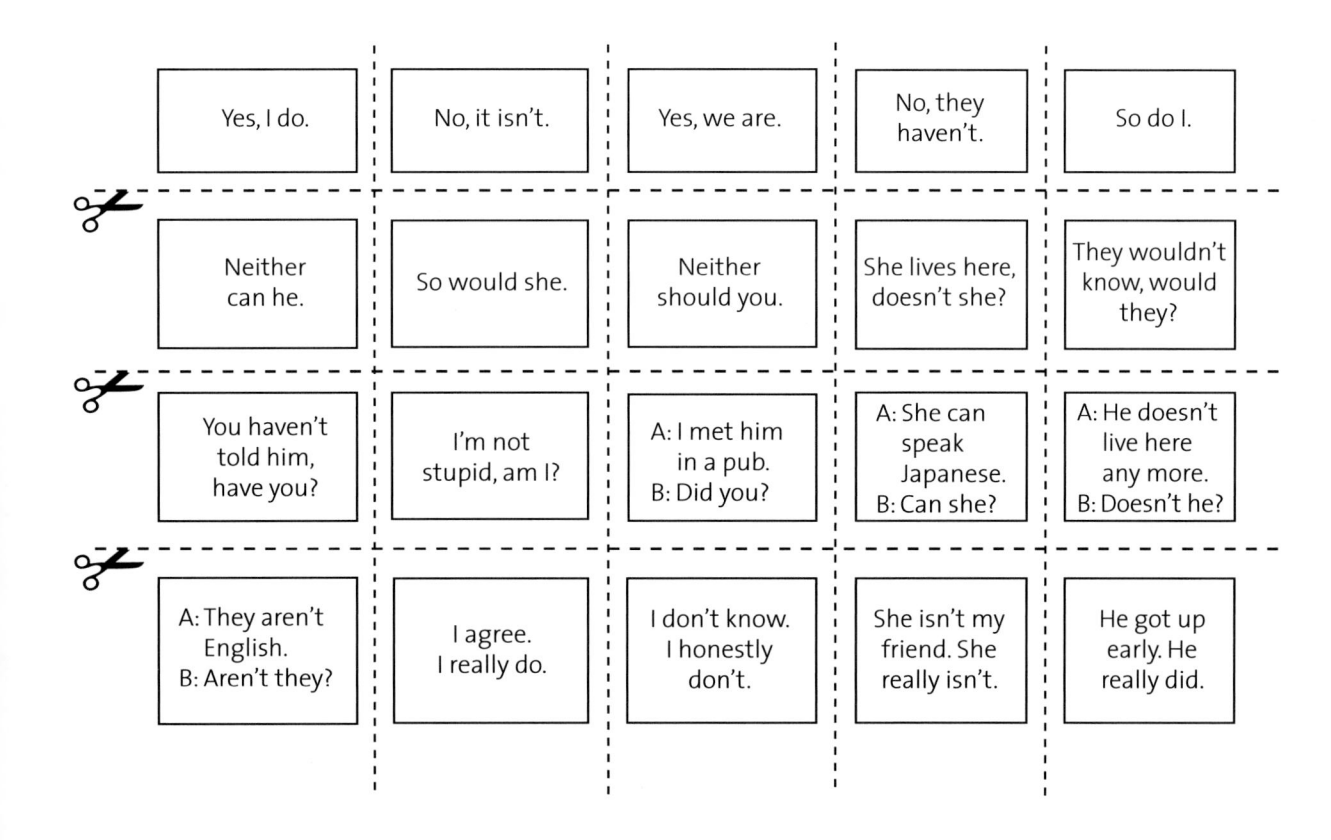

Yes, I do.	No, it isn't.	Yes, we are.	No, they haven't.	So do I.
Neither can he.	So would she.	Neither should you.	She lives here, doesn't she?	They wouldn't know, would they?
You haven't told him, have you?	I'm not stupid, am I?	A: I met him in a pub. B: Did you?	A: She can speak Japanese. B: Can she?	A: He doesn't live here any more. B: Doesn't he?
A: They aren't English. B: Aren't they?	I agree. I really do.	I don't know. I honestly don't.	She isn't my friend. She really isn't.	He got up early. He really did.

Yes, I do.	No, it isn't.	Yes, we are.	No, they haven't.	So do I.
Neither can he.	So would she.	Neither should you.	She lives here, doesn't she?	They wouldn't know, would they?
You haven't told him, have you?	I'm not stupid, am I?	A: I met him in a pub. B: Did you?	A: She can speak Japanese. B: Can she?	A: He doesn't live here any more. B: Doesn't he?
A: They aren't English. B: Aren't they?	I agree. I really do.	I don't know. I honestly don't.	She isn't my friend. She really isn't.	He got up early. He really did.

9A FIND SOMEONE LIKE YOU

	You	Another student
1. Where are you living at the moment – in a first, second, third floor flat? In a house? Other?	_____	_____
2. When and where are you next going on holiday?	_____	_____
3. How long have you been learning English?	_____	_____
4. What were you doing between 7 p.m. and 9 p.m. last night?	_____	_____
5. What will you be doing at this time next Saturday?	_____	_____
6. What kind of things do you most like being given?	_____	_____

✂ -

	You	Another student
1. Where are you living at the moment – in a first, second, third floor flat? In a house? Other?	_____	_____
2. When and where are you next going on holiday?	_____	_____
3. How long have you been learning English?	_____	_____
4. What were you doing between 7 p.m. and 9 p.m. last night?	_____	_____
5. What will you be doing at this time next Saturday?	_____	_____
6. What kind of things do you most like being given?	_____	_____

✂ -

	You	Another student
1. Where are you living at the moment – in a first, second, third floor flat? In a house? Other?	_____	_____
2. When and where are you next going on holiday?	_____	_____
3. How long have you been learning English?	_____	_____
4. What were you doing between 7 p.m. and 9 p.m. last night?	_____	_____
5. What will you be doing at this time next Saturday?	_____	_____
6. What kind of things do you most like being given?	_____	_____

✂ -

	You	Another student
1. Where are you living at the moment – in a first, second, third floor flat? In a house? Other?	_____	_____
2. When and where are you next going on holiday?	_____	_____
3. How long have you been learning English?	_____	_____
4. What were you doing between 7 p.m. and 9 p.m. last night?	_____	_____
5. What will you be doing at this time next Saturday?	_____	_____
6. What kind of things do you most like being given?	_____	_____

© Heinle, Cengage Learning 2012

9B Job interviews

Interviewee

You are at an interview for a job in an advertising company. The interviewer will ask you some questions about your experience and skills, and will explain what the job entails Ask for more information about the job and the conditions. Make sure you ask about:

- Crèche / childcare facilities
- Perks – subsidised travel, holidays, company car
- How much notice you have to give
- Flexitime and compassionate leave
- Salary, commission, bonuses and pay rises

Interviewee

You are at an interview for a job in an advertising company. The interviewer will ask you some questions about your experience and skills, and will explain what the job entails Ask for more information about the job and the conditions. Make sure you ask about:

- Crèche / childcare facilities
- Perks – subsidised travel, holidays, company car
- How much notice you have to give
- Flexitime and compassionate leave
- Salary, commission, bonuses and pay rises

Employer

You are interviewing someone for a job in your advertising company. Ask about their experience and skills and answer their questions. Explain that the job involves:

- Coming up with new strategies
- Inputting new information / ideas
- Overseeing new campaigns
- Networking with new and old contacts
- Troubleshooting any problems

Employer

You are interviewing someone for a job in your advertising company. Ask about their experience and skills and answer their questions. Explain that the job involves:

- Coming up with new strategies
- Inputting new information / ideas
- Overseeing new campaigns
- Networking with new and old contacts
- Troubleshooting any problems

10A Body cards

Set A

flutter	raise	kick	stroke	clap	pat someone	wipe
clutch	click	your shoulders	your fist	your legs	beats	fast
your arm	in the stomach	your back	your food out	your head	rises and falls	your hand

Set B

your eyelashes	your eyebrows	the ball	the cat	your hands	on the back	your forehead
wanders	your chest	your fingers	shrug	clench	stretch	your heart
scratch	punch someone	support	spit	nod	your belly	raise

Set A

flutter	raise	kick	stroke	clap	pat someone	wipe
clutch	click	your shoulders	your fist	your legs	beats	fast
your arm	in the stomach	your back	your food out	your head	rises and falls	your hand

Set B

your eyelashes	your eyebrows	the ball	the cat	your hands	on the back	your forehead
wanders	your chest	your fingers	shrug	clench	stretch	your heart
scratch	punch someone	support	spit	nod	your belly	raise

© Heinle, Cengage Learning 2012

10B Bad patients role-play

> **Useful language**
> You should / shouldn't have done / been doing
> You might / could have done / been doing
> You must have done / been doing
> You can't have done / been doing

Symptoms
Chest infection
Advice
- get plenty of rest
- drink lots of fluids
- don't drink or smoke
- inhale eucalyptus and menthol
- suck lozenges

Symptoms
Headaches
Advice
- don't drink coffee or alcohol
- eat a balanced diet with plenty of fresh fruit and vegetables
- have your eyesight checked
- don't use a computer or watch TV too much
- get plenty of sleep

Symptoms
Insomnia
Advice
- don't eat a big meal after 7 p.m.
- don't drink coffee or alcohol
- get plenty of fresh air and exercise
- have a milky drink or herbal tea before bed
- don't watch TV just before bed

> **Useful language**
> You should / shouldn't have done / been doing
> You might / could have done / been doing
> You must have done / been doing
> You can't have done / been doing

Symptoms
Chest infection
Advice
- get plenty of rest
- drink lots of fluids
- don't drink or smoke
- inhale eucalyptus and menthol
- suck lozenges

Symptoms
Headaches
Advice
- don't drink coffee or alcohol
- eat a balanced diet with plenty of fresh fruit and vegetables
- have your eyesight checked
- don't use a computer or watch TV too much
- get plenty of sleep

Symptoms
Insomnia
Advice
- don't eat a big meal after 7 p.m.
- don't drink coffee or alcohol
- get plenty of fresh air and exercise
- have a milky drink or herbal tea before bed
- don't watch TV just before bed

© Heinle, Cengage Learning 2012

11A Finish my sentence

Student A

Beginnings	Endings
1 Although it was raining,	A ... otherwise, we'll be relegated.
2 Our team will be promoted,	B ... they will lose, whether they score or not.
3 We left early	C ... it will be upheld.
4 They keep on playing penalties	D ... whether they score or not.

Student B

Beginnings	Endings
1 Unless they bring on a substitute,	A ... so as to get a good seat.
2 We really need to improve;	B ... as long as they win the next match.
3 Even if they challenge the decision,	C ... until one team misses one.
4 They are going to get thrashed	D ... we carried on playing.

Student A

Beginnings	Endings
1 Although it was raining,	A ... otherwise, we'll be relegated.
2 Our team will be promoted,	B ... they will lose, whether they score or not.
3 We left early	C ... it will be upheld.
4 They keep on playing penalties	D ... whether they score or not.

Student B

Beginnings	Endings
1 Unless they bring on a substitute,	A ... so as to get a good seat.
2 We really need to improve;	B ... as long as they win the next match.
3 Even if they challenge the decision,	C ... until one team misses one.
4 They are going to get thrashed	D ... we carried on playing.

Student A

Beginnings	Endings
1 Although it was raining,	A ... otherwise, we'll be relegated.
2 Our team will be promoted,	B ... they will lose, whether they score or not.
3 We left early	C ... it will be upheld.
4 They keep on playing penalties	D ... whether they score or not.

Student B

Beginnings	Endings
1 Unless they bring on a substitute,	A ... so as to get a good seat.
2 We really need to improve;	B ... as long as they win the next match.
3 Even if they challenge the decision,	C ... until one team misses one.
4 They are going to get thrashed	D ... we carried on playing.

Student A

Beginnings	Endings
1 Although it was raining,	A ... otherwise, we'll be relegated.
2 Our team will be promoted,	B ... they will lose, whether they score or not.
3 We left early	C ... it will be upheld.
4 They keep on playing penalties	D ... whether they score or not.

Student B

Beginnings	Endings
1 Unless they bring on a substitute,	A ... so as to get a good seat.
2 We really need to improve;	B ... as long as they win the next match.
3 Even if they challenge the decision,	C ... until one team misses one.
4 They are going to get thrashed	D ... we carried on playing.

© Heinle, Cengage Learning 2012

11B Odd one out

Find and replace the odd one out.

1 shuffle	tackle	lay	deal
2 double fault	deuce	rally	goal
3 hearts	clubs	trumps	spades
4 substitute	keeper	crossbar	penalty
5 chess	backgammon	bridge	monopoly
6 deck	ace	hand	dice
7 board	counter	king	piece
8 blackjack	scrabble	poker	roulette
9 suit	jack	joker	queen
10 sent off	cheated	booked	suspended

Find and replace the odd one out.

1 shuffle	tackle	lay	deal
2 double fault	deuce	rally	goal
3 hearts	clubs	trumps	spades
4 substitute	keeper	crossbar	penalty
5 chess	backgammon	bridge	monopoly
6 deck	ace	hand	dice
7 board	counter	king	piece
8 blackjack	scrabble	poker	roulette
9 suit	jack	joker	queen
10 sent off	cheated	booked	suspended

Find and replace the odd one out.

1 shuffle	tackle	lay	deal
2 double fault	deuce	rally	goal
3 hearts	clubs	trumps	spades
4 substitute	keeper	crossbar	penalty
5 chess	backgammon	bridge	monopoly
6 deck	ace	hand	dice
7 board	counter	king	piece
8 blackjack	scrabble	poker	roulette
9 suit	jack	joker	queen
10 sent off	cheated	booked	suspended

Find and replace the odd one out.

1 shuffle	tackle	lay	deal
2 double fault	deuce	rally	goal
3 hearts	clubs	trumps	spades
4 substitute	keeper	crossbar	penalty
5 chess	backgammon	bridge	monopoly
6 deck	ace	hand	dice
7 board	counter	king	piece
8 blackjack	scrabble	poker	roulette
9 suit	jack	joker	queen
10 sent off	cheated	booked	suspended

© Heinle, Cengage Learning 2012

12A SIMILE STORIES

Set A

Once there was a man who was [1]very, very old. He went out one evening and the sky was [2]very black. He decided to have a cigarette – he [3]smoked a great deal. As he was smoking, he heard a roaring sound behind him. He was terrified. He turned [4]very white and ran into his house [5]very fast. When his wife asked him what was the matter, he didn't remember. He had [6]a very bad memory.

| as white as a sheet | as black as night | a memory like a sieve |
| as quick as a flash | smoked like a chimney | as old as the hills |

Set B

Last week I went to an awful party. I felt [1]very uncomfortable as me and the other people there were [2]so different from each other. Also there was a woman there who I was at university with, who I usually [3]try my very best to avoid. She was [4]really hard and [5]really cold. Then I ended up stuck talking to someone who was explaining the rules of bridge to me, which were [6]horribly confusing.

| as hard as nails | avoid like the plague | as clear as mud |
| like a fish out of water | like chalk and cheese | as cold as ice |

Set A

Once there was a man who was [1]very, very old. He went out one evening and the sky was [2]very black. He decided to have a cigarette – he [3]smoked a great deal. As he was smoking, he heard a roaring sound behind him. He was terrified. He turned [4]very white and ran into his house [5]very fast. When his wife asked him what was the matter, he didn't remember. He had [6]a very bad memory.

| as white as a sheet | as black as night | a memory like a sieve |
| as quick as a flash | smoked like a chimney | as old as the hills |

Set B

Last week I went to an awful party. I felt [1]very uncomfortable as me and the other people there were [2]so different from each other. Also there was a woman there who I was at university with, who I usually [3]try my very best to avoid. She was [4]really hard and [5]really cold. Then I ended up stuck talking to someone who was explaining the rules of bridge to me, which were [6]horribly confusing.

| as hard as nails | avoid like the plague | as clear as mud |
| like a fish out of water | like chalk and cheese | as cold as ice |

© Heinle, Cengage Learning 2012

12B Jumbled sentences

Set A
1 No sooner had I arrived than the party ended.
2 Never before had he met such an amazing person.
3 Not only were they the best but they were also the cheapest. (or … the cheapest … the best)
4 Not until you explain will I let you leave.
5 idea heard silly never I have a such. ....
6 I think couldn't no time escape at did we. ....
7 realise he loved much did her after left she only how. ....
8 sight seen else she seen such beautiful nowhere had a. ....

✂---

Set B
1 arrived party the I had ended sooner no than. ....
2 he had never met an person before such before amazing. ....
3 they the cheapest were best only also but the only were not they. ....
4 I leave not you let explain you until will. ....
5 Never have I heard such a silly idea.
6 At no time did I think we couldn't escape.
7 Only after she left did he realise how much he loved her.
8 Nowhere else had she seen such a beautiful sight.

✂---

Set A
1 No sooner had I arrived than the party ended.
2 Never before had he met such an amazing person.
3 Not only were they the best but they were also the cheapest. (or … the cheapest … the best)
4 Not until you explain will I let you leave.
5 idea heard silly never I have a such. ....
6 I think couldn't no time escape at did we. ....
7 realise he loved much did her after left she only how. ....
8 sight seen else she seen such beautiful nowhere had a. ....

✂---

Set B
1 arrived party the I had ended sooner no than. ....
2 he had never met an person before such before amazing. ....
3 they the cheapest were best only also but the only were not they. ....
4 I leave not you let explain you until will. ....
5 Never have I heard such a silly idea.
6 At no time did I think we couldn't escape.
7 Only after she left did he realise how much he loved her.
8 Nowhere else had she seen such a beautiful sight.

© Heinle, Cengage Learning 2012

13A Just a minute!

Start / Finish	freedom of the press	broadsheets	headlines	invasion of privacy	Sunday supplements	harassment	tabloids
free							political bias
international news		**Just a minute!**					being a journalist
I							being a war reporter
celebrity interviews	paparazzi	your favourite magazine	your favourite newspaper	horoscopes	reviews	film	the sports pages

------- ✂ -------

Start / Finish	freedom of the press	broadsheets	headlines	invasion of privacy	Sunday supplements	harassment	tabloids
free							political bias
international news		**Just a minute!**					being a journalist
I							being a war reporter
celebrity interviews	paparazzi	your favourite magazine	your favourite newspaper	horoscopes	reviews	film	the sports pages

© Heinle, Cengage Learning 2012

152 Outcomes

13B Reporting verbs

Student A

The other day, Bobby's mother accused him of breaking a vase. Bobby hotly denied it, but his mother blamed the breakage on him and urged him to tell the truth. Bobby acknowledged that he had picked up the vase, but he refused to admit to something he hadn't done. His mother assured him that if she discovered he hadn't been honest, he would be severely punished.

1 Kate: I'm sorry, but I don't agree with that.
2 Julie: Have you been doing lots of exercise?
3 Kate: Thanks!
4 Julie: I think you should be careful not to overdo it.
5 Kate: Well, I'm not eating any less than usual
6 Julie: I'm a bit concerned about you – you look so thin.
7 Kate: I have started going to the gym every day.
8 Julie: Well, I admire your determination

Student B

Last time Julie saw her best friend, Kate, she expressed concern about how much weight she had lost. Kate claimed she was eating exactly the same as usual. Julie asked her if she had been taking much exercise and Kate confirmed that she had started to go to the gym on a daily basis. Julie warned her to take it easy but Kate rejected her advice. Julie praised her for her sticking power and Kate thanked her sarcastically.

1 Bobby: Well, OK, I did pick it up....
2 Mother: OK, but if I find out you've lied, you'll be sorry!
3 Bobby: No, I didn't, I really didn't.
4 Mother: Well, someone has broken it and I think it was you.
5 Bobby: ...but I absolutely won't admit to doing something I didn't do.
6 Mother: I think you broke this vase.
7 Bobby: I'll say it again – I didn't do it.
8 Mother: I really think you should tell the truth.

Student A

The other day, Bobby's mother accused him of breaking a vase. Bobby hotly denied it, but his mother blamed the breakage on him and urged him to tell the truth. Bobby acknowledged that he had picked up the vase, but he refused to admit to something he hadn't done. His mother assured him that if she discovered he hadn't been honest, he would be severely punished.

1 Kate: I'm sorry, but I don't agree with that.
2 Julie: Have you been doing lots of exercise?
3 Kate: Thanks!
4 Julie: I think you should be careful not to overdo it.
5 Kate: Well, I'm not eating any less than usual
6 Julie: I'm a bit concerned about you – you look so thin.
7 Kate: I have started going to the gym every day.
8 Julie: Well, I admire your determination

Student B

Last time Julie saw her best friend, Kate, she expressed concern about how much weight she had lost. Kate claimed she was eating exactly the same as usual. Julie asked her if she had been taking much exercise and Kate confirmed that she had started to go to the gym on a daily basis. Julie warned her to take it easy but Kate rejected her advice. Julie praised her for her sticking power and Kate thanked her sarcastically.

1 Bobby: Well, OK, I did pick it up....
2 Mother: OK, but if I find out you've lied, you'll be sorry!
3 Bobby: No, I didn't, I really didn't.
4 Mother: Well, someone has broken it and I think it was you.
5 Bobby: ...but I absolutely won't admit to doing something I didn't do.
6 Mother: I think you broke this vase.
7 Bobby: I'll say it again – I didn't do it.
8 Mother: I really think you should tell the truth.

Student A

The other day, Bobby's mother accused him of breaking a vase. Bobby hotly denied it, but his mother blamed the breakage on him and urged him to tell the truth. Bobby acknowledged that he had picked up the vase, but he refused to admit to something he hadn't done. His mother assured him that if she discovered he hadn't been honest, he would be severely punished.

1 Kate: I'm sorry, but I don't agree with that.
2 Julie: Have you been doing lots of exercise?
3 Kate: Thanks!
4 Julie: I think you should be careful not to overdo it.
5 Kate: Well, I'm not eating any less than usual
6 Julie: I'm a bit concerned about you – you look so thin.
7 Kate: I have started going to the gym every day.
8 Julie: Well, I admire your determination

Student B

Last time Julie saw her best friend, Kate, she expressed concern about how much weight she had lost. Kate claimed she was eating exactly the same as usual. Julie asked her if she had been taking much exercise and Kate confirmed that she had started to go to the gym on a daily basis. Julie warned her to take it easy but Kate rejected her advice. Julie praised her for her sticking power and Kate thanked her sarcastically.

1 Bobby: Well, OK, I did pick it up....
2 Mother: OK, but if I find out you've lied, you'll be sorry!
3 Bobby: No, I didn't, I really didn't.
4 Mother: Well, someone has broken it and I think it was you.
5 Bobby: ...but I absolutely won't admit to doing something I didn't do.
6 Mother: I think you broke this vase.
7 Bobby: I'll say it again – I didn't do it.
8 Mother: I really think you should tell the truth.

14A Crossword – economy and business

Across ➡

4 In times of difficulty, a company may have to make serious .... (3, 5)
5 We are going to .... the company on the stock market
6 To be successful a company needs a .... client base.
8 Notes taken at a meeting.
10 Companies declare themselves bankrupt if they .... (2, 5)
13 List of items to be discussed at a meeting.
14 A legal agreement to buy or sell products.
17 Time of financial slowing down.
18 There has been a sharp .... in profits.
19 If a product is successful, it is a ....

Down ⬇

1 Dismiss an employee for economic reasons. (4, 7, 9)
2 Bid for a ....
3 Customers give you their ....
4 A person who buys your products or services.
5 Another word for inundate.
7 Another word for 16 down.
9 When one company buys up another. (4, 4)
11 Another way to describe 1 down (3, 3)
12 To be successful, you need to be able to .... the books.
15 After a recession, things tend to .... (4, 2)
16 The company is .... to Bristol.

© Heinle, Cengage Learning 2012

154 Outcomes

14B DEFINITIONS GAME

Student A

Election	Referee	Military coup
Crèche	Early retirement	Bandage

a time when...   a person who...
a situation in which...   a place where...
a situation in which...   a thing which....

Student B

Underdog	An orphan	A scholarship
A privileged background	An evacuee	A gorge

a team or player who...   someone whose...
something which...   a situation in which...
a person who...   a place where...

Student A

Election	Referee	Military coup
Crèche	Early retirement	Bandage

a time when...   a person who...
a situation in which...   a place where...
a situation in which...   a thing which....

Student B

Underdog	An orphan	A scholarship
A privileged background	An evacuee	A gorge

a team or player who...   someone whose...
something which...   a situation in which...
a person who...   a place where...

Student A

Election	Referee	Military coup
Crèche	Early retirement	Bandage

a time when...   a person who...
a situation in which...   a place where...
a situation in which...   a thing which....

Student B

Underdog	An orphan	A scholarship
A privileged background	An evacuee	A gorge

a team or player who...   someone whose...
something which...   a situation in which...
a person who...   a place where...

Student A

Election	Referee	Military coup
Crèche	Early retirement	Bandage

a time when...   a person who...
a situation in which...   a place where...
a situation in which...   a thing which....

Student B

Underdog	An orphan	A scholarship
A privileged background	An evacuee	A gorge

a team or player who...   someone whose...
something which...   a situation in which...
a person who...   a place where...

© Heinle, Cengage Learning 2012

15A Spot the difference

15B Prepositions snakes and ladders

31 She's working there in a temporary basis.	32	33 I know I can rely on him.	34	35 FINISH
30	29 They were chosen at random.	28	27 They bombarded me with questions.	26
21 He is as a brother to me.	22	23 They are terribly at debt.	24	25 On the long term, things are sure to change.
20	19 The book was translated from French.	18	17 Besides studying, I also work part-time.	16
11 I've been living by my own.	12	13 I'm working up to 8 p.m. this evening.	14	15 It's grown to a very big company.
10	9 On leaving university, he found a job.	8	7 This style has been popular during many years.	6
1 START	2	3 You did that in purpose.	4	5 I'm very fond of him.

16A Accident and emergency dictation

Student A

The other day I had a really stupid accident. I was cutting vegetables and I foolishly [1] sliced part of my finger off. I was in [2] absolute agony and blood was [3] pouring out of my finger. I started to [4] freak out and then I must've [5] fainted because the next thing I knew was I [6] came to and my friend had wrapped my finger in a bandage and poured me a stiff brandy!
tear　　　　　　　break　　　　　　whack scald　　　　　　　profuse　　　　　cut

Student B

I was running downstairs the other day when I tripped and fell. I [1] hit myself on the arm and heard something [2] snap. My elbow was bleeding heavily, there was a [3] gash on my arm, and one of my finger nails was almost [4] ripped off. Worst of all, though, I'd been carrying a hot cup of coffee, which of course went all over me and [5] burnt my leg.
terrible pain　　regain consciousness　　panic pass out　　　　stream　　　　　　　　cut

✂ -

Student A

The other day I had a really stupid accident. I was cutting vegetables and I foolishly [1] sliced part of my finger off. I was in [2] absolute agony and blood was [3] pouring out of my finger. I started to [4] freak out and then I must've [5] fainted because the next thing I knew was I [6] came to and my friend had wrapped my finger in a bandage and poured me a stiff brandy!
tear　　　　　　　break　　　　　　whack scald　　　　　　　profuse　　　　　cut

Student B

I was running downstairs the other day when I tripped and fell. I [1] hit myself on the arm and heard something [2] snap. My elbow was bleeding heavily, there was a [3] gash on my arm, and one of my finger nails was almost [4] ripped off. Worst of all, though, I'd been carrying a hot cup of coffee, which of course went all over me and [5] burnt my leg.
terrible pain　　regain consciousness　　panic pass out　　　　stream　　　　　　　　cut

✂ -

Student A

The other day I had a really stupid accident. I was cutting vegetables and I foolishly [1] sliced part of my finger off. I was in [2] absolute agony and blood was [3] pouring out of my finger. I started to [4] freak out and then I must've [5] fainted because the next thing I knew was I [6] came to and my friend had wrapped my finger in a bandage and poured me a stiff brandy!
tear　　　　　　　break　　　　　　whack scald　　　　　　　profuse　　　　　cut

Student B

I was running downstairs the other day when I tripped and fell. I [1] hit myself on the arm and heard something [2] snap. My elbow was bleeding heavily, there was a [3] gash on my arm, and one of my finger nails was almost [4] ripped off. Worst of all, though, I'd been carrying a hot cup of coffee, which of course went all over me and [5] burnt my leg.
terrible pain　　regain consciousness　　panic pass out　　　　stream　　　　　　　　cut

✂ -

Student A

The other day I had a really stupid accident. I was cutting vegetables and I foolishly [1] sliced part of my finger off. I was in [2] absolute agony and blood was [3] pouring out of my finger. I started to [4] freak out and then I must've [5] fainted because the next thing I knew was I [6] came to and my friend had wrapped my finger in a bandage and poured me a stiff brandy!
tear　　　　　　　break　　　　　　whack scald　　　　　　　profuse　　　　　cut

Student B

I was running downstairs the other day when I tripped and fell. I [1] hit myself on the arm and heard something [2] snap. My elbow was bleeding heavily, there was a [3] gash on my arm, and one of my finger nails was almost [4] ripped off. Worst of all, though, I'd been carrying a hot cup of coffee, which of course went all over me and [5] burnt my leg.
terrible pain　　regain consciousness　　panic pass out　　　　stream　　　　　　　　cut

© Heinle, Cengage Learning 2012

16B Agree / disagree

	agree strongly	agree with reservations	disagree with reservations	disagree strongly
1 We are bound to run out of oil before the end of this century.				
2 There is a distinct possibility we will go to war over water in the future.				
3 Chinese is set to become the next international language.				
4 Brazil is on the verge of becoming the next superpower.				
5 The odds are that the economy will be in recession for several years.				
6 The European Union Community is highly likely to collapse in the near future.				
7				
8				

----

	agree strongly	agree with reservations	disagree with reservations	disagree strongly
1 We are bound to run out of oil before the end of this century.				
2 There is a distinct possibility we will go to war over water in the future.				
3 Chinese is set to become the next international language.				
4 Brazil is on the verge of becoming the next superpower.				
5 The odds are that the economy will be in recession for several years.				
6 The European Union Community is highly likely to collapse in the near future.				
7				
8				

GRAMMAR REFERENCE

01 CITIES

PERFECT TENSES

Exercise 1
1a haven't called   b don't call
2a was done up   b it's been done up
3a had been struck   b was struck
4a to curb   b to have curbed
5a will have changed b will change
6a Having seen   b seeing
7a pump   b have pumped
8a were   b had been

Exercise 2
1 he won't **have** finished
2 correct
3 the country's **been** emerging
4 they may **win**
5 correct
6 you **have played**
7 **having** invested all that money
8 correct

02 CULTURE AND IDENTITY

EMPHATIC STRUCTURES

Exercise 1
1 amazes + amount
2 frustrates + lack
3 upset + seeing
4 disturbs + stance
5 drives + way
6 concerns + number
7 worries + level
8 angers + not

Exercise 2
(slight variations possible)
1 What surprised me was that the city is (was) very (so) cosmopolitan.
2 What disturbs me is that he can be very nationalistic.
3 What concerns me is the growing wealth gap between rich and poor.
4 What really scares me is the fact that the whole society is ageing at an alarming rate.
5 What really angers me is that people assume that I must love football just because I'm Brazilian.

Exercise 3
1 It
2 that
3 not
4 who / that
5 fact

03 RELATIONSHIPS

WOULD

Exercise 1
1 I'd completely agree with you on that.
2 I'd say it was your own fault, to be honest.
3 I'd imagine they'll buy a new one.
4 I'd expect it to arrive sometime next week.
5 I would have thought he was just trying to lighten the mood.
6 I wouldn't have thought it could be done.

Exercise 2
1 correct
2 I **used to** have
3 correct
4 I wish my nose **wasn't / weren't** so big.
5 Would you mind me **sitting** here?
6 I wouldn't be here if I **hadn't had** the surgery.
7 correct
8 correct
9 I knew **he'd** say that.

160 OUTCOMES

Exercise 3
1 get
2 been
3 added
4 bother
5 thought
6 react
7 taking
8 to explain

04 POLITICS

CONDITIONALS

Exercise 1
1 it triggered
2 would've wanted
3 I told
4 I'd told

Exercise 2
1 don't
2 going
3 would
4 should
5 never
6 keeps / continues
7 knew, don't
8 be, had

Exercise 3
1 If we don't get support, we won't achieve anything.
2 If I wasn't / weren't in a hurry, I'd stop and talk.
3 They would've won by a landslide, if they'd changed their leader.
4 I'd vote for them, if they had a different stance on education.
5 He might still be president if he hadn't got / been mixed up in that scandal.

05 NIGHT IN, NIGHT OUT

NOUN PHRASES

Exercise 1
1 Joel Riley gives a talk
2 photography was swept along = no object
3 The parents are seeking an amount of damages

Exercise 2
1 Visit the awe-inspiring cathedral, designed by the architect Antonio Gaudi.
2 I read a fascinating article in the paper by the novelist Ann Tyler.
3 The exhibitions held in the centre are accompanied by workshops suitable for all ages.
4 There is a wealth of exhibits on show, dating back thousands of years.
5 The number of people going to the cinema is far fewer than the number currently attending theatre performances.

Exercise 3
1 The six-week course provides guidelines for losing weight.
2 The disposal of nuclear waste is a matter often causing controversy.
3 There's widespread opposition to the abolition of car tax.
4 The erection of the statue celebrated the centenary / 100th anniversary of his birth.

GRAMMAR REFERENCE

06 CONFLICT

I WISH / IF ONLY

Exercise 1
1 could
2 wasn't / weren't
3 had, mentioned
4 would stop
5 had said
6 could have
7 would, get
8 wouldn't do
9 was / were

Exercise 2
1 If only I could stop smoking.
2 If only I had given him my mobile number.
3 If only he would ask me before taking things from my room. / If only he wouldn't take things from my room without asking.
4 If only you weren't so selfish.
5 If only you'd listen to me when I'm trying to talk to you.
6 If only I'd remembered / I hadn't forgotten to lock the front door when I left.

Exercise 3
1 had
2 could
3 hadn't
4 was / were
5 weren't

07 SCIENCE AND RESEARCH

PASSIVES

Exercise 1
1 has been achieved
2 was given an injection
3 is believed to be
4 had one of my wisdom teeth (taken) out
5 funding from the / to be funded by the
6 be underpinned by
7 being employed by
8 is believed to be caused by

Exercise 2
1 is being carried out
2 affected, have been vaccinated
3 undertaking, be produced
4 be caused, being exposed to
5 being extracted, was tested
6 has set back, is hoped, prevent

08 NATURE

AUXILIARIES

Exercise 1
1 I did
2 It doesn't
3 We will
4 It does
5 It is

Exercise 2
1 That fish does look weird.
2 I did like the country …
3 My son does really enjoy going to the zoo.
4 The female of the species does participate in the raising of the young …
5 Tigers did use to be quite common …
6 He does interrupt a bit …

Exercise 3
1 are
2 do
3 did
4 does
5 wouldn't
6 shouldn't
7 hadn't, did
8 wasn't / weren't, can't
9 should
10 haven't, will
11 will
12 was, may / might / could

09 WORK

CONTINUOUS FORMS

Exercise 1
1a have drawn up   b have been drawing up
2a had been losing   b lost
3a is dealing with /   b will deal with
   will be dealing with
4a were having   b had had
5a are processed   b is being processed
6a wouldn't be sitting   b wouldn't sit
7a was being interviewed   b was interviewed

Exercise 2
1 correct
2 He must've **been doing**
3 it's being **done** up
4 supposed **to be** taking on
5 I **see**
6 she's **come up** with
7 correct
8 **I'll sort** out

162 OUTCOMES

GRAMMAR REFERENCE

10 HEALTH AND ILLNESS

MODAL VERBS

Exercise 1
1 That must've been painful.
2 He should have stopped smoking earlier.
3 It can't be that hard to do.
4 They couldn't have done any more to help.
5 It can't have been cheap.
6 He shouldn't have been taking those pills.
7 You may / might / could need three or four operations.
8 He must've been lying about his diet!
9 She may / might / could have picked up the bug from my son.
10 If he managed to get to hospital in time, everything must have been fine.

Exercise 2
1 would be, might have seen
2 may have suffered, should have carried out, would stop
3 must be, should go, could be
4 shouldn't be playing, could have been killed, wouldn't have had
5 can't be, must weaken / be weakening, might get
6 must have, would have screamed, could remain / could've remained

11 PLAY

LINKING WORDS

Exercise 1
1 and then
2 Even if
3 although
4 so as not to
5 if
6 until
7 in order to
8 so long as
9 otherwise

Exercise 2
1 so
2 otherwise
3 provided
4 if
5 case
6 as
7 even
8 but / although

12 HISTORY

DRAMATIC INVERSION

Exercise 1
1 Only when it became obvious it could no longer be contained, did he admit his involvement in the scandal.
2 Never before had we witnessed an international relief operation on such a scale.
3 Not until 1996 did the first women's team come into existence.
4 At no time did anybody try to prevent the tragedy.
5 Nowhere else in the world can you combine business and pleasure quite so well.
6 They made it very clear that under no circumstances could I move; otherwise, they'd shoot me.
7 Only after America rebelled against the high import taxes imposed on tea, did coffee become more popular.
8 Not only was he an artist and poet, he was also a military leader.
9 No sooner had they taken office than the government put up taxes.
10 Only once in our recent history have we had an honest leader.

Exercise 2
1 **did** so few people do
2 **did** she campaign
3 **does** it start
4 No sooner *had* the **truce been** called
5 **was** corruption finally tackled
6 on no account **would** foreigners be allowed

GRAMMAR REFERENCE

13 NEWS AND THE MEDIA

REPORTING AND VERB PATTERNS

Exercise 1
1 cited
2 urged
3 refused
4 blamed
5 announced
6 instructed
7 pleaded
8 boasting

Exercise 2
1 anger at the tax
2 to me to having
3 to have it done
4 urged us to visit
5 expressed concern that the situation
6 threatened me with the sack
7 acknowledged that the rescue plan had been

Exercise 3
1 encouragement for students to apply for university
2 criticism for / about his decision
3 the invitation to work
4 an announcement that they were getting married last week

14 BUSINESS AND ECONOMICS

RELATIVE CLAUSES

Exercise 1
1 We have to identify the areas where / in which improvements can be made.
2 My boss, whose office is next to mine, heard everything.
3 In January we borrowed ten thousand euros, most of which has already been spent.
4 Deals can depend on the way in which you approach negotiations.
5 For the starting point of our study, we chose 2004, when our president / which was the year our president submitted the highest budget.
6 I wanted to explore the extent to which large corporations influence the economic health of nations.
7 The meeting in 2008 was a very important one, when we realised we could no longer work as allies.
8 We have over 9000 employees, the vast majority of whom are based in China.
9 We found ourselves expected to pay large bribes to local officials, which was a very difficult situation.
10 We've reached a crucial point, where we can't cut costs any further without having to lay people off.

Exercise 2

A
1f after whom the company is named
2e without whom we would never have survived this difficult year
3c with which we are all satisfied
4a about which we currently know very little
5b from whom I've learned a huge amount
6d with which we surround ourselves

B
1 who the company is named after
2 who we would never have survived without
3 we are all satisfied with
4 which we currently know very little about
5 who I've learned a huge amount from
6 we surround ourselves with

GRAMMAR REFERENCE

15 FASHION

PREPOSITIONS

Exercise 1
1 for
2 up
3 On
4 in
5 by
6 into
7 from
8 for
9 On / After
10 from
11 off
12 until

Exercise 2
1 the game on purpose to
2 as regards to the overall design
3 to his arrival
4 reducing the costs, we have enabled
5 on a daily basis
6 in the long term
7 accounts for

16 DANGER AND RISK

OTHER FUTURE FORMS

Exercise 1
1 *probable* not correct
2 both correct
3 both correct
4 both correct
5 both correct
6 *chance*s not correct
7 both correct
8 *likely* not possible

Exercise 2
1 of
2 in
3 for
4 on
5 for
6 at

Exercise 3
1 is to be overseen by
2 is sure to damage
3 believe they are on the point of finding
4 are about to be evicted
5 success is bound to follow
6 are highly likely to rise this year

AUDIO TRACK LISTING

CD1

track	content	
1	titles	
2	1.1	1
3		2
4	1.2	
5	1.3	1
6		2
7		3
8	1.4	1
9		2
10		3
11	2.1	1
12		2
13	2.2	
14	2.3	1
15		2
16		3
17	3.1	1
18		2
19		3
20	3.2	1
21		2
22		3
23		4
24		5
25	4.1	1
26		2
27	4.2	1
28		2
29		3
30	4.3	1
31		2
32		3
33		4
34		5
35	R1.1	1
36		2
37		3
38		4
39		5
40	5.1	1
41		2
42	5.2	
43	5.3	

CD2

track	content	
1	titles	
2	6.1	1
3		2
4	6.2	
5	6.3	1
6		2
7		3
8	7.1	1
9		2
10	7.2	
11	7.3	1
12		2
13		3
14		4
15		5
16	7.4	1
17		2
18		3
19		4
20		5
21	8.1	1
22		2
23	8.2	
24	8.3	
25	8.4	1
26		2
27	R2.1	
28	9.1	
29	9.2	
30	9.3	
31	9.4	1
32		2
33		3
34		4
35		5
36	10.1	1
37		2
38	10.2	
39	10.3	
40	10.4	
41	11.1	1
42		2
43		3
44	11.2	
45	11.3	1
46		2
47		3
48		4
49		5

CD3

track	content	
1	titles	
2	12.1	
3	12.2	
4	12.3	1
5		2
6		3
7		4
8	R3.1	1
9		2
10		3
11		4
12		5
13	13.1	1
14		2
15		3
16		4
17		5
18	13.2	
19	13.3	
20	13.4	
21	14.1	1
22		2
23	14.2	
24	14.3	
25	15.1	1
26		2
27		3
28		4
29	15.2	1
30	16.1	1
31		2
32	16.2	
33	16.3	
34	16.4	
35	16.5	
36	16.6	
37	R4.1	

NOTES

NOTES